ABSORPTION NARRATIVES

Absorption Narratives

Jewishness, Blackness, and Indigeneity in the Cultural Imaginary of the Americas

STEPHANIE M. PRIDGEON

UNIVERSITY OF TORONTO PRESS
Toronto Buffalo London

© University of Toronto Press 2025
Toronto Buffalo London
utorontopress.com
Printed in the USA

ISBN 978-1-4875-2771-6 (cloth)   ISBN 978-1-4875-2773-0 (EPUB)
                                   ISBN 978-1-4875-2772-3 (PDF)

Library and Archives Canada Cataloguing in Publication

Title: Absorption narratives : Jewishness, blackness, and indigeneity in the cultural imaginary of the Americas / Stephanie M. Pridgeon.
Names: Pridgeon, Stephanie, 1986– author
Description: Includes bibliographical references and index.
Identifiers: Canadiana (print) 20240455711 | Canadiana (ebook) 20240455797 | ISBN 9781487527716 (cloth) | ISBN 9781487527723 (PDF) | ISBN 9781487527730 (EPUB)
Subjects: LCSH: Latin American fiction – History and criticism. | LCSH: Jews in literature. | LCSH: Black people in literature. | LCSH: Indigenous peoples in literature. | LCSH: Race relations in literature. | LCSH: Ethnic groups in literature.
Classification: LCC PQ7082.N7 P75 2025 | DDC 863/.0093529 – dc23

Cover design: Val Cooke
Cover image: iStock.com/Nattima Cheechang; iStock.com/tomograf

We wish to acknowledge the land on which the University of Toronto Press operates. This land is the traditional territory of the Wendat, the Anishnaabeg, the Haudenosaunee, the Métis, and the Mississaugas of the Credit First Nation.

This book was published with funds from Bates College, including from the Bates Faculty Development Fund.

University of Toronto Press acknowledges the financial support of the Government of Canada, the Canada Council for the Arts, and the Ontario Arts Council, an agency of the Government of Ontario, for its publishing activities.

 Canada Council for the Arts / Conseil des Arts du Canada

 ONTARIO ARTS COUNCIL / CONSEIL DES ARTS DE L'ONTARIO — an Ontario government agency / un organisme du gouvernement de l'Ontario

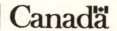 Funded by the Government of Canada / Financé par le gouvernement du Canada

 MIX Paper | Supporting responsible forestry — FSC® C016245

Contents

Acknowledgments   vii

1 Absorption Narratives: Jewishness, Blackness, and Indigeneity in the Cultural Imaginary of the Americas   3

2 "There's No Jews on the Reservation": Jewish–Indigenous Encounters in Fiction of the Americas   37

3 "What Is It We Absorb?": Fictional Genealogies of Hybridity between Jewishness and Indigeneity   80

4 Accidents of Racism: Passing and Absorbing Blackness into Jewishness   119

5 Creole Dreams: Blackness and Jewishness in Urban Spaces throughout the Americas   150

6 Queering Ethnic Rites of Passage   178

   Epilogue: Can Fiction Unite the Ununitable?   197

Notes   203

Works Cited   219

Index   235

Acknowledgments

I first drafted most of this book in 2020 during the pandemic lockdown and my fall 2020 pre-tenure leave. The world felt broken and more uncertain than it ever had to me, and I found solace, hope, and humour in the beautiful, provocative words of the works that I explore in these pages. If the experience of writing this book was particularly isolating, this book is also the result of many people who inspired and challenged me. Throughout 2020, my writing was sustained through daily Zoom check-ins with a lively bunch of colleagues: Karen Melvin, Paqui López, Alison Melnick Dyer, Melinda Plastas, Anelise Hanson Shrout, Tiffany Salter, Margaret Creighton, and Beth Woodward. I'm grateful to the reviewers of the manuscript for their formative feedback and to my editor at University of Toronto Press, Mark Thompson. This book also owes greatly to inspiration from Phyllis Graber Jensen, Claudia Aburto Guzmán, David George, Baltasar Fra Molinero, Laura Fernández, Jon Cavallero, Brittany Longsdorf, Justin Moriarty, Mike Rocque, Emily Kane, Tyler Harper, Josh Rubin, Michael Sargent, Paul Schofield, Joe Hall, Cynthia Baker, Charles Nero, Marcelle Medford, Mary Rice-DeFosse, Kirk Read, Laura Balladur, Alex Dauge-Roth, Justine Wiesinger, Keiko Konoeda, Raluca Cernahoschi, Jakub Kazecki, Rebecca Herzig, Erica Rand, Clarisa Pérez Armendáriz, Sonja Pieck, Erik Bernardino, Carolina González Valencia, Lucy Britt, Andrea Trumble, Megan Boomer, Jacqueline Lyon, Jake Longaker, Caroline Shaw, Anne Garland Mahler, Nanci Buiza, Rebecca Janzen, Emily Hind, Estelle Tarica, Marilyn Miller, Hazel Gold, Ignacio Sánchez Prado, Dalia Kandiyoti, Erin Graff Zivin, Stephen Silverstein, Karen Stolley, Naomi Lindstrom, Adriana Brodsky, David Koffman, Margaret Boyle, Irina Popescu, Nadia Celis, Javier Cikota, Ana Almeyda-Cohen, Ben Fallaw, Tiffany Miller, Nico Ramos-Flores, Katherine Ostrom. And Dara Goldman, may her memory be a blessing.

viii Acknowledgments

This book is dedicated to Archer. In Mexico City in summer 2022, I felt a flutter move across my abdomen, and the next day as I stood in the Museo Memoria y Tolerancia looking at a map tracing the movement of Holocaust refugees across Europe and to the Americas, I thought about all of the migrations and all of the movements across geographical and biological spaces that led to that flutter. Parentage, memory, and life have taken on new meanings. Finally, these pages would not exist if not for Josh; I cannot recall exactly how I managed to revise this manuscript substantively in the blur of those post-partum months, but I do know that it was because of Josh's devoted, selfless caring for Archer – and for me – that I was able to write.

Finally, I would like to acknowledge that this book received financial support from the Bates Faculty Development Fund and that a section of chapter 2 appeared in *Revista Canadiense de Estudios Hispánicos* 42.1 as "Silences Between Jewish and Indigeneity in Eduardo Halfon's *Mañana nunca lo hablamos*," and an earlier version of chapter 6 was published *in Multiethnic Literatures of the United States* 47.1.

ABSORPTION NARRATIVES

1 Absorption Narratives: Jewishness, Blackness, and Indigeneity in the Cultural Imaginary of the Americas

James Baldwin remarked in a 1967 *New York Times* opinion piece that, while one may draw parallels between the atrocities of slavery and those of the Holocaust, these historical truths mean different things for Black folks than for Jews in the United States (US) because, whereas the US fought against the Axis forces, the same nation enslaved Black people. At the heart of Baldwin's objection is the relationship between oppressed groups' memories, their places of refuge, and the sites of their oppression. This relationship has guided the construction of racialized discourse throughout the Americas since the Spanish Conquest and bears indelibly on the ways that race continues to be understood and articulated. Categories of racial difference have come to be understood through individuals' and groups' shifting relationships to the spaces they inhabit in the present and to the memory of spaces inhabited by prior generations of their families and communities. Baldwin goes on to state that "it is bitter to watch the Jewish storekeeper locking up his store for the night, and going home. Going, with your money in his pocket, to a clean neighborhood, miles from you, which you will not be allowed to enter" (n.p.). In Baldwin's essay, to be Jewish in the Americas is to benefit from the upward social mobility that allowed the shopkeeper to move out of Harlem, where Black neighbours remained. For Baldwin, the Jew is *absorbed* into middle-class white America.[1] The phenomenon that Baldwin observed in 1967 is so because, despite the very real and atrocious oppressions that Jews escaped to come to the Americas, Jewish presence in nations throughout the Americas is a function of settler colonialism and immigration policies in nations that allowed entry to white immigrants. Many of these nations are characterized by paradigms of racial mixture – cosmic race in Mexico, racial democracy in Brazil – that absorb racial difference into an amalgamated model of mixture that underscores national identity. These models dominate society and undergird the ways that Jewish, Black, and Indigenous people understand how they and others belong (or do not belong) in their nations.

While, in Harlem in 1967, James Baldwin noted the bitter feeling of watching the Jewish shopkeeper leave for a ritzier neighbourhood, a fictional representation of Bom Retiro in São Paulo, Brazil, set three years later shows a young Jewish boy remarking that he wants to "be Black and to fly" in Cao Hamburger's film *The Year My Parents Went on Vacation*. Hamburger conveys a Jewish fascination with Afro-Brazilian identities that verges on appropriation – the absorption of the Afro-Brazilian into the Jewish imaginary. For Baldwin, Jews were afforded the upward social mobility of whiteness by being absorbed into white spaces, while for Hamburger's young protagonist, Jewish belonging in 1970 in the *pais de futebol* (football country) in Pelé's heyday involved a desire to be Black. In the latter scenario, the young Jewish child desires to absorb Black difference into his own identity. In both cases, absorption in Jewish–Black relations is a function of Jewish access to whiteness.

Literature from throughout the Americas has used the term "absorption" explicitly to reference co-optation, assimilation, and appropriation in Jewish encounters with racial alterity. Guatemalan American Jewish author Francisco Goldman's 1992 novel has its *mestiza* Jewish character Flor ask, "Guatemala, in what we like to think of as its deepest self, is Mayan. We, who aren't actually Indian, what is it we absorb?" (242). This character uses "absorption" to speak of the ways in which Black and Indigenous encounters with Jews throughout the Americas are bound up in particularities of individual and collective connections to the past and of disparate relationships to the land and to urban spaces within the Americas. Whereas Goldman voiced a mestiza-Jewish Guatemalan's concerns about what she and others who "aren't actually Indian" "absorb" from the Maya, US novelist Philip Roth later also focused on absorption through his creation of the fictional "Office of American Absorption" in his 2004 novel *The Plot Against America*. At its core, the novel (like its 2020 adaptation as an HBO miniseries) is a dystopic fantasy whose central conceit is the catastrophic effects of "absorption" – in this case, forced assimilation.[2] The absorption narrative of Roth's storyline echoes the nineteenth-century forced removal of Native American groups from the Southeastern US that pushed them into the Midwest. The story of Jewish displacement co-opts (absorbs) the historical trauma visited upon Native Americans. Roth's dystopic ideation of the anti-Semitic effects of absorption functions inversely to this historical event, insofar as the so-called Trail of Tears separated

Native Americans from white settlers, whereas the "Office of American Absorption" seeks to forcibly assimilate Jews into the US heartland. Absorption works in contradictory ways: Jewishness is sometimes absorbed into middle-class whiteness, and Jewishness also absorbs Indigeneity through co-optation. Jewish communities have been both objects and agents of absorption.

As we begin to observe from the above examples, absorption is present in multiple, contradictory ways in Jewish–Black and Jewish–Indigenous encounters in the Americas. Often, Jews are absorbed (assimilated) into whiteness while other minority groups do not pass as white. By extension, Jews become complicit, or absorbed, in settler colonialism and racial capitalism. Jews can "absorb" elements of Indigenous or Black identities – paradoxically, often as a way of attaining and maintaining their status as white. The etymology of "absorption" explains much of the paradox of how absorption functions: the "ab" signals separation, the "sorb" signals introjection. Absorption involves both separation and joining. The term also evokes ideas of liquidity, perpetuated across generations through the fluidity of racialized memory, and porosity, which is problematized by the very different notions of "mainstream" culture throughout the Americas. Absorption simultaneously problematizes yet maintains ideas about racial purity – which, as I show throughout, are particularly significant for conversations about Jewishness and race in the Americas given the historical meaning of blood purity used both to fuel anti-Semitic and anti-Muslim policies in fifteenth-century Iberia and as a framework for coetaneous and later ideas about racial mixture in the Spanish colonies. Absorption also conjures such notions as the "one-drop rule" in the twentieth-century US and Native American blood quantum. In their own ways, both concepts are predicated on the degrees to which the blood of ancestors of different races is or is not absorbed.

Despite these stories that speak to the phenomenon of absorption, no existing scholarship has considered how Jewishness commingles with Blackness or Indigeneity in geographical contexts from North, Central, and South America. Jewish encounters with Black and Indigenous communities in both rural and urban spaces are bound up in complicated understandings of whiteness (and white supremacy) and racial mixture, a phenomenon that has been studied more in North American contexts than in Latin America. In *How Jews Became White Folks*, anthropologist Karen Brodkin examines her own Jewish family – specifically, her immigrant grandmother's embrace of racist language and attitudes to refer to Black people – and concludes, paraphrasing Toni Morrison, that her grandmother's racism shows that "one could

6   Absorption Narratives

become an American by asserting one's own white superiority over African Americans" (19). For Brodkin, the Black-white binary understanding of race in the US often compels Jews into white supremacist attitudes and behaviours. I further Brodkin's line of enquiry to explore how Jewish complicity in white supremacy continues to bear on Jewish relations with non-white racial groups throughout the Americas. Similarly, historian Eric Goldstein has shown that racial paradigms in the US leave Jews few options other than to avow whiteness, because Black and white are often the only identifications available. In Latin America, in contrast, historian Jeffrey Lesser argues, "studies of Jewish 'whiteness' (or the lack thereof) that have become so central to the study of Jews (and other ethnic groups) in the US, has [sic] been generally ignored in the Latin American case" (7). Nonetheless, as Lesser rightly notes, just as Goldstein and Brodkin have argued that Jewishness has salient implications for racial categories in the US, convergences among Jewishness, Blackness, and Indigeneity in other parts of the Americas also shed light on how race is understood. *Absorption Narratives* fills this critical lacuna that Lesser names through a sustained consideration of how Jewishness comes into contact with Blackness and Indigeneity in nations that are codified racially through the cultural emphasis placed on *mestizaje* and racial mixture in Latin America. Put another way, if taking critical account of Jewish investment in whiteness has telling implications for how racial paradigms are constructed and understood, then an understanding of how Jewishness factors into these varied racial paradigms throughout the Americas allows further understanding of how race is constructed.[3] Works of fiction from throughout the Western hemisphere underscore how Jewish encounters with Blackness and Indigeneity question the construction of race. While the topic may appear somewhat niche, I engage a vast, diverse array of fiction that conceptualizes the complex convergences of these identity categories. My comparative approach to race and ethnicity throughout the Americas destabilizes US-centric critical practices by "reading North by South" (Larsen). In so doing, we come to see that US-focused models for thinking about racial alterity vis-à-vis Jewishness are limiting and that the story of race relations in the Americas must necessarily be told and analysed as a hemispheric story rather than from US perspectives.

To begin to think about absorption between Jewish groups and Indigenous and Black groups throughout the Americas, I first introduce the concept of syncretic spaces. Jewish encounters with Black and Indigenous communities throughout the Americas take place within "contact zones" understood as "the space of imperial encounters, the space in which peoples geographically and historically separated come into contact with each other and establish ongoing relations, usually involving conditions of coercion, radical inequality, and intractable conflict" (Pratt 2008, 8). These spaces chronicle the convergence and blending of ethnicities and religious practices from different cultures that have long characterized racial and spiritual paradigms in Latin America. Syncretism – predicated upon the maintenance of certain elements of the cultures of origin – has a long and complicated history in the Americas. Syncretism is often used to refer to religious practices and, in Latin American contexts, nearly always connotes a blending of religious and racial components. I consider syncretism as a conceptual model predicated on the preservation of elements of cultures and identities that are maintained after cultures come into contact with one another and are hybridized. Iconic examples of syncretism in Latin America – such as Afro-Cuban *santería* and the Mexican figure of Virgen de Guadalupe – are characterized by an enmeshment between spiritual practices and ethnic identifications. In santería, the Yoruba religion is blended with Catholicism to give way to such phenomena as the La Virgen de la Caridad del Cobre and Ochún, the patronesses of Cuba. In Mexico, the Virgen de Guadalupe is often discussed as a function of syncretism because she – an apparition of the Catholic Virgin Mary – appears phenotypically mestiza and spoke to Juan Diego (the man before whom she appeared) in Nahuatl. These syncretic figures blend ethnicity and spirituality in ways that have come to emblematize national identities in Cuba and Mexico, respectively. Syncretism is useful when thinking about Jewish encounters with Blackness and Indigeneity in the Americas beyond Latin America because the concept brings together ethnic and spiritual identifications related to Blackness and Indigeneity.

Considering syncretism in the context of Jewishness in the Americas is necessary because (1) like syncretism, Jewishness connotes both religious identification and ethnicity and (2) Jewishness comes into contact with other syncretic practices in meaningful ways. And yet syncretism can also be a limiting category insofar as the very preservation of difference can also absorb and appropriate difference, particularly when models of syncretism are used to underscore national identity. Nonetheless, syncretism can be approached through a critical lens that focuses on the maintenance of difference. As Cuban scholar Antonio Benítez Rojo argued in his groundbreaking 1986 essay *The Repeating Island*, syncretism has implications that reach far beyond the purely religious. Benítez Rojo defines a syncretic artifact as "not a synthesis, but rather a signifier made of differences" (22). Syncretism allows for thinking about mixture in ways that resist the absorption of difference. In thinking about contact zones throughout the Americas as syncretic

8   Absorption Narratives

spaces, *Absorption Narratives* focuses on these sites of contestation as spaces of ethno-religious negotiations.

In addition to the importance of syncretism as a signifier made of difference, Jewishness connects with other categories of racial alterity in very different ways in Latin America and the Caribbean than in the US and Canada due to paradigms of mestizaje. Understood broadly as the racial mixture that has long characterized societies throughout Latin America dating back to the Conquest, mestizaje has exceeded the category of race to become an organizing principle for societies throughout Latin America. Beginning with the *casta* – "caste" – system in the seventeenth century, the concept of mixture between white Europeans, Black enslaved people, and Indigenous groups throughout Latin America served as a way to categorize individuals and their status in society according to the degrees and types of racial mixture in their lineage. Concepts of mestizaje extended beyond the biological or phenotypical to encompass the cultural and the spiritual. Paradigms of mestizaje continued to pervade cultural, political, and spiritual understandings of national identity well into the twentieth century through such enduring (though contested and, increasingly, debunked) ideas as Mexican José Vasconcelos's "cosmic race" and Brazilian Gilberto Freyre's "racial democracy."

Vasconcelos's model, introduced in the homonymous 1925 essay, celebrates the creation of a "fifth race" through the mixture of European, African, Indigenous American, and Asian races as a new spiritual ("cosmic") force in Mexico and throughout Latin America. For his part, Freyre's 1933 *The Masters and the Slaves* touted the positive effects of racial mixture between Europeans and enslaved Africans as the foundation of a harmonious, racially mixed society in Brazil. After decades of debate and controversy, these ways of thinking have largely fallen out of fashion, due in no small part to the fact that they eschew (absorb) racial difference. Nonetheless, mestizaje continues to pervade the ways in which race is conceptualized throughout most Latin American nations, unlike in the US where a binary racial paradigm informs much thinking about race. For this reason, and because ideas of mestizaje and understandings of Jewishness are predicated upon ideas of racial mixture, we cannot fully understand Jewishness or the construction of racial categories without understanding how Jewishness comes into contact with both Blackness and Indigeneity in the Americas. *Absorption Narratives* is directed to experts in US literature so that paradigms of Latin American literary analysis may nuance discussions of racial mixture, and to specialists in Latin American literature so that considering Jewishness vis-à-vis racial alterity may broaden conversations in Latin American literary and cultural studies.

Because of the importance of both ethnicity and spirituality for Jewishness, both mestizaje and syncretism must be taken into account in order to understand Jewishness and race in an inter-American context. In a similar vein, Sarah Phillips Casteel (*Calypso Jews*) has argued that Black–Jewish dynamics in the Americas "cannot be interpreted through the lens of Black-Jewish relations in the US" and that the tradition is "informed by an awareness of the deep historical presence of Sephardic Jews in the Caribbean as well as more recent moments of Caribbean-Jewish encounter" (5). I agree with Casteel that Sephardism must be foregrounded for a robust and holistic understanding of Black–Jewish relations in the Americas. Similarly, Jonathan Freedman focuses on Jewishness in relation to Blackness and Latinidad in the US in *Klezmer America*. I argue that Casteel's and Freedman's shared focus on Sephardism begs for analysis of the role of racial and ethnic identities in Latin America beyond the Caribbean that account for mestizaje and syncretism in these matrices of ethno-religious identities. Moreover, Freedman and Casteel do not centre mestizaje in their discussions of how Jewishness engages with Blackness and Latinidad in the Americas, leaving the fundamental racial paradigm out of view, despite the provocative ways in which mestizaje bears on these encounters between races. Focusing on both the opportunities and limits that mestizaje and syncretism present, *Absorption Narratives* offers comparative discussions of texts from throughout the Americas and reads North American Jewish texts through conceptual lenses from Latin America and the Caribbean. *Absorption Narratives* decentres the geographical and linguistic heritages that existing scholarship has tended to privilege. In this way, this book serves to reimagine the meaning of Jewishness in the Americas as well as the place of Spanish-language texts in comparative hemispheric studies and in comparative literature. This approach is necessary, I maintain, because of the shared histories – part and parcel of Iberian imperialism in the Americas – of racialization and discrimination towards Jewish, Indigenous, and Black individuals in the Americas dating back to the Spanish Conquest. These shared histories – and the divergent trajectories that they have all taken – continue to inform encounters today between Jewish, Indigenous, and Black communities.

How does *fiction* account for the complexities and tensions that characterize these syncretic spaces? Often, the voices of racial Others become absorbed in moments of convergence. The works that I study here at times take account of and at times contest this absorption of voices. Anna Deavere Smith's *Fires in the Mirror* is the most overt example of such contestation of absorption. Brooklyn's Crown Heights

10 Absorption Narratives

neighbourhood witnessed one of the most intense Black–Jewish confrontations in the history of the Americas (and the world) in 1991 after a rabbi's motorcade struck and killed a Guyanese child playing on the sidewalk. The incident continues to live on in the cultural imaginary as an exemplary case of Black–Jewish relations. Non-Jewish Black playwright Anna Deavere Smith's documentary-style one-woman play *Fires in the Mirror* captures these complexities by listening to and parlaying the voices of those directly and indirectly affected by the riots. Premiered in 1992, the play was recently performed off Broadway in fall 2019 to critical acclaim. In both Smith's performance through which she originated the play and in Michael Benjamin Washington's 2019 revival of the role, Black US-born actors take on the voices of Guyanese immigrants, Hasidic Jews, the Reverend Al Sharpton, and a litany of other characters to tell an aggregate story about being Jewish or Black in 1991 Brooklyn. It is through taking on other voices that self-expression, if not mutual understanding, can happen. In her play, Anna Deavere Smith ventriloquizes the subjects whom she interviewed about the Crown Heights debacle in an attempt to "represent as precisely as possible not just what they've said, but how they've said it" in order to explore "the relationship between speech and identity" ("In Conversation with Anna Deavere Smith"). That is, Smith showed in 1992 – and the new production of her play again emphasized – that the written word, the spoken word, and individual identities are necessarily bound together when communities come into contact and tension with one another in "contact zones," such as Crown Heights. In order to understand the convergence of difference in Crown Heights, it is necessary to understand how people speak about themselves and how their words imagine the Other. Further, for Smith, this type of theatre disrupts racism. Through embodying other voices, authors refigure how race converges in these spaces of exchange. This ventriloquism is a form of absorption that allows for dialogue across racial categories.

In order for ventriloquism to resist co-optation, speakers must first listen deeply to the Other. In these works of fiction from throughout the Americas, speaking for racial Others is never as simple as mere appropriation (although it certainly can be appropriative). Rather, speaking for the Other in these cases is predicated on listening to the Other. I liken this model of listening to deceased philosopher María Lugones's model of "faithful witnessing," which Lugones maintains is key to coalition-building among people who are differently and multiply repressed. She argues, "a faithful witness witnesses against the grain of power, on the side of resistance" (7). Michael Chabon's 2012 novel *Telegraph Avenue* employs Chabon's third-person narration – authored by a white Jewish author – of Black protagonist Archy Stallings's friendship and business partnership with white Jewish Nat Jaffe. The novel is narrated by a third-person, omniscient narrator who is voiced by Black actor Clarke Peters in the audiobook version. A review of the audiobook makes note of this particular function of speaking for the racial Other: "Many of these voices are black, and Chabon seems second only to Richard Price among white novelists who have a convincing ear for urban vernacular" (Walton, *Michael Chabon's "Telegraph Avenue" Is Rich, Funny*). In the reviewer's estimation, Chabon's novel lends itself to being voiced by a Black narrator because of Chabon's deftness in articulating Black voices, attributed to the author's "ear" for urban vernacular. That is, Chabon is successful at speaking through Black voices because he is adept at listening to them.[4] For his part, Goldman in his aforementioned *The Long Night of White Chickens* has the narrator and the narrator's best friend discuss character Flor de Mayo's "right to hold long monologues with herself" (179). The Jewish Guatemalan narrator is an interlocutor for these "long monologues" that he recounts to readers. Listening is necessary for narrators to speak for characters and functions as a specific type of absorption.

Here, I focus on how Jewish, Black, and Indigenous voices listen to and speak through one another to reimagine the place of Jewishness in the construction of race in the Americas and the role of Spanish-language cultural productions in Jewish studies and comparative literature. The layers and exchanges of voices question power and privilege but do not erase the stratification and power differentials among different groups; voices speaking for other groups also run the risk of effacing individual agency. Nonetheless, as cultural productions from throughout the Americas have shown, instances in which Jewish, Black, and Indigenous voices take on one another's voice are vital to understand belonging in a nation or in specific urban spaces. In these instances, taking on the voice of another becomes vested with significance for religion, ethnicity, and national belonging. Layers of ventriloquism and speaking for one another articulate a complex, contradictory sense of what it means for different characters to belong or not in a broader panorama of national and regional identities.

Ventriloquism can be understood within the framework of Bakhtinian heteroglossia, in which each character possesses its own belief system. For Bakhtin, "the language used by characters in a novel, how they speak, is verbally and semantically autonomous; each character's speech possesses its own belief system, since each is the speech of another in another language; thus, it may also refract authorial intentions and consequently may to a second degree constitute a second language

12 Absorption Narratives

for the author" (315). As Bakhtin notes, in the schema of heteroglossia the stratification that comes to characterize speech in the novel is directly informed by ideology. It is important to note that heteroglossia also creates racial stratifications in which, although there are exchanges and hybridity, the privilege and power from which (predominantly white) authors benefit never ceases to function. Dorothy J. Hale has argued that we are well served as critics to think of Bakhtinian double speech in terms of Du Bois's double consciousness, insofar as both are "defined by a negative capability: [the subject's] self-consciousness about the social identities contained in language allows him to be more than the social languages that define him – but that greater identity formulated through the activity of distanciation, possesses no positive value of its own" (448). Du Bois famously describes, "It is a peculiar sensation, this double-consciousness, this sense of always looking at one's self through the eyes of others, of measuring one's soul by the tape of a world that looks on in amused contempt and pity" (*The Souls of Black Folk* chapter 1). In the context of Iberian literature, Nicholas Jones's *Staging habla de negros* draws from Bakhtinian heteroglossia in his focus on "the way in which practitioners of Africanized Castilian utilize their black characters to simultaneously reify and contest prevailing stereotypes while also speaking with an inherent expressive power" (6). Jones's emphasis on the racialized implications of heteroglossia bridges ideology, speech, and race in ways that both affirm and oppose racial stereotypes. Racial anxieties rooted in the Atlantic world and the early modern Spanish empire would come to be co-constitutive of both anti-Jewish notions of *pureza de sangre* and the racial caste systems that characterized Spain and its colonies for centuries. These paradigms continue to undergird the construction of racial categories throughout the Americas. Despite the appropriation inherent to speaking through the voices of other racial categories, authors' use of voices of racial alterity creates systems of speech marked by exchange across racial and cultural difference. Heteroglossia and double consciousness allow possibilities for absorption – voices into narrations, individuals into mainstream society – without the loss of what makes those voices and individuals unique.

Both Black literature and Jewish literature of the Americas have been analysed as wandering signifiers, a critical approach that links the two groups' literary histories. In his consideration of the trickster figure in African American fiction in *The Signifying Monkey*, Henry Louis Gates considers Cuban and, by extension, New World models of signification. In his contemplation of *nganga* (a term which has multiple interpretations, the most productive of which, for Gates, is that of "interpreter"), Gates notes,

> The significance of nganga suggests a multiplicity of meanings, each of which informs the KiKongo-Cuban survival. Most dramatically of all, Rodillo figures the nganga "forever floating over the waves of water" like a wandering signifier, suggesting perpetually its range of meanings from its Bantu roots, even – or especially – in its New World setting. We may take this sort of perpetual, or wandering, signification as an emblem of the process of cultural transmission and translation that recurred with startling frequency when African cultures encountered New World-European cultures and yielded a novel blend. (19)

Gates considers Blackness in the Americas in relation to the wandering signifier (as Erin Graff Zivin does also in the case of Jewishness in Latin American literature, as I address later). The "novel blend" of which Gates speaks allows us to think anew about forms of racial hybridity in the syncretic spaces created by encounters between African cultures and New World–European groups. Specifically, the mixture that Gates considers in *The Signifying Monkey* calls for new forms of reading in the Americas. Gates discusses, in particular, the god Esu and the way his meaning morphs in specific contexts in the New World: "This most common myth of Esu has been glossed in several ways, as if its encoded indeterminacy has blinded even the most astute commentators to a meaning even more fundamental than any literal rendering of its allegory allows. For this myth ascribes to Esu his principal function of the indeterminacy of interpretation" (35).[5] The "indeterminacy of interpretation" with which Gates concludes his reading of Esu allows for more multiplicity than specific tropes (namely, the literal rendering of its allegory, as Gates names here) would allow. If the "master tropes" of Bloom, de Man, Vico, Nietzsche, and Burke are irony, metonymy, synecdoche, metaphor, hyperbole, litotes, and metalepsis, Gates posits that to that list must be added: "aporia, chiasmus, and catachresis, all of which are used in the ritual of Signifyin(g)" (52). In particular, Gates's insistence on chiasmus in the ritual of signifying is crucial to my readings of texts in which the grammar of the analogies between racial groups and their relationship to place is often chiastic. Gates underscores throughout *The Signifying Monkey* that this relationship to language has everything to do with Black folks' geographical displacement from Africa to the New World.

In what follows, I advocate for a praxis of reading culture from throughout the Americas that depicts Jewish encounters with Blackness

14   Absorption Narratives

and Indigeneity in what I term a "spirit of chiasmus." That is, if syntactical chiasmus does not abound is these works, there is nonetheless a chiastic relationship depicted between distinct racial groups that forms the ground for empathy or – at the very least – awareness of the Other. In turn, my geographical pairings of works from different regions of the Americas in each chapter establish chiastic conversations, nations, and regions to discern more clearly the reliefs of racialized discourse. The chiasmus is particularly provocative if we think of literary expressions of oppression along racialized lines as mirror images: both same and yet reversed. In a chiasmus, the order – and thus the logic – of the things in relation to one another is reversed. Within the context of the multivalent, multilayered nature of absorption in the texts discussed here, differing groups are shown as reliefs of one another in ways that mirror yet also distort similarities between each other. We see this phenomenon of chiasmus most clearly in the line from Chippewa author Louise Erdrich's novel *The Master Butchers Singing Club* from which I take chapter 2's title, "There's no Jews on the reservation." That is, the Native American character who utters this sentence does not articulate an analogy to explain his own lack of awareness of Jews and European Jews' lack of awareness of Native Americans. Rather, he applies a chiastic logic to Jews' and Native Americans' lack of awareness of one another by suggesting that European Jews did not know about him *because* he as a Native American did not know about them.

Beyond chiasma, voices speak through one another using a variety of other literary tropes and figures. Relationships between identities – individual and community – and place are registered through a variety of tropes and figures. At their most fundamental level, these literary figures – allegory, aporia, catachresis, chiasmus, metaphor, metonymy, simile, and synecdoche – have to do with the distance between the literal and the figurative as well as the space between narrator and subject. They also have to do with the distance – both literal and figurative – between individuals and their places of origin and with the spaces between racial and ethnic categories. These relationships between the literal and the figurative are also predicated on the degree to which one is (or is not) absorbed into the mainstream. At the heart of encounters between Jewishness, Blackness, and Indigeneity in the Americas are the historical and current conditions of rootedness in the land, exile, forced migrations, and enslavement. The historical realities of Jewish exile, the African slave trade, and Indigenous uprooting from the land characterize these respective groups. Drawing from these historical conditions, figurative language used to depict categories of racial and ethnic identifications is often connected to relationship to the land. The ubiquitous moniker "wandering Jew" speaks to the lack of connection to the land that has characterized Jewish exile and wandering. Meanwhile, demonyms used to refer to tribes in Africa as well as Indigenous groups throughout the Americas often signal traits of the land from which they hail, despite being displaced or uprooted. Figurative language also serves to denote difference between groups as well as degrees of hybridity and the absorption of difference.

Allegory, in particular, often functions to absorb the specificities of difference insofar as Jewishness is often represented in literature as an allegory of difference. Daniel Itzkovitz has noted that "Jewishness explains difference, but Jewish difference is never explained" (178). That is, Jewishness has often been accepted as a stand-in for alterity writ large. This phenomenon is often registered through allegorical depictions. For this reason, Jewishness has often been depicted as all but interchangeable with other categories of difference (as Graff Zivin notes, in *The Wandering Signifier*, that authors throughout Latin America have done). A vague model of difference, as Itzkovitz has noted, drawing from the Boyarin brothers, has often led to the allegorization of Jewishness itself. The Boyarins trace the allegorization of Jewishness to the Bible, arguing that "'real Jews" ended up being only a trope ("Diaspora" 697). The Boyarins argue that moving past this reading of the Bible in which "real Jews" are "only a trope" holds salient possibilities for anti-racism (707). Ultimately, for the Boyarins, the question of how Jewish difference is conceptualized has to do with the relationship to the land: "It is profoundly disturbing to hear Jewish attachment to the Land decried as regressive in the same discursive situations in which the attachment of Native Americans or Aborigine in Australia to their particular rocks, trees, and deserts is celebrated as an organic connection to the Earth that 'we' have lost" (714–15). For the Boyarins, the lack of analogy – that is, the distinction – between Jewish connection to the land as "regressive" and Indigenous connection to the land as "celebrated as organic" is illogical if one considers both Jews and Indigenous peoples in the context of uprootedness. As I elaborate further in my discussion of *destierro* later in this chapter, there are ways of thinking about Jewish uprootedness vis-à-vis Indigenous relations to the land that allow for more solidarity between Jews and Indigenous Peoples. The Boyarins do insist, however, that such a perspective of Jewish connection to the land is productive as a self-critical and self-aware approach to the subject matter: "Traditional Jewish attachment to the Land, whether biblical or post-biblical, thus provides a self-critique as well as a critique of identities based on notions of autochthon" (715). I thus read the Boyarins' intervention as tacitly distinguishing between self-allegorization

16 Absorption Narratives

and self-critique along the conceptual axis of questioning attachment to the land. This questioning, as they have shown, applies to Jews, Afro-descendants, and Indigenous peoples and brings up a litany of complexities surrounding how all three relate to the land, rootedness, and uprootedness. Drawing from the Boyarins' analysis, I read Jewish authors with an emphasis on questioning Jewish attachment to the land as a way of contesting Jewish absorption of racial difference.

Elsewhere, Jewishness and racial alterity in the US have been analysed within the framework of a move from synecdoche to metonymy, as Jonathan Freedman notes in his discussion of the function of Emma Lazarus's poem – inscribed on the Statue of Liberty – in the US cultural imaginary in *Klezmer America*. Freedman posits that, in the late-nineteenth and early-twentieth centuries, "Jewish-specific images, sites, experiences have become broadly representative of that social moment itself – a culturally validated synecdoche, to put it in rhetorical terms, for the experience undergone by all immigrants to America. ... What seems to be synecdoche ... rapidly transformed itself into a set of metonymies ... to project these narratives onto something else" (7–8). As Freedman notes, we continue to observe this move from synecdoche to metonymy in such concepts as the "Jewish Lower East Side," which functions both as a synecdoche of Jewish US life and as metonymy for immigrant experiences writ large. That is, the neighbourhood is both part of the whole Jewish experience and adjacent to other immigrant experiences that it comes to signify, and it is the adjacency that, primarily, it has come to signify. This phenomenon holds true also throughout Latin America and informs Jeffrey Lesser's historical analysis of "How the Jews Became Japanese" in Brazil and San Francisco. Lesser's article interrogates the reasons for which Jews, Arabs, and the Japanese have almost always been discussed alongside one another in Brazilian studies. A metonymic function of Jewishness applies to minority immigrant groups, such as Asians and Italians, as Lesser and Freedman note. But the same metonymic phenomenon of Jewishness does not hold true with Black groups in nearby spaces in New York, São Paulo, or San Francisco; nor is it the case for Jewish vis-à-vis Indigenous groups. Moreover, as Lesser notes in the above-mentioned article, studies of Jewish whiteness like those in the US have not generally been undertaken in Latin American contexts. This lack of critical attention, I argue, is precisely because Jewishness does not function metonymically in relation to Blackness or Indigeneity in the same way that it does in relation to other immigrant groups.

Despite this general lack of critical attention, there have been some important references to Jewishness vis-à-vis Indigeneity in myths of national identities. Doris Sommer's groundbreaking 1991 study *Foundational Fictions: The National Romances of Latin America* argues that, in the Colombian novel *María* (1867) by Jorge Isaacs, "Both lovers are apparently white, if Jews can be legitimately white in a nineteenth-century code that generally equates ethnicity with race, or in any other code for that matter" (*Foundational Fictions* 186). As with all of the novels that Sommer discusses in *Foundational Fictions*, *María* serves as an allegory of national identity predicated on a love relationship between individuals of different ethnic backgrounds.[6] Also like the other novels Sommer discusses, this national allegory is an imperfect one that attempts to "resolve" national problems (and problems of race) through a seemingly harmonious blending of difference. The fraught allegorical model is thus, for Sommer, related to Jewish whiteness in the case of Isaacs's novel. In Sommer's terms, Jews are "apparently" white in the schemata of racial mixture that sustain national identities in these "foundational" narratives. To function (even if imperfectly), these national allegories absorb racial and ethnic difference. In the US (though not in the context of literature), similar narratives of foundational myths were observed in 1969 by Native American rights activist Vine Deloria, Jr. Deloria named the preponderance of white US citizens who claimed to have Native American ancestry – specifically, maternal ancestors who were noble. As Deloria notes, "Whites claiming Indian blood generally tend to reinforce mythical beliefs about Indians" (3). Deloria emphasizes that, in common discourse of everyday life, white US citizens absorb noble Native American princesses into their own genealogies. Deloria goes on to add, however, "Only among the Jewish community, which has a long tribal-religious tradition of its own, does the mysterious Indian grandmother, the primeval princess, fail to dominate the family tree" (4). As he noted, in the late 1960s Jewish Americans had not absorbed Native American identities in the way that non-Jewish white Americans had in everyday folklore. Yet, as we shall see, Jewish American voices would come to appropriate Indigenous identities in other ways.

Elsewhere in the Americas, metaphors of racial mixture define the literary figure of Argentine gaucho, the skilled cowboy of the Argentine plains, in everyday discourse and literary depictions. Alberto Gerchunoff's 1910 novel *Los gauchos judíos/Jewish Gauchos* tells a fictionalized version of Jewish settlers on the pampas. To do so, the novel has Jews absorb the identity of the gaucho, who may be of any race but who is archetypically mestizo. Anthropologist Judith Noemí Freidenberg argues, "At one level, the metaphor [of the Jewish gauchos] is emblematic of a mode of immigrant incorporation, where assimilation is a survival strategy but does not entail complete acculturation" (147).

18   Absorption Narratives

For Friedenberg, this iconic text and the archetype of the Jewish gaucho that it inspired constitute a metaphor that allows Jews to assimilate as gauchos while maintaining their Jewish identities. Friedenberg goes on to add, "the Jewish gaucho is an icon of a hybrid identity: rather than being pure types, each is open to transformation into the Other. Instead of an opposition of "civilized" versus "barbarian," there is the pairing of a helpful gaucho and a foreigner eager to learn" (149).[7] Thus, despite the absence of "complete acculturation" that Friedenberg notes, the model of the Jewish gaucho nonetheless suggests an impulse to absorb the best qualities of two marginalized groups and homogenize them, similar to the models of cosmic race and racial democracy. Jewish Argentine author Ricardo Feierstein furthers this metaphor in his 1988 novel *Mestizo* by using the term "mestizo" to denote his own dual identity as Jewish and Argentine. Ilan Stavans notes in the introduction to Feierstein's novel that the author "clearly refers to a cross-fertilization that is cultural and not hereditary. For him the word *mestizo* denotes a person with Jewish ancestry born to Jewish immigrants in Argentina and almost paralyzed by the duality" (xi). In Feierstein's novel, the metaphor of mestizaje is appropriated to refer to a particular convergence of geography and ethnicity experienced by Jews in the Americas, evidencing Jewish absorption of European–Indigenous mixture.

The challenges presented by the abovementioned metaphor of the Jewish gaucho and mestizo speak to a central concern in my study: the fact that Jewish presence in the Americas is often a function of settler colonialism, even if Jews were arriving to these places seeking refuge from persecution; yet, neither Jewish presence on American lands nor Indigenous experiences in Latin America are considered within the context of settler colonialism, with few exceptions. As historian David S. Koffman (*The Jews' Indian*) has argued, situating Jewish presence in the US and Canada within the framework of settler colonialism moves beyond the celebratory narratives of belonging that often characterize understandings of Jewish life in the Americas, allowing us to think of Jewish complicity in such phenomena as manifest destiny. Within literary and film studies, this framework changes how we might think of beloved works such as *The Jewish Gauchos* or the 1991 US animated film *Fievel Goes West*. A growing corpus of scholars have emerged to argue for a critical framework of settler colonialism to disrupt the utopic and eugenicist narratives in which mestizaje is often presented as undergirding ethno-national identities in a variety of Latin American contexts. To this point, M. Bianet Castellanos has noted, "Conceived as a nationalist whitening project rooted in hierarchical colonial race relations, *mestizaje* erases indigeneity by absorbing it into the body politic. At the same time, this concept is contingent on remembering ... the Indian. The Indian is continually hailed throughout Latin America as a way to assert national belonging and thus can never be fully absorbed into the nation" (778). Lorenzo Veracini also considers absorption in the context of settler colonialism. In his case, he contrasts absorption to assimilation: "The term 'assimilation' ... also means 'absorption': ... it is the settler body politic that needs to be able to absorb the indigenous people that have been transformed by assimilation (in some contexts, assimilation is referred to as 'incorporation', which confirms a bodily metaphor). But absorption and assimilation are not the same: one focuses on the settler entity, the other on the indigenous collective" (38). As both Bianet Castellanos and Veracini underscore, absorption is a paradoxical function in which Indigenous groups are paradoxically "incorporated" into the body politic of the nation. To think of Jewish presence in the Americas as a function of settler colonialism, I argue, may serve further to contest such "absorption" of difference into the body politic by disaggregating and reconceptualizing the parts that have been absorbed into homogeneous notions of mestizo national identities as a result of unexamined functions of settler colonialism throughout the Americas.

Metaphors of settler colonialism have also proven integral to critical discussions about decolonization and Indigenous studies. Eve Tuck and K. Wayne Yang have argued in a now very well-known article that "decolonization is not a metaphor." They discuss the metaphorization of Indigeneity that allows settler colonists to exculpate themselves from the stealing of Indigenous lands by absorbing the discourse of decolonization:

> Decolonization in a settler context is fraught because empire, settlement, and internal colony have no spatial separation. Each of these features of settler colonialism in the US context ... make it a site of contradictory decolonial desires. Decolonization as metaphor allows people to equivocate these contradictory decolonial desires because it turns decolonization into an empty signifier to be filled by any track towards liberation. (7)

Tuck and Yang's analysis of decolonization draws from an extensive reading of James Fenimore Cooper's series of novels that "fantasize the foundation and expansion of the US settler nation by fictionalizing the period of 1780–1804, distilled into the single narrative of one man" (15). In contrast, I focus on the ways in which Jewish voices metaphorize Indigenous figures as a way of connecting Jewish presence to settler colonialism, resisting such "distillation," to use Tuck and Yang's term.[8] Taking into account both allegorical and metaphorical depictions of

20   Absorption Narratives

identities while recognizing the limits and misappropriations inherent to these representations, Dean Franco takes up the question of how metaphor functions vis-à-vis Jewish and other groups' respective connections to the land. He notes, "If metaphorical identification is embedded in history as a raft of beliefs, practices, or folkways carried over though time, metonymical identity is more synchronic and more spatially determined" (15). Franco's model posits a relationship between synchronicity and metonymy, on the one hand, and diachronicity and metaphor on the other. To conclude his intervention, Franco advocates for a praxis of reading and neighbourly solidarity that melds metaphor and metonymy. In essence, his focus on metonymy and metaphor also has to do with speaking for the Other in microscopic recognitions of sameness and difference, as he notes through his reading of Levinas. Franco argues: "neighbors, for Levinas, remain neighbors precisely because of unassimilable difference. Levinas's neighbor is never part of a 'we,' and the ethics pertaining to his neighbor always open outward into the strangeness of the other. Put another way, Levinas sustains nearness, which implies an approach as well as a gap – simultaneity without sameness" (117). In the convergences and contiguities that Franco discusses in Los Angeles, engaging both metaphorical and metonymic possibilities makes way for interpretive models in which differences can coexist without being erased or absorbed.

Adjacency is particularly significant in thinking about metaphor and metonymy. The two tropes register different degrees of absorption: whereas metonymy suggests sameness on the basis of adjacency, still recognizing that the signifier and signified are adjacent to one another (i.e., separate), metaphor absorbs the boundary between the two altogether.[9] W.E.B. Du Bois's concept of the colour line sets up a metonymic model of oppression along racialized lines. Yet, the colour line becomes blurred for Du Bois in his reflections on Jews prompted by his visit to Warsaw. Seeing the persecution of Jews made him think about racialized oppression – specifically, slavery in the US – beyond the colour line in his 1952 essay "The Negro and the Warsaw Ghetto." Du Bois reflected, "the problem of slavery, emancipation, and caste in the U.S. was no longer in my mind a separate and unique thing as I had so long conceived it. It was not even solely a matter of color and physical and racial characteristics, which was particularly a hard thing for me to learn, since for a lifetime the color line had been a real and efficient cause of misery" (15). If the colour line is a metonymy ("the real and efficient cause of misery"), in light of Du Bois's account of how his visits to Warsaw changed his understanding of slavery in the US, bringing metonymy into conversation with other tropes and figures allows us to

Absorption Narratives 21

think through the relationship between Jewish oppression worldwide and the oppression of people of colour in the Americas specifically.[10] Put another way, the comparative and overlapping oppression of Jewish and Black people upon which Du Bois reflected after visiting the Warsaw ghetto problematizes the metonymic function of the colour line.

These literary tropes are used to contest representation by a speaker or author who vests themselves with the authority to speak on the Other's behalf. Yet literary imaginations of racial Others also explore how Jewish, Indigenous, and Black presence in the Americas occupies space and geography throughout the hemisphere. Recognizing the difficulties of analogizing discrete racial categories' lived experiences, I venture that Tuck and Yang's "decolonization is not a metaphor" finds conceptual affinity with the Boyarins' and Itzkovitz's rejections of allegories of Jewishness. These differing models have in common that they are diachronic, taking root in past generations while very much manifest in the present. Similarly, speaking through the voice of the Other is another way of acknowledging difference while absorbing it. I thus propose a praxis focused on the differential ways that voices speak for the Other so as to move past these absorptions of difference while acknowledging possibilities for affinity and identification.

In opposition to speaking for the Other, the importance of speaking for oneself as a subaltern subject has been explored, notably, in Gayatri Spivak's work. Spivak, drawing from Marx, parses out *vertreten*, "rhetoric as persuasion" and *darstellen*, "rhetoric as trope." In Spivak's reading of Marx, the distinction between rhetoric as persuasion and as trope is integral to the distinction between the individual and discursive representation within a social stratification. Spivak asserts, "The complicity of *Vertreten* and *Darstellen*, their identity-in-difference as the place of practice ... can only be appreciated if they are not conflated by a sleight of word" (72). Spivak emphasizes the particularities of rhetoric as trope in her broader argument distinguishing between "speaking for" others and "listening to" others, opting for a preferred praxis of "speaking to" others. In Spivak's reading of Marx, the use of tropes is fundamental to the phenomenon of self-representation in a stratified society, as I also identify here in fiction's depictions of categories of racial alterity.

Subaltern speech has been a subject of enquiry for scholarship that has sought to decolonize and emancipate Native American and Chicanx studies. Through a focus on the self-representation of speaking for oneself, ethnic studies scholar Arturo Aldama has advocated for a critical understanding of Chicanx and Native American identities focused on subjects' speech as a way of negotiating decolonial space. Aldama proposes, "By mapping the model of the subject-in-process to consider

22   Absorption Narratives

the enunciative powers of multiple, hybrid, mestiza, and Indigenous mixed-race subjects, the epistemic possibilities of the subject-in-process as an interpretive model can liberate our understanding of subaltern subjectivity and signifying acts of cultural and political productions" (33). Aldama's model pushes Kristeva's understanding of the speech act – fundamental to ventriloquism and to speaking for oneself – to further emancipatory possibilities through a focus on multiplicity in subaltern subjectivities. Focusing on these emancipatory possibilities, I explore how Black and Indigenous voices imagine Jewishness and vice versa as a way of forging alliances among multiply and differently oppressed communities throughout the Americas.

While speaking for oneself is obviously tied to identity, speaking for other racial groups has also been shown to be integral to group identities. Instances of speaking for racial others have been shown to be fundamental to Jewish self-understanding and to relationships between Jews and racial others in US literary productions from throughout the Americas. While the same phenomenon has not been explored in Latin American contexts, it nonetheless is an important element of cultural productions. In her book *Borrowed Voices*, Jennifer Glaser explores the phenomenon of US Jewish authors who have ventriloquized racial others. She wonders, "If speaking for another is often a form of silencing, how do we understand both the Jewish interest in acting as a mouthpiece for other racial and ethnic groups ... and Jewish writers' and artists' related interest in identifying with or understanding themselves as 'Jews' (a vexed identity category if there ever was one) through their relationship to other others?" (loc. 159). Similarly, in a Latin American context, Graff Zivin (*The Wandering Signifier*) has articulated a critical model of Jewishness as a "wandering signifier" that serves to take on different valences throughout history and across the Latin American region depending on the context. The elasticity with which Graff Zivin vests "Jew" as a signifier has particular meaning for the construction of racial categories in a variety of geographical contexts.[11] I bring Graff Zivin's notion of the wandering signifier into conversation with Daniel Itzkovitz's model of Jewish "racial chameleonism" in a US context to argue that Jewishness takes on different valences in a variety of geographical contexts throughout the Americas.

Latin American cultural studies are useful to consider for the analysis of Jewishness and race elsewhere in the Americas because Jewishness has always been a factor in hegemonic understandings of race in Latin America. The particular affinities and investments that Jewishness has towards Indigeneity and Blackness may be traced to the Spanish Conquest of the Americas and to the important role that racial mixture – mestizaje – played therein. Mestizaje has a particular relationship to both Jewishness and anti-Jewishness. The expulsion of the Jews from the Iberian Peninsula in 1492 and the beginning of the Spanish Conquest of the Americas during the same year, much more than mere temporal coincidence, are in fact part and parcel of one another and of Spanish attitudes that sought to perpetuate a hierarchy of Catholic white supremacy over other ethnoreligious groups. Thus, the categories that undergirded caste systems in Latin America are laden with the paradigms of *pureza de sangre* (blood purity) that provided the impetus for the expulsion of Jews from the Iberian Peninsula and that would later be integral to the Spanish Inquisition. Preoccupations with Jewishness have undergirded categories of racial difference in Latin America since the very inception of these categories. In this vein, historian María Elena Martínez's *Genealogical Fictions* "undermines the view ... that the problem of *limpieza de sangre* was primarily an Iberian preoccupation as well as the contention that it can be separated from that of race. Furthermore, it problematizes the conceptual division that the literature on race sometimes makes between colonial racism and anti-Semitism" (13). Martínez focuses specifically on the importance of narratives surrounding racial difference and their origins in Latin America through her emphasis on the term "genealogical fictions," which she glosses as "ideological constructs based on religious and genealogical understandings of difference that despite their invented nature were no less effective at shaping social practices, categories of identity, and self-perception" (61). Similarly, historian Ben Vinson notes that "the Iberian grade of inquest used to discern Christian background would not be replicated in Spanish America, since Jews and Moors were forbidden from traveling to Spain's colonies (though small numbers trickled through). Nevertheless, the ideas and principles that underwrote limpieza de sangre successfully made the journey across the Atlantic" (44). Vinson emphasizes the primacy in Iberia placed on not having any Jewish or Moorish ancestry and the legacy of this idea throughout the former Spanish Empire.

Thus, attitudes towards Jews and racial mixing became an organizing principle in the Conquest of the Americas. Just as Martínez and Vinson trace the construction of these "fictions" on which racial caste systems are predicated to the lack of Jewishness (the main tenet of Spanish blood purity), I show throughout my analysis of recent cultural productions that preoccupations with Jewishness (and with its absence) are shown to be integral to foundational understandings of racial difference throughout the Americas. Vinson cites an entry from the *Archivo General de la Nación* that notes that "in *this* kingdom, limpieza

24   Absorption Narratives

de sangre consists of not having any mixture of *castas* [castes]" (54, emphasis original). In this way, an emphasis on excising Jewishness, the organizing principle of Spain's understanding of limpieza de sangre, travelled to the New World and morphed into a model in which social capital was placed not only on being white per se but on the absence of racial mixture. Jewishness and racial mixture thus shared a similar marginality in Iberia and its colonies at this time. Yet, by the 1700s, Vinson notes, distinctions between *raza* (race) and *casta* became blurred as a result of "the reduced zeal in trying to excise Jewish and Islamic heresies, combined with the circulation of new racial ideas from other parts of Europe and the New World" (59). Racialized marginalization would come to characterize Jews and mixed-race individuals alike in the Spanish colonies.[12]

I am certainly not the first scholar to foreground limpieza de sangre as a historical paradigm through which to reach present-day Jewish racial identifications in an inter-American context. Melanie Kaye/Kantrowitz invokes the historical implications of limpieza de sangre to explore the question "Are Jews white?" in a US context. She notes, "The experience of the Sephardi *conversos*, whose difference came to be seen as more and more racial in their lack of *limpieze* [sic] *de sangre* despite their actual or pretended acceptance of Christianity, suggests the increasingly frenetic intertwining of racial and religious bigotry as the modern age unfolds" (13). While she does not focus much on Sephardim or the Spanish-speaking world, Kaye/Kantrowitz invokes the racialization of Sephardim that underscored the principle of limpieza de sangre in the Early Modern period as a way of conceptualizing Jewish racialization in contemporary US contexts. For Jonathan Freedman, the expulsion of Jews from the Iberian Peninsula in 1492 "saw the first emergence of [the assimilating Jew], challenging both the religious-based norms of established Jewish communities and the proto-racialism of the Spanish Crown who insisted on limpieza de sangre – purity of blood – as a sine qua non for social acceptance and privilege" (10). To be sure, my approach to Jewishness by no means assumes Jewish whiteness. Some of the works that I study here depict Jewish characters who do not present as white. Yet my main interest is not to question whether Jews are white, or even how white Jewishness comes into contact with other racial categories; rather, my interest is to foreground the ethnic and racial hybridity that is constitutive of the relationship between Jewishness and racial alterity.

Because of the importance of imperial notions of blood purity, the figures of the *marrano* and the *converso* have salient implications for racial identifications in Latin America and the Latinx diaspora. In his discussion of *Days of Awe* and *Spirits of the Ordinary* – two novels I study here – Jonathan Freedman argues, "the discourse on the nature and fate of conversos and Marranos, New Christians and crypto-Jews in the Americas is of further significance ... it's used, as the idiom and history of Jews and Jewishness so frequently are deployed, as a metonym for ethnic otherness itself, especially as that discourse attempts to distinguish between race and culture as determinants of identity" (216). For Freedman, the "idiom" of crypto-Jewishness that resulted from paradigms of blood purity takes on a metonymic function that connects narratives of passing (whether Black folks passing as white or Jews passing as gentiles) in ways that bring together Canadian, US, and Spanish American paradigms of race. As one discerns through the above examples that Kaye/Kantrowitz and Freedman provide, understandings of race and empire that undergirded the caste system throughout the Spanish viceroyalties were bound up in preoccupations of Jewishness. In this vein, they shed critical light on the ways in which Jewishness, Blackness, and Indigeneity come into contact with one another throughout the Americas. To do so is not only to bring together existing conversations on Jewishness, Blackness, and Indigeneity as separate categories but also to disentangle categories of particularity that have historically been absorbed by discourses on mestizaje.

The Sephardic Jews who were ousted from the Iberian Peninsula were ethnically and linguistically similar to Catholic Iberians and distinct from other Jewish groups, particularly Eastern European Ashkenazi Jews. Just as the paradigm of mestizaje has crucial implications for how we may approach the role of settler colonialism in Jewish life in the Americas, the same concept also takes on particular significance for critical understandings of Sephardism. While there are significant Sephardic presences in the US and Canada, Sephardism is itself an important category to bear in mind vis-à-vis ethno-religious paradigms that bear on Jewishness across the Americas, given the history of Sephardic immigration to the continent.

More than mere geographical overlap, Sephardic and mestizo histories in the Americas can never be fully extricated from one another insofar as the two categories mutually informed one another throughout the formation of Latin America and both are key components of the Iberian diaspora in the Americas. Dalia Kandiyoti explored this issue in her book chapter "Sephardism in Latina Literature," wherein she productively concludes that "thinking through *and* beyond comparison can help us reconstruct Latino/a and Jewish narratives by producing new elective and creative affinities informed by shared and overlapping Jewish and Latino destinies in the conflict zones of the Americas,

26 Absorption Narratives

rather than based on parallel-and-distinct participation in the American dream" (255). Responding to Kandiyoti's call, *Absorption Narratives* thinks "through and beyond comparison" in order to approach a more holistic understanding of how Jewishness, Indigeneity, and Blackness converge and diverge in the cultural imagination of the Americas. Rather than simply conceptualize how Otherness is imagined between and among groups, I focus on parallel, analogous conversations articulated along the lines of mutual (yet distinct) experiences of Othering, marginalization, and difference that may be accounted for in a way that also does justice to overlapping categories. To do so requires constant awareness that these overlaps are not merely the product of two categories coincidentally superimposed onto one another; rather, as Kandiyoti shows, they are indicative of an intersection that is itself the product of a long history of enmeshed ethno-religious identifications. To think "through *and* beyond comparison," I submit, requires recognizing and scrutinizing how different figures and tropes are used to talk about difference. My primary interest here is not in Sephardic literature per se (although I do analyse some texts that centre on Sephardic characters) but to point out that the importance of Sephardic culture that other scholars have noted begs for more comprehensive understandings of Iberian American racial paradigms as they relate to Jewish presence in the Americas.

Preoccupations of race and difference have long been at the fore of critical models of literature and cultural productions in Latin America and the Caribbean in ways that are valuable for considering inter-American models of race in literature. As I outline below, these discussions differ from critical accounts of race in the US in ways that have crucial implications for how we think about Jewishness vis-à-vis race.[13] Existing ideas of hybridity in the Caribbean have mapped out crucial critical paradigms of which I take account here. Cuban anthropologist Fernando Ortiz describes the tobacco plant and its process of transculturation that "necessarily involves the loss or uprooting of a previous culture" followed by "the consequent creation of new cultural phenomena" (103). Ortiz posits that this process leads ultimately to something akin to biological reproduction in which "the offspring always has something of both parents but is always different from each of them" (103). Stuart Hall engages Ortiz's model of transculturation in his discussion of Creolization processes in the Caribbean, the Americas, and throughout the world. Hall contemplates Edouard Glissant's assertion that "the whole world is becoming Creolized" and disclaims that Glissant is speaking metonymically rather than metaphorically in saying so. This characterization delineates different types of mixture (*créolité*)

Absorption Narratives 27

based on geographical locations – the Francophone Caribbean, the Americas, and Europe. Hall asks whether the concept of "créolité" can be applied to any form of cultural mixture or whether it is specific to the French Caribbean – paying particular attention to the role of "America" (in the sense both of the US and of the Americas). In so doing, he takes account of créolité's specificity to the French Caribbean both in its original meaning of linguistic hybridity and in its use to refer to racial hybridity. This relationship between linguistic mixture and racial mixture – namely, the distinct implications of speaking metonymically versus metaphorically – is a vital element of speaking for the racial Other. Hall's distinctions between rhetorical forms show specific tropes to cleave to different relationships to margin and periphery as racial and cultural groups converge in various contact zones.

The metaphor of transculturation has also been taken up to theorize Jewishness and Blackness in the Caribbean. Stephen Silverstein takes interest in Ortiz's model, specifically his metaphor of the Caribbean stew known as *ajiaco*, to talk about the coexistence of Jews and Afro-Cubans. Silverstein submits, "it was in this *ajiaco* of entangled anxieties, exclusions, and desires that Cuban anti-Semitism and Negrophobia came to flavor one another" (5). Ortiz introduces his neologism *transculturación* drawing from Polish Jewish anthropologist Branislow Malinowski's model of acculturation. The Cuban author is even sure to stipulate in his description of his new term that Malinowski – in his "unimpeachable authority" – instantly approved of Ortiz's term (1995, 103). Venezuelan anthropologist Fernando Coronil's introduction to the English translation of *Cuban Counterpoint* characterizes Ortiz's first chapter as a "utopian allegory" (à la Jameson, in Coronil's view) through which "Ortiz envisioned national unity attained by the making the productive relations established under colonialism the basis of Cuban culture" (xxiv).[14] For Coronil, Ortiz's "suggestion of utopian allegory" is nuanced by his subsequent articulation of transculturation. Thus, in Coronil's reading of Ortiz, if allegory absorbs difference, transculturation is a model of identities that accounts for hybridity that still retains difference.

Drawing from Ortiz's genealogy of transculturation, Uruguayan literary critic Ángel Rama considered how this type of hybridity has informed literature and national identities in Latin America in his iconic 1982 book *Transculturación narrativa en América latina*, (English title: *Writing across Cultures: Narrative Transculturation in Latin America*). Specifically, Rama outlines how appropriation of the figures of Black and Indigenous people came to undergird national identity through literary productions. Rama posited that "Latin American letters fanned the demagogic zeal of the *criollos* ... who repeatedly called on a pair of themes – the destitute Indian, the cruelly punished black slave – as pretexts to justify their own bill of grievances against the colonizers" (2012, 4). This absorption of Indigenous and Black plight would become integral to the emergence and flourishing of Latin American letters whose originality, as Rama argues, was predicated on "literature's ability to represent the region that gave rise to it" (5). That is, Latin American cultural productions coalesced around a logic of writing the nation – an endeavour that necessarily centred the figures of the "destitute Indian" and "cruelly punished black slave" as ways of creating national and regional identities that contested Spanish imperialism. In this way, Jewish authors' engagement with these racial categories is part of a broader trajectory of Latin American culture. To read Jewish investment with Black and Indigenous identities in literary productions throughout the Americas thus serves to think further about how race figures into literary traditions and cultural identities throughout the Americas.

Furthering Rama's model, critic Antonio Cornejo Polar explored transculturation as a theoretical lens through which to understand mestizo literature. Cornejo Polar submitted, "Transculturation would imply, in the long run, the construction of a syncretic plane that finally incorporates in a more or less unproblematical [sic] totality (in spite of the conflictive character of the process) two or more languages, two or more ethnic identities, two or more aesthetic codes and historical experiences" (117). Cornejo Polar takes issue with this notion of the "unproblematical [sic] totality" and concludes that in order to theorize mestizo literature, conceptual approaches that de-emphasize syncretic functions are necessary. To achieve such approaches, Cornejo-Polar turns to Bakhtinian dialogism. Cornejo-Polar disputes syncretism because of its capacity as a hegemonizing force, noting that a focus on dialogism may help to resist such a force. Dialogism in literature allows us to disentangle some of what becomes subsumed by cultural understandings of racial hybridity. Furthermore, the dialogism for which Cornejo-Polar calls also dovetails with existing critical models of US Jewish fiction's ventriloquism of Black and Indigenous voices. A focus on hybridity in speech acts serves to disaggregate an "unproblematized" understanding of Indigeneity and racial mixing.

Ideas of racial mixture in the Americas are often complicated by the legacies of chattel slavery, the Holocaust, and Native American genocide, issues often manifest in literary studies of these respective groups. An abundance of fraught attempts to analogize or to quantify Jewish, Indigenous, and Black experiences of genocide have, at times, provided a point of departure for thinking through relationships among these groups.[15] Studying Jewishness alongside Blackness and Indigeneity almost necessarily evokes a plethora of analogies. A useful framework to contextualize Holocaust analogies is Zygmunt Bauman's term of the Holocaust's "normality and uniqueness." For Bauman, "The *possibility* of the Holocaust was rooted in certain universal features of modern civilization; its *implementation* on the other hand, was connected with a specific and not at all universal relationship between state and society" (82). This combination of normality and uniqueness, of the universality of possibility and the specificity of implementation, can be observed to varying degrees in virtually all instances of oppression along racialized lines. Collective relationships to space create different theatres of oppression that converge and diverge over time to define racialized experiences throughout the Americas. Within these spaces, voices imagine their own place vis-à-vis the Other in the present and in relation to their nations' and communities' histories.

Comparisons between the Atlantic slave trade and the Holocaust led Michael Rothberg to introduce the productive concept of "competitive memory." Rothberg (2009) describes this phenomenon in the following terms: "many people assume that the public sphere in which collective memories are articulated is a scarce resource and that the interaction of different collective memories within that sphere takes the form a zero-sum struggle for preeminence" (2–3). As a way of moving past "competitive memory," Rothberg introduces the possibility of "multidirectional memory": "Far from being situated – either physically or discursively – in any single institution or site, the archive of multidirectional memory is irrevocably transversal; it cuts across genres, national contexts, periods, and cultural traditions" (18). Whereas Rothberg focuses primarily on the multidirectionality between Europe and North America, with some discussions of Africa, I propose to think about memory's movement throughout Latin America to continue Rothberg's endeavour on the basis of "shared histories of racism, spatial segregation, genocide, diasporic displacement, cultural destruction, and – perhaps most importantly – savvy and creative resistance to hegemonic demands" (23). I take multidirectional memory to be characterized by the convergence of a polyphony of voices and a variety of figurative tropes to imagine and represent alterity in literature as well as in audiovisual narrative forms. My approach to multidirectional memory foregrounds the chiastic relationship between race and geographical origins.

The convergence and divergence among Indigenous, Black, and Jewish experiences in the Americas has everything to do with each group's experiences with dispossession of land. In Spanish, the term "destierro"

30 Absorption Narratives

means both exile (which can also be communicated through the English cognate "exilio") and displacement. "Destierro" – which translates to English literally as "dis-landing" – denotes similarity between Indigenous people ousted from their lands, exiled Jews, and Africans taken from their lands to be brought as enslaved people to the Americas. Yomaira Figueroa argues that "destierro is a term that can capture the complex and multiple forms of dispossession and impossibilities of home for Afro and Indigenous descended peoples in the modern world. Thinking about and through destierro enables us to push decolonial thought further toward liberatory practices, and map different forms of dispossession and resistance across intersecting identities" (5). In keeping with Figueroa's focus on destierro as a decolonizing tool, I propose here – and expand further in my reading of Obejas's novel in chapter 4 – that we may acknowledge the shared exilic and diasporic conditions that have characterized Jewish, Black, and Indigenous experiences in the Americas in a way that does not efface racial and class differences. The uprooting or destierro that Jewish, Black, and Indigenous peoples all experienced (in different ways and at different points over the course of the history of the Americas) continues to characterize their respective relations to the land and to national belonging. Like Ortiz puts forth in his schema of transculturation, this destierro brings about the mixture of these groups' identities with those of others, creating new ethnoreligious hybridity. Nonetheless, the particularities of Jewish presence in the Americas must also be taken into account within the framework of white settler colonialism, even if this presence has come about through being exiled.[16]

Because of the pervasiveness of exile, Jewish experiences with a lack of belonging come to inform – at times even define – Jewish presence in the Americas. Exile, for Jews, often comes to connote a lack of belonging in a variety of circumstances. Within this framework, Jewish presence in the Americas and the notions of a lack of belonging therein can be fraught with a possible wilful self-separation on the basis of racialized difference. Similarly, Estelle Tarica argues in her discussion of Leo Spitzer's *Hotel Bolivia* that the sense of social alienation on the part of Jewish refugees living among Indigenous Bolivians was "a dearly held belief, one that their time in Bolivia appeared to strengthen rather than mitigate" (20).[17] Tarica relates this tendency to hold onto Jewish feelings of not belonging to resistance strategies forged in the context of Holocaust persecution. She notes, "But Spitzer takes his account a step further, not only describing but also justifying the refugees' Eurocentric beliefs. He argues that these were part of a creative – perhaps even laudable – response to the difficulties of their situation against the backdrop of the Holocaust, a sign of Jewish resistance to extermination" (20). This characterization of Spitzer's Eurocentrism prefigures Figueroa's discussion of exile as bourgeois and colonialist. Here, the conflicting vulnerabilities of different ethnic groups in the Americas come into sharper relief against one another. The relationship among marginalized groups, the geographical places where their repression was codified, and the lands where they currently find themselves creates a variegated matrix of identity and belonging (or lack thereof). Tarica's position that Jewish feelings of not belonging are "dearly held" in Latin America also connects with Jennifer Glaser's point about the advent of Jewish ventriloquism of racial others prompted by Jews' loss of their own othered status. Glaser refers to "the culture wars of the 1980s and 1990s, when Jewish American writers contended with their increasingly canonical status alongside the perceived whitening of an identity that just a few decades earlier had been distinctly other" (loc. 376). I would venture that the Jewish feelings of not belonging that Tarica points out prompt similar anxieties – decades later and in a different geographical context – to speak through the voices of racial others that Glaser points out. In Spitzer's case, the encounter with Indigenous Bolivians, a group that is Othered, prompts a similar questioning of Jewish alterity.

In the geographical context of the US–Mexico border, we find further instances in which displacement is racialized. Gloria Anzaldúa focuses on the ways in which destierro is racialized in her iconic text *La frontera/Borderlands*. She considers the destierro that occurred in the Mexican–American war to think about racial mixture so as to resist the hegemonic and racial supremacist narratives of mestizaje and to place embodied identities at the fore of conversations of the body politic. Anzaldúa notes, "The Gringo, locked into the fiction of white superiority, seized complete political power, stripping Indians and Mexicans of their land while their feet were still rooted in it. *Con el destierro y el exilio fuimos desuñados, destroncados, destripados* – we were jerked out by the roots, truncated, disembodied, dispossessed, and separated from our identity and our history" (7–8).[18] Anzaldúa connects destierro to "the fiction of white superiority" and explores the ways in which the uprooting of Indians and Mexicans robbed these populations of their identities. Anzaldúa is tacitly writing against José Vasconcelos's model of the cosmic race, in which Jewishness is absorbed into the mestizo ideal. In his essay, Vasconcelos eschews the particularity of difference that makes up the cosmic race. For Vasconcelos, "Judaic striae can be seen that have hidden themselves in Castilian blood since the days of the cruel expulsion; the Arab's melancholies are a trace of the sickly

32   Absorption Narratives

Muslim sensuality; who among us doesn't have some of all of that or doesn't desire to have it?" (17). Vasconcelos takes Jewishness into account but that does so in a way that does not recognize or allow for Jewish difference, as Vasconcelos also does with other categories of ethnic difference.

We thus observe the need to make space for Jewish difference in cultural models, such as Vasconcelos's cosmic race (as Anzaldúa has done). Anzaldúa advocates for a model of mestizaje that is quite different from that put forth by Vasconcelos. As Theresa Delgadillo has noted, "Although *Borderlands* invokes José Vasconcelos's notion of the cosmic race, of the *mestizo* as the ultimate and desired racial subject, a mixture of all races, Anzaldúa's theory of a mestiza consciousness does not suggest a positivistic fusion nor the 'eventual hybrid homogeneity' brought about by 'generalized miscegenation'" (12). For Delgadillo – and Anzaldúa – mestizaje is a generative framework in which to conceptualize race so long as one avoids the impulse towards homogeneity that undergirds ideas such as Vasconcelos's model of the cosmic race. Similarly, Diana Taylor's 2003 *The Archive and the Repertoire* also advocates a critical approach to mestizaje that does not reproduce Vasconcelos's model as a way of furthering our understanding of cultural memory: "Rather than turn to the language of blood and heredity that theorists such as Vasconcelos used in the 1920s, we would need to think about memory, ethnicity, and gender in terms of the double-codedness of linguistic, epistemic, and embodied practices associated with mestizaje" (88). *Absorption Narratives* draws from Delgadillo's and Taylor's delineation between Vasconcelos's and Anzaldúa's models of mestizaje predicated on homogeneity and heterogeneity, respectively, by paying close attention to the role of Jewishness in racial mixture throughout the Americas.[19]

It is not a coincidence that Anzaldúa's emphasis is on the feminine "mestiza" consciousness. Gender is integral to conceptualizing race and spirituality in radical ways. In many of the works that I discuss here, sexuality plays a pervasive role as characters grapple with their encounters with racial alterity and as they forge an understanding of their own identity. Even in works in which sexuality is not explicitly treated, sexual and romantic relationships between individuals from distinct categories are nonetheless presented as paradigms of encounters between groups and the convergence of different experiences. Moreover, gender categories are shown to bear indelibly on the processes through which characters identify or do not identify with the religious and spiritual groups with which they come into contact. Gender and spirituality are inexorable from one another; Judaism, Christianity, and Indigenous religions all avow specific rites and beliefs to which gender is integral. The aforementioned Virgen del Cobre and Virgen de Guadalupe are but two examples of how Catholic Marianism has come to undergird syncretic spiritualities throughout the Americas. In recent years, gender has been shown to be specifically salient when it comes to such issues as Black Catholic masculinities and Jewish sexual orientations. Eve Kosofsky Sedgwick's foundational *Epistemology of the Closet* discusses Queen Esther's coming out as Jewish to her husband in relation to coming out as queer. Sedgwick concludes that "male and female gay identity have crossed and recrossed the definitional lines of gender identity with such disruptive frequency that the concepts 'minority' and 'gender' themselves have lost a great deal of their categorizing (though certainly not of their performative) force" (82). Taking cues from Sedgwick and from Anzaldúa, gender and sexuality are woven throughout my readings of these texts in ways that further underscore the fluidity of identities.

Bringing together these ideas of how spirituality, race, and ethnicity converge, chapter 2, "There's No Jews on the Reservation," discusses Indigenous and Jewish portrayals of one another, focusing both on the affinities and the points of divergence between Jewishness and Indigeneity in Eduardo Halfon's *Mañana nunca lo hablamos* (*Tomorrow We Never Did Talk About It*), Victor Perera's *Rites: A Guatemalan Boyhood*, Kathleen Alcalá's *Spirits of the Ordinary*, and Louise Erdrich's *The Master Butchers Singing Club*. In my discussions of these works, I focus on how Jewish and Indigenous voices imagine one another as ways of reckoning with national identities and belonging. While there are ways in which discourses surrounding Jewishness vis-à-vis other ethnic categories diverge between Latin America and the US, settler colonialism offers a framework through which to explore the commonalities of Jewish–Indigenous encounters throughout the Americas. David S. Koffman has noted that the framework of settler colonialism destabilizes the "celebratory narrative" that underwrites many critical and popular conceptualizations of the Jewish presence in the US. Recent critical studies have begun to discuss settler colonialism in Latin American as a way of upsetting the ways in which mestizaje has often been understood in Latin American racial paradigms (Castellanos, "Introduction"). I further these lines of enquiry so as to reconceptualize the relationship between Jewish presence and mestizaje, a conceptual relationship that is further bolstered by my focus on syncretism.

Chapter 3 focuses on novels that depict hybridity between Indigenous, mestizo, and/or Jewish identities. I take into account both assimilation and the preservation of difference within these experiences

34 Absorption Narratives

in my discussions of Michael Chabon's *The Yiddish Policemen's Union*, Francisco Goldman's *The Long Night of White Chickens*, Gerald Vizenor's *The Heirs of Columbus*, and Mordecai Richler's *Solomon Gursky Was Here*. The hybridity of ethnicities and religious beliefs that characterizes syncretism comes into its sharpest relief in this chapter. Goldman's novel, for example, includes a reflection on behalf of its character Flor de Mayo about what she – an Indigenous Guatemalan woman raised in Boston by a Jewish man and a *Ladina* woman – has "absorbed" from the Maya: "So OK, Guatemala, in what we like to think of as its deepest self, is Mayan. We, who aren't actually Indian, what is it we absorb? Not that supposed Indian lack of egocentrism, that community and cosmos first stuff, that's for sure" (242). Flor's self-definition as "not actually Indian" and her lamentation that non-Mayas haven't "absorbed" the spiritual aspects ("lack of egocentrism" and "community and cosmos first") underscore the ways in which spirituality and ethnicity inform models of racial mixture in ways that prompt Jewish Guatemalans to reflect on these models. For his part, the same novel's narrator, Roger, has been described by critics as "confused about his identity to a degree that encourages him to live vicariously through others" (Gräbner, "But How to Speak" 55). This characterization resonates with Glaser's US-based model of "borrowed voices" and with Graff Zivin's model of the "wandering signifier" in Latin American Jewish fiction. I focus on the multiplicity of ways in which subjects come to understand themselves as ethnically and spiritually hybrid.

The fourth chapter focuses on hybridity between Blackness and Jewishness in Philip Roth's *The Human Stain*, Achy Obejas's *Days of Awe*, and Clarice Lispector's "The Smallest Woman in the World." I introduce Lispector's 1960 short story as a way to think about how the Jewish author imagined middle-class, urban responses to the image of a diminutive Black woman "discovered" in Africa by a European explorer. Roth's novel somewhat infamously has its African American protagonist pass as Jewish after returning from World War II and enjoy a life of success on the basis of the privilege of passing as Jewish rather than African American, only to be foiled late in life by 1990s campus political correctness when a comment he makes is interpreted as an anti-Black slur. Obejas's acclaimed novel recounts its Cuban-born narrator's process of learning about her family's crypto-Jewish roots as she comes into contact with racial alterity in the US and in her country of birth and considers whether her family is "inevitable Jews" in dialogue with anthropologist Ruth Behar's autobiographical documentary *Adió, Kerida* in which she describes her Jewish family's presence in Cuba as an "accident of racism." I argue that, taken together, these works offer meaningful reflections on the place of Jewishness within considerations of racial politics in social and academic registers.

The fifth chapter discusses the convergence of Blackness and Jewishness in urban spaces throughout the Americas as depicted in novel, film, and theatre. My approach to Jewish–Black relations in the US and Latin America destabilizes understandings of the topic through a comparative, transnational perspective. Works discussed in this chapter include Cao Hamburger's *The Year My Parents Went on Vacation*, Anna Deavere Smith's *Fires in the Mirror*, and Michael Chabon's *Telegraph Avenue*. Drawing from conversations about divergence and convergence between Black and Jewish communities, the chapter focuses on negotiations between the two in urban spaces in the US and Brazil. Hamburger's film explores Jewishness and so-called *futebol mulato* in São Paulo's Bom Retiro neighbourhood. Smith's *Fires in the Mirror* is a one-woman play prompted by the debates and tensions between Black and Jewish communities in the US following the 1991 Crown Heights riots; a November 2019 off-Broadway production of the play (over twenty-five years after it was written) was reviewed in *The New York Times* as "the most compelling and sophisticated view of racial and class conflict that one could hope to encounter." For its part, *Telegraph Avenue* – set in a record store on the homonymous artery that divides Berkeley from Oakland – focuses on the friendship between the store's Jewish and Black co-owners. The contradictions between convergence and divergence call for a critical exploration of how Jewishness and Blackness come into contact with one another in urban spaces throughout the Americas.

Finally, the sixth chapter furthers the previous chapter's focus on urban spaces to analyse queer rites of passage in Latinx and Jewish contexts in Los Angeles as depicted in recent television programs *Transparent* and *One Day at a Time* and the documentary *East LA Interchange*. In summer 2018, a kosher deli in Los Angeles's Boyle Heights neighbourhood was boycotted over the owner's xenophobia towards Latinx populations. Responses to the case highlighted the neighbourhood's welcoming of Jewish immigrants in the 1930s and the expectation that the Jewish community extend the same hospitality towards other immigrant and minority groups. Similarly, in her 2016 documentary, *East LA Interchange*, director Betsy Kalin includes accounts from community members who assert that the Jewish community in Boyle Heights avowed strong support for Latinx civil rights in the 1960s as an expression of affinity and solidarity. Such stories are certainly not limited to the Boyle Heights neighbourhood; many urban spaces boast histories of various immigrant groups' having occupied them at different times. Boyle Heights has featured in recent cultural depictions of Jews through

36   Absorption Narratives

the popular series *Transparent*. Although the series does not seize on the opportunity to engage with the present-day Latinx inhabitants of the neighbourhood, we nonetheless observe depictions of assimilation and identity negotiations on behalf of queer Jews in a way that dovetails with recent media depictions of queer Latinx experiences. The Netflix reboot of *One Day at a Time*, set nearby in Los Angeles's Echo Park neighbourhood, depicts queer Cuban coming-of-age stories in a way wholly similar to *Transparent*'s treatment of queer coming-of-age in a Jewish setting. These programs focus on gendered rites of passages – the Latinx *quinceañera* and the Jewish *bat mitzvah* – in a way that shows queer identifications and ethnicities sitting uncomfortably with one another among second-generation queer adolescents.

To conclude, I briefly discuss a short story, "Sabra" (1994), by Chicana author Luz Alma Villanueva, and a recent film, *You People* (2023), that, as I show, suggest possible models for understanding race and memory in the Americas. These possibilities, in keeping with the works I discuss throughout this monograph, in many ways further complicate – rather than resolve – the complexities of the points of convergence between Jewishness, Blackness, and Indigeneity. Yet it is through fiction that continually revisits and further interrogates these contact zones, I argue, that we glean some understanding of how race and memory converge in the various nations that make up the Americas.

2 "There's No Jews on the Reservation": Jewish–Indigenous Encounters in Fiction of the Americas

On Monday nights in the early 1990s, CBS aired *Northern Exposure*, in which recent medical school graduate Joel Fleischman was the lower forty-eight Everyman – an unmistakably Jewish Everyman – among Native Americans in Alaska. The contrasts between him and the Native Americans come into clearest relief in the show's Thanksgiving episode from the fourth season (1992). Aired during the year that marked the five-hundredth anniversary of Columbus's arrival in the New World, the Thanksgiving episode begins with Joel Fleischman commenting that he loves Thanksgiving because "it's the only holiday that's for everyone. There's no theological strings attached. Christians, Muslims, Jews" (*Northern Exposure*, "Thanksgiving," season 4, ep. 8). He is greeted by half Native American Ed, who pelts him with a tomato. Bemused and irate as he tries to clean the tomato stains from his shirt once inside his medical office, Joel comments to his receptionist Marilyn, who is Native American, that he does not understand why Ed would do such a thing, and Marilyn responds that Native Americans have a lot of anger towards white people because it is Thanksgiving. From Joel's perspective, he is not white (and is, as he avows, "an innocent bystander") because his people have faced oppression. As a Jew in the US, he loves the holiday because, unlike Christian holidays, it is "for everyone." His claim denies the reality of this holiday for Native Americans. He seeks Marilyn's empathy as a fellow member of an oppressed group by insisting that "the Cossacks would ride through regularly" when his ancestors lived on the shtetl. This utterance in Alaska in the days leading up to Thanksgiving in the year commemorating the five-hundredth anniversary of Columbus's arrival to the Americas negates the importance of place.[1] Fleischman's characterization of Thanksgiving and shared oppression absorbs the differences between himself and Marilyn in an imprecise analogy between the oppression

38 Absorption Narratives

against his ancestors in the shtetl and the oppression of Native Americans, an analogy that he (wrongly, comically) interprets to mean that he is "a fellow person of color."[2]

The same year, Jonathan Boyarin took up this very question of analogizing Jewish and Native American experiences in Europe and North America, respectively. He asked in his 1992 article "Europe's Indian, America's Jew," "to what extent can we consider the Jew in Europe as analogous to the Indian in the Americas?" (197). Boyarin notes that asking this question "would cancel out the specifics of each term in both matched pairs on either side of the double colon" (197). Because of the limits of the premise of the analogy, Boyarin wonders instead, "To what extent have Jews fulfilled the same function for the imagination of Europe as Indians have in the invention of America?" (197). Furthering Boyarin's rejection of an attempt to analogize Jewish experiences in Europe to those of Native Americans in the Americas, I argue for a chiastic approach to Jewish–Indigenous encounters in the Americas, an approach that does not analogize Indigenous peoples' experiences in the Americas to those of Jews in Europe. A chiastic approach foregrounds the ways in which these distinct experiences – in specific geographic locales and based on ethnic particularities – necessarily inform encounters between these two groups. Mexican anthropologist Claudio Lomnitz, raised in Peru, also recently contemplated the possibilities for analogizing Jews in Europe to Indigenous people in Peru in his academic memoir *Nuestra América*. Lomnitz cogently argued that any attempt to analogize Jewish and Indigenous experiences is vexed by differing possibilities for passing and assimilating. Lomnitz posited, "*Las posibilidades del disimulo para el indio en el Perú estaban sujetas a restricciones que se parecían más a las del judío en Rumania, donde era bien complicada la asimilación, que a las del judío en que se podía confundir con un europeo cualquiera*" ("The options for dissembling for the Peruvian Indian were subject to restrictions that more closely mirrored those imposed on Jews in Romania, where assimilation was quite complicated, than those imposed on the Jew who could be confused with any other European," my translation; 103). Lomnitz thus delineates contexts in which being Jewish in Europe was and was not like being Indigenous in South America based on the specific temporal and geographical contexts that have (not) allowed for assimilation. These contextual specifics mean that analogies necessarily do not work.

Also in a Peruvian context, novelist and 2010 Nobel Prize laureate Mario Vargas Llosa explored Jewish absorption of Indigeneity in the Amazons in his 1987 novel *El hablador* (*The Storyteller*). Vargas Llosa identifies neither as Jewish nor as Indigenous Amazonian; for this reason,

I do not dedicate great length to his exploration of Jewish–Indigenous encounters. *The Storyteller*'s Jewish protagonist (and sometimes narrator), Saúl Zuratas, goes to live among the Machiguenga tribe in the Peruvian Amazons and becomes a storyteller among them under the name Mascarita. Vargas Llosa's novel employs a narrative structure in which the main narrator (an alter ego of Vargas Llosa himself) narrates some chapters from Europe while others are voiced through Saúl/Mascarita. The narrator speculates, as a way of concluding his story, about how Saúl became a storyteller among the Machiguenga: "I believe that his identification with this small, marginal, nomadic community had ... something to do with the fact that he was Jewish, a member of another community which had also been a wandering, marginal one throughout its history, a pariah among the world's societies, like the Machiguengas in Peru" (159). Susan Antebi interprets this speculation on the narrator's behalf: "It is the insistence on Saúl's fascination with the Machiguengas, rather than textual references to his family roots and his [Jewish] father's beliefs, that most clearly marks him as Jewish" (274). Put another way, in *The Storyteller*, fascination with Indigeneity is so closely associated with Jewishness that this fascination connotes Jewishness. In the Amazon, Jewish Saúl becomes the storyteller, a mouthpiece for an Indigenous group, while the novel's principal narrator recounts the story to readers from Europe. Vargas Llosa thus creates a multilayered narrative through which metropole and periphery, Jewishness and Indigeneity are explored in relation to one another.

Encounters between Indigenous peoples and Jews throughout the Americas tell stories of a common condition of marginalization and nomadism, yet the two groups are shown to inhabit separate, almost parallel, worlds. In the novels I discuss in this chapter, these worlds converge in unexpected ways (for their characters as well as for us as readers) that show Jewishness and Indigeneity as reliefs of one another. This relationship further complicates a simple, analogized model, articulating a chiastic paradigm of Indigenous–Jewish relations in the Americas. For the crypto-Jewish protagonist of Kathleen Alcalá's *Spirits of the Ordinary*, the wandering and secrecy of crypto-Judaism defines serves as a point of identification with the Indigenous peoples he encounters in northern Mexico. *The Master Butchers Singing Club* is non–Jewish Native American German author Louise Erdrich's fictional account of the child of a World War I soldier who immigrates to the US and reimagines her own German grandfather as a secret Jew, borrowing from tropes of crypto-Judaism as she also tells of Jewish involvement in settler colonialism. In *Rites: A Guatemalan Boyhood* and *Tomorrow We*

40   Absorption Narratives

Never Did Talk About It, respectively, Guatemalan-born Jewish authors Victor Perera and Eduardo Halfon create largely autobiographical (and autofictional) accounts of their childhood years in Guatemala – Perera in the 1940s and 1950s and Halfon in the 1970s – in ways that emphasize their outsider status, often in relation to other categories of marginalization, particularly Indigenous characters. As I underscore in my readings of these four novels, Jewish and Indigenous wandering and lack of belonging are presented as a chiasmus – rather than as analogies or mirror images – because of the reality of settler colonialism.

To be sure, experiences of displacement and dispossession are bound up in particularities of privilege and belonging that shift over time. In the case of Jewish presence in the Americas outside of urban centres, the recent past of pogroms and Holocaust or the much more distant experience of the Inquisition and expulsion from the Iberian Peninsula bear on Jewish encounters with Indigenous groups in the Americas. As Estelle Tarica has noted of Leo Spitzer's *Hotel Bolivia* – in which she shows that Jewish sense of being out of place in Bolivia was a "dearly held belief," as I discussed in the introduction – even an acknowledgment of Jewish racism in Bolivia may still ultimately serve to entrench further this distinct otherness. Tarica submits that, "despite the fact that he himself is highly critical of the racist strands of Jewish culture in Bolivia, he participates in the construction of Bolivia as an alien, unknown and ultimately impenetrable place to which it would be difficult, if not impossible, for a middle-European Jewish refugee to belong" (20). Yet Tarica develops a praxis of reading Spitzer that convincingly argues that Jewish racism is not the only interpretation of Jewish experience in Bolivia by questioning what Spitzer leaves out through his focus on Bolivia as a place of Jewish transience, determined a priori by his emphasis on Bolivia as a "hotel" rather than a "home." Likewise, in my following readings of Jewish accounts of their experiences among Indigenous peoples and of Indigenous peoples' accounts of Jews in Mexican, Guatemalan, and US contexts, I focus on ways in which authors reject or embrace the foregone conclusion of Jewish alterity and alienness vis-à-vis Indigenous populations in the Americas.

My focus on Jewish encounters with Indigeneity throughout the Americas furthers two key recent trends in scholarship: first, the growing work on settler colonialism in Latin America and, second, settler colonialism as a conceptual framework to account for Jewish presence in the Americas. M. Bianet Castellanos's recent call to conceptualize Indigeneity in Latin America in line with settler colonialism acknowledges that "the Indian is continually hailed throughout Latin America as a way to assert national belonging and thus can never be fully

"There's No Jews on the Reservation"   41

absorbed into the nation, even in the Southern Cone, where the push to-ward racial homogenization led to the mass elimination of Indigenous communities" (778). For Bianet Castellanos, the focus – both critical and popular – placed on mestizaje in Latin America eschews this very real way in which, because of a framework of coloniality predicated on settler colonialism, Indigenous figures are hailed as a way for non-Indigenous individuals and groups to claim national belonging. Bianet Castellanos focuses on the extent to which Indigenous people are never "fully absorbed" precisely because they are hailed as an icon of national belonging. In some cases, Jewish immigrants (and their children and grandchildren) to nations throughout the Americas, in an attempt to assimilate into the mainstream of the nation, have found in Indigenous people a way of claiming national identity and thus become absorbed into mainstream whiteness. This paradox of absorption creates a chiastic model between Jewishness and Indigeneity in encounters between the two groups.

Speaking to this relationship of Jewish involvement in settler colonialism, David Koffman has argued, "Settler colonialism offered a range of opportunities for Jews. Immigrant Jews transformed themselves into pioneer Jews through their interactions among Native Americans and whites vis-à-vis Indians and by subsequently writing about these interactions, memorializing them, and eventually canonizing them in local Jewish history" (*The Jews' Indian* 25). As Koffman goes on to underscore, Jewish immigrants to the US were settlers, like other white inhabitants of rural parts of the US, because they envisioned and imagined the frontier and their place in it. Jewish fascination with Indigeneity thus both informed the Jewish imaginary of the Americas before immigrating and continued to characterize many Jews' understanding of place long after their arrival. It is because of this phenomenon that Indigenous people, such as the characters in *Northern Exposure*, would throw tomatoes at Joel Fleischman "because he is white." He is white, from their perspective, not because of his skin but because of his complicity in settler colonialism.

"Why Guatemala?" *Rites: A Guatemalan Boyhood*

Rites emphasizes its Jewish narrator's status as an outsider in his native country. As the subtitle "A Guatemalan Boyhood" suggests, Perera and his narrator both spent only their childhood years in Guatemala before immigrating to the US. His parents were also immigrants to Guatemala, so that being Guatemalan was more of a temporary condition than a permanent characteristic for Perera. Nonetheless, the political

42 Absorption Narratives

climate and racial landscape of the nation bear indelibly on the narrator's self-understanding. Notably, the author writes in English for an English-speaking audience. Alastair Reid, on the back cover of *Rites*, notes that "Victor Perera is one of those rare writers who need never suffer the uncertainties of translation, for besides his fluency in both English and Spanish, he has both a Latin American and a North American sensibility. *Rites* is another fine example of how affectingly he can cross from one to the other, bringing all his insights with him." Perera's ability to move from one context – linguistic or geographical – to another speaks to a cosmopolitanism that is a function of, on the one hand, privilege and, on the other, an uneasy lack of belonging that affects his presence in various places around the world. Throughout the novel, set predominantly in the 1940s and 1950s, Perera's fictionalized account of his childhood years in Guatemala seems to acknowledge that his lack of belonging – while difficult to navigate as a child – was also a function of privilege. *Rites* emphasizes the racial differences between its Sephardic protagonist and Indigenous Guatemalans as a way of reflecting on national belonging.

While the political happenings of the 1940s and 1950s in Guatemala are crucial to orient narrator Jaime's coming-of-age, Perera himself has noted that, once he returned to Guatemala in the 1980s, the harsh political realities – specifically the violence against Indigenous people – were new and foreign to him. In his memoir *The Cross and the Pear Tree*, Perera compares the nation in which he grew up to political realities he had observed in Europe and India:

> Nothing in my education or my years in Europe and India had prepared me for this level of violence, which turned neighbor against neighbor, friend against friend, and provoked respectable heads of family to hire contract killers to rid themselves of an offending relative over a petty argument or political disagreement. In the highlands, the army's war of counterinsurgency against three guerrilla organizations had cost the lives of more than 40,000 Guatemalans, the great majority Indians of Mayan descent. (252)

Perera narrates a trajectory that moves from his own lack of familiarity with Guatemala (emphasizing his years in Europe and India) to a recognition that most victims of this state violence had been Indigenous Guatemalans. This dynamic evokes complicated questions about the role of Jewish immigrants to the nation in such a moment of patently ethnic violence. Notably, the Guatemalan-born author describes his time in Europe and India as his origin story, approaching the violence that he witnessed in Guatemala in the 1980s as if he were a complete outsider to the nation.

The study of Jewish Central American literature problematizes critical understandings of Central American literature and Jewish Latin American literature. Specifically, as Arturo Arias posits in *Taking Their Word: Literature and the Signs of Central America*, Central American culture is "marginalized both by the cosmopolitan centre and by countries exercising hegemony in Latin America" (xii). While Arias does not name these "countries exercising hegemony" explicitly, countries that have traditionally been the foci of Latin American Jewish studies – Argentina, Brazil, Mexico, and Cuba – have for decades also been editorial and cinematic powerhouses, exerting a certain amount of cultural hegemony over the rest of Latin America. At the same time, as Jorge Luis Borges once remarked, the Latin American Jew is doubly marginalized by virtue of being both Latin American and Jewish. Perera thus presents a particular challenge to critical considerations of positions of hegemony and power, because his narrator enjoys the privileges afforded by being non-Indigenous and wealthy within Guatemala, yet is also Guatemalan and Jewish and thus marginalized on both counts within Latin America. We are reminded of the nuances of the narrator's seemingly privileged position by his exposure at a young age to anti-Semitism and to the violence that affects his country, whereby we are left to wonder: what are the points of contact between his identities as Jewish, Guatemalan, and non-Indigenous?[3]

As a Sephardic Jew, Perera has a complicated ethnic identity in a nation where ethnic categories are difficult to define. Anthropologist Kay Warren advocates for a constructivist approach to race in Guatemala in which "the Guatemalan categories *indio*, *indígena*, *natural*, or *maya* may be contrasted with *ladino*" but that "there is no Maya or Ladino except as identities are constructed, contested, negotiated, imposed, imputed, resisted, and redefined in action" (72–3). In light of the elasticity of the term *Ladino*, accounts such as Perera's (and, as I continue to study later in this chapter and in the following, Halfon's and Goldman's novels) raise the question of how Jews relate to the category of Ladino within a cultural paradigm in which Ladino or Indigenous (which Perera's narrator assuredly is not) are often presented as the only options available for racial identification. Here, I note a terminological challenge that is particularly relevant to Perera as a Sephardic Guatemalan: in Guatemala, "Ladino" is a term for non-Indigenous people and includes mestizo people, but the term carries a strong connotation of upward social mobility and assimilation into non-Indigenous sectors of society (sometimes even connoting the denial of Indigenous components

44   Absorption Narratives

of one's identity and ancestry). These works' consideration of the place of Jewish children in Guatemala's political landscape raise questions about Jewish relationships to the state and to national belonging.

Perera's autobiographical narrator, Jaime Nissán, tells readers that he wondered as a child why his parents had chosen to immigrate to Guatemala of all places: "Why Guatemala? Father never explained this to my satisfaction" (*Rites* 9). The question of how Jewish immigrants belong (or do not) in Guatemala becomes a point of tension in the father-son relationship. Perera depicts Jewish presence in Guatemala as happenstance or arbitrary, whereby his protagonist struggles to find belonging. Early in the novel, Perera tells of a fellow outsider in the school, a French Protestant boy named Coco whom he describes as being "as much a foreigner in the school" as Jaime himself (26). Perera thus posits being non-Catholic (Protestant or Jewish) as being a specific type of outsider: foreign. This characterization is particularly important for Perera's own situation as an outsider and for the very different forms of marginalization that characterize his retrospective account of the violence visited upon the nation's Indigenous populations.

In addition to recognizing a certain form of white privilege from which he benefits, Perera also explicitly discusses the differences between different ethnic groups of Jews. Namely, he addresses how his Sephardic family perceives itself as different from Ashkenazim. Specifically, he does so in terms of what he terms a "caste." Jaime reflects, "I was very early inculcated with the gospel of Sephardic caste. If all other Jews were Chosen, we were the Elect. We Sephardim were the sole heirs to a remote but glorious Golden Age whose legacy we could batten on, without any effort on our part, until the Day of Judgment" (*Rites* 74). His reflection on a Sephardic "caste" recalls the shared origins of ideas of both blood purity and miscegenation in the Spanish Empire. Later in the novel, his aunt and uncle ask why he is not friends with the other Jewish kids, to which he responds that there is only one. His uncle balks: "Potorowski? The son of Jaime Potorowski? The Polack who sells cloth in the Chinese quarter? ... Better goyim than a Potorowski" (112). Unlike the narrator's description of mestizo and Indigenous characters' physical appearances, there is no reference to the phenotypical markers of ethnic difference between various groups of Jews. Yet awareness of the Sephardic "caste" nonetheless influences Jaime's own Jewish identity.

Rites details mixed-race and Indigenous characters' physical appearances, often in ways that tacitly fetishize these characters. The narrator describes a childhood friend: "a mestizo named Eduardo Rodriguez. Eduardo's complexion was a lustrous walnut. Against it were set

"There's No Jews on the Reservation" 45

intense black eyes with long curling lashes that already won him special indulgences from one of our female teachers" (48). His description of Eduardo sexualizes and fetishizes the young mestizo boy through triangulated desire in the depiction of the female teacher. The teacher's fetishizing of the young boy here foreshadows Perera's unsettling account of Eduardo's losing his virginity to his aunt. *Rites* describes Eduardo as "part of a tiny but growing mestizo middle class" (53). The novel incorporates class in its fetishized discussion of mestizo sexuality in describing what finally became of Eduardo: "At eighteen he realized the prime mestizo dream of knocking up the white boss's daughter" (61). Retrospectively, the narrator seems to have realized that Eduardo's father might have been partly Black: "Eduardo's father was the darkest man I'd ever seen. His complexion was a polished rosewood to Eduardo's walnut and [Eduardo's mother] Pilar's blond maple. It didn't occur to me that he might be part Negro, chiefly because I had never seen a black man up close. Nearly all of Guatemala's blacks live on the Atlantic coast – West Indian Caribs hired by the United Fruit Co." (57). Jaime includes this lengthy, racist description of Eduardo's father to explain why he was astonished when he first met him. His astonishment – along with his description decades later – connotes a patent racism that the narrator ironically seeks to exculpate through an appeal to a "colour-blind" justification for his Othering of Eduardo. Of note here is the fact that his explanation for never having seen a Black person before was that Black Guatemalans lived mainly on the Atlantic coast, a claim that explicitly couples race with geographical location. The narrator does not explain, however, whether he knew as a young boy meeting Eduardo's father that most Black people in the country lived on the coast or that was something he came to learn later. Perera's description of Eduardo and his family couples race with location in a way that presents Black Guatemalans as geographically marginalized.

Perera shows his narrator's fascination with racial alterity before he is even five years old during a scene at the national fair in 1938. Edna, one of Jaime's nannies, tells him about the Lacandons, and he asks Edna whether she is Indian after comparing her to an Indigenous woman whom he sees is weaving at the fair: "I had noticed [Edna's] wide, flat nose and high cheeks were like the weaving woman's, though her skin wasn't as brown" (119–20). By his own account, Jaime has already been made aware of phenotypical traits associated with race from an early age. Edna responds, however, that she is not Indian but rather mestiza and explains to Jaime that mestiza is "like café con leche" (120). Edna's simile – voiced through the Sephardic Jewish narrator recounting his childhood decades later and from the US – repeats one of the

46   Absorption Narratives

more problematic tropes of mestizaje commonly uttered when speaking about racial mixture in Latin America. Unlike his description of Eduardo as part of the growing mestizo middle class, however, his description of Edna supposes that she is more Indigenous than white, whereas it had not occurred to him that Eduardo's family was partly Black. In this way, Perera shows vague understandings of Indigeneity to inform default assumptions about racial identities and belonging in Guatemala.

Besides Edna, who describes herself as "like café con leche," the other domestic employee whom Jaime describes (and often Others) is Chata, his nanny from a young age. Similar to Jaime's fetishized depiction of Eduardo, his descriptions of Chata (before her death) also sexualize Indigenous bodies in ways that are both patently racist and inappropriate for the age of the characters. In this case, he describes Chata, who "would gently tease me into fondling her firm round breasts under the thin blouse" (23) as a five-year-old child. Here, Perera's fetishized and sexualized account of his narrator's relationship to his caretaker somewhat inverts the way that he speaks of the schoolteacher's fetishized favouring of the partly Black Eduardo. After Chata is killed, her sister Elvira takes her place. Jaime speaks not only of Chata and Elvira's racial difference from him and his family but also of Elvira's Catholicism and her attempts to take him to mass. Elvira says to him, "You must pray to our Lord to be forgiven for your ancestors' sins against him. That way you can go to Heaven, even if you're not Catholic" (28). Perera presents Jaime as being Othered by the domestic workers in his home as a child, bringing class, race, and religious alterity into tension with one another. Jaime certainly benefits from many forms of privilege compared to these workers, yet he also is faced with their anti-Semitic comments. Yet these anti-Semitic statements are also a function of the Catholic hegemony that imposed itself on Indigenous peoples in the Americas.

Perera describes his narrator and other white children of immigrants as being marginalized in ways that are patently different from the marginalization faced by Indigenous and Black characters in the novel. In *Rites*, one child, whom the other children dub "Frenchie," is presented as being equally out of place as Jaime. The child has the nickname "Coco" "because his head was round and hard like a coconut. Even his curly blond hair resembled a coconut. He was as much a foreigner in the school as I was. He was Protestant" (26). Perera couples whiteness (blondness) with religious alterity by comparing his own foreignness as a non-Catholic to Coco's. Perera uses the equation "as much as" to underscore his and Michel's alterity as non-Catholics at the same time

"There's No Jews on the Reservation"   47

that he mentions the child's blond curls. However, Jaime and his family move to Brooklyn, whereas Coco is given a post in Jacobo Árbenz's administration in which he is in charge of the land-reform program and becomes caught up in the political tumult of the country throughout his early adulthood. Perera's story thus represents the Jewish character as more of an outsider to Guatemalan politics than the French Protestant character, despite their phenotypic similarities and their shared condition of being non-Catholic.

Perera tacitly contrasts Jewish otherness to racial alterity among Indigenous and mestizo characters through focusing on Indigenous and mestizo characters' avowal of Christianity. His narrator notes that, in his kindergarten days, a classmate accuses Jews of having killed Christ. In a moment of comical childhood innocence, Jaime recalls first wondering who Christ was and then thinking to himself, "I remembered stepping on a cockroach once, and stomping on ants in the kitchen. Maybe I had killed Christ by accident" (25). Perera uses the innocence in Jaime's childhood perspective to create a comical anecdote in which his protagonist is completely unaware of who Christ was until other children accuse him of having killed Christ. In response, Jaime asks his father that evening at home why his family is Jewish. Ada Savin (1998) notes of this moment in the novel, "As a kindergarten boy, he already feels that he does not belong" (229). Perera's novel thus engages with a common anti-Semitic trope throughout the world in which Jews are referred to as the killers of Christ.[4] The narrator describes the boy who accuses him of killing Christ: "Arturo, a dark, thickset boy with hooded eyes and hairy legs below his short trousers" (24–5). The narrator's description of Arturo's skin colour belies his own ignorance of racial difference at this age. Put another way, before he is fully conscious of his own awareness of Jewish difference, Jaime already shows racialized thinking and describes darker-skinned children in overtly racial terms. Arturo's comment to Jaime that his mother told him that the Jews killed Christ makes Jaime feel Othered, yet his description of Arturo's appearance Others Arturo.

Elsewhere in the novel, Perera evokes the Conquest and conflicts between European and Mayan characters in his description of encounters between Jewishness and Indigeneity in his own childhood years, a reference that also characterizes parts of Goldman's novel, which I discuss in the next chapter. Jaime recalls, "I begrudged Becky the pampering she got from Father's salesgirls and from our housemaids, who called her *canche* in the reverent tones the Mayas had accorded Cortez's blond, bearded captain, Pedro de Alvarado, even as he plundered their cities and temples" (86). Their father's salesgirls and housemaids were

48   Absorption Narratives

predominantly darker-skinned mestiza and Indigenous women. Here, he talks about their pampering of his sister in terms of her whiteness as contrasted to their own racial appearance – and evokes the Conquest to do so. Perera ventriloquizes voices of mestiza and Indigenous characters, repeating their use of the term "canche" (used in Central America to refer to a person who is white and usually blond) as a way of fetishizing his sister's whiteness. Unlike the sexualized terms in which he couches adult females' encounters with male children, here he begrudges only Becky's "pampering." Nonetheless, in light of the racialized and sexualized terms with which he describes children's encounters with adults, Perera suggests a gendered element to the young boy's begrudging the attention that his sister receives from older, mestiza, and Indigenous women.

The narrator describes his own difference on the basis of gender and ethnicity, further complicating the points of contact between Jewishness, race/ethnicity, and national belonging for Jewish Guatemalans. The novel begins with an account of the *second* time he was circumcised as a child (the first time, we learn, the rite was performed incorrectly). The circumcision takes on particular significance in light of the novel's title, "Rites," of which the circumcision is the first emphasized in the novel. Through the subtitle "A Guatemalan Boyhood," Perera suggestively links national belonging (or perhaps more accurately the process of grappling with possible national belonging), Jewishness, and gender in his novel's first pages. *Rites* begins, "I was not quite six when I was circumcised for the second time because the first job, performed by a Gentile doctor, was pronounced unclean" (3). Describing this harrowing childhood memory, the narrator finally goes on to speak of "the bitter, sinking knowledge that I would never be whole again" (4). Perera speaks of the rite of circumcision not within the context of the purity it is thought to bring but in the framework of being left empty. What is striking is that in a novel subtitled "A Guatemalan Boyhood," Perera makes no mention in this prologue (titled "Initiation") of Guatemala, although he does include geographical references to refer to the mohel: "Rabbi Isaac Toledano, summoned from Turkey to be the first pastor of our growing Jewish community" (4). The prologue thus, without naming Guatemala, introduces the narrator's childhood within a framework of temporality: the period of his early life during which he was, in his mother's terms, "part heathen" for not being properly circumcised, and the time to which the "growing Jewish community" was bound in that country. The rabbi was "summoned from Turkey" and duly sought not only to help the Jewish community thrive but also correct the unclean, partial circumcision said to have been performed by a gentile

"There's No Jews on the Reservation" 49

doctor. With these opening pages, Perera underscores the importance of Jewish embodiment and Jewish diaspora.

Here, Perera also provocatively couples circumcision and Jewish presence in Guatemala, evoking allegorical notions of nationalism and Jewish masculinity. In a variety of geographical contexts throughout the Americas, we see similar narratives about Jewish masculinities bound up in preoccupations of national belonging – from US author Philip Roth's breakthrough 1969 novel *Portnoy's Complaint* to Argentine director Daniel Burman's 2004 *El abrazo partido* and surrealist Chilean filmmaker Alejandro Jodorowksy's 2013 film *La danza de la realidad*.[5] Similarly, as Dean Franco has argued in his reading of *Portnoy's Complaint*, circumcision in Jewish literature links race and sexuality. Franco submits: "Circumcision is the peculiar mark of Jewish racialization, the retroactive racialization of the Jewish male body that thereby folds the Jewish male child into the clan. Circumcision thus supplements matrilineal genetic descent with cultural descent, with the mother ambiguously poised between race and culture" (92). In Franco's reading, circumcision serves as a topic through which Roth's novel explores generational shifts and tensions surrounding Jewish racialization and Jews' relations to racial politics. Likewise, Perera's novel begins with a meditation on his narrator's second circumcision couched within a reflection on his family's belonging (or lack thereof) in a new nation in which they were racially different from others.

Despite the fact that the novel is subtitled "A Guatemalan Boyhood" and centres predominantly on Jaime's childhood, the author incorporates a few notable leaps to reflect on what became of specific characters (such as Coco and Eduardo) in their adult years and also to discuss the particular tumult of the 1970s in Guatemala. As Perera states towards the novel's end, "The differences between the violence of '71 and the bloodshed of winter '81 were more than statistical, as more and more Indians joined underground peasant unions and guerrilla groups, and appeared on anti-Communist 'death lists' in regional newspapers" (183). Perera's description of the 1981 counterinsurgency, in its patently didactic tone, is written with an eye towards educating non-Guatemalan (and English-speaking) readers about the country's recent history. As I will discuss further in this chapter in the case of Halfon's novella, both authors present their Jewish families' experiences with exile and diaspora as creating an outsider mentality that pervades their relationship to Guatemala even before they leave the country. Yet, as we have seen in these specific moments of Perera's text, the vivid detail and awareness with which he recalls categories of difference and the ways in which other children are shown to belong (or not belong, as the case

50   Absorption Narratives

may be) in Guatemala convey a leitmotif of reckoning with race and Otherness throughout his childhood years in the country as a way of pondering for himself, as an adult looking back, the very question that his father never answered satisfactorily: "Why Guatemala?"

"We Too Believe in Four Worlds": *Spirits of the Ordinary*

Kathleen Alcalá was born in the Western US to a Mexican American family. In the 1990s, she was inspired to write a novel about a Mexican American family and began a thorough archival project to learn as much about her own family and about nineteenth-century Mexico as possible. When she discovered hints of her own family's crypto-Jewish past, she centred that part of her ancestry in the story she tells in the first part of the trilogy: *Spirits of the Ordinary*. *Spirits of the Ordinary* offers a unique model for ethno-religious identities in the US–Mexico borderlands. Set in the nineteenth century, the novel not only rewrites the last two centuries of Mexican American experiences but indeed re-envisions the entirety of Spanish, crypto-Jewish, and Indigenous presences in the Americas. In Alcalá's novel, the mixture between Indigenous, Catholic, and Jewish belief systems is constitutive of a new syncretic order that undergirds border identities. While existing criticism has situated *Spirits of the Ordinary* within US Chicanx literature and US Jewish literature, I explore a reading of this novel within the framework of Mexican and Latin American literary and cultural history to expand understandings of Jewishness, borders, and the Americas.

Within the tradition of ethnicity and nationalism in Mexico, Alcalá's treatment of the encounters between Jewishness and Indigeneity tacitly evokes the thinking of Mexican cultural leader José Vasconcelos, whose controversial (indeed, eugenicist) ideas about mestizaje – racial mixture – puts forth an ethnonational model of the "fifth race" created by the mixture of European, Indigenous, Asian, and Black races in Mexico, as I discussed in the introduction. Vasconcelos takes Jewishness into account but in a way that does not recognize or allow for Jewish difference, vertiginously absorbing Jewish difference as he does other categories of ethnic difference in order to articulate a model of "cosmic" mixture. Seeking to shed light on these Jewish elements that have remained "hidden," here I trace Alcalá's treatment of crypto-Jewishness in the borderlands. For Vasconcelos, a model of national identity predicated on racial mixture obliquely acknowledges difference but ultimately absorbs it into the mestizo "cosmic race." While the role of Jewishness in Vasconcelos's model remains critically underexplored, Jewish Mexican author and critic Ilan Stavans has addressed the role

"There's No Jews on the Reservation" 51

of Jewishness in mestizaje. Stavans notes that Latin American societies are "homogeneously mestizo" in such a way that "the particular is continually being devoured by the monstrous whole [and] the Jews are ... part of that particular" ("Introduction" in *Tropical Synagogues* 1). For Vasconcelos, mestizaje is not only an ethnic category but a spiritual and nationalistic concept. As Stavans reminds us here, Jews are absorbed within this "monstrous whole," as Vasconcelos himself noted through the hidden Jewish striae. As a way of bringing "that particular" to the fore of the conversation and resisting the absorption of these Jewish striae into the homogeneously mestizo body politic, here I explore how Alcalá creates a narrative that focuses on the particularities of Jewishness as it comes into contact with Indigeneity.

Despite critical attention to racial mixture in *Spirits of the Ordinary*, the model of the cosmic race has not been explored in relation to Alcalá's novel. Drawing from Cornejo Polar's and Gloria Anzaldúa's respective uses of Vasconcelos's "cosmic race," crypto-Judaism in and of itself in Latin America is paradigmatic of syncretic practices (in terms of the blending of outward avowal of Christian practices and inward embrace of Judaism). However, as Cornejo Polar has shown, syncretism itself can also be a limiting category insofar as it acknowledges difference but ultimately absorbs it. Similarly, Vasconcelos's image of "Jewish striae" as an inscription of Jewish ethnicity in cultural and critical models of Mexican ethnic identities marginalizes the role of Jewishness within this amalgamated "cosmic race." In contrast to Vasconcelos's notion, I seek here to contest prevailing conceptualizations of centre and periphery by bringing Jewishness to the fore in discussions of ethnonational identities. In my reading of Alcalá's novel, I centre her narrative of Mexican American crypto-Jewishness as it relates to models of Mexican national identity while still in dialogue with US Latinx and US ethnic literatures.

If Vasconcelos depicts Jewishness as striae that have hidden themselves in Castilian blood, notions of crypto-Jewishness also find affinity with Anzaldúa's model of the borderland's "new mestiza consciousness." Theresa Delgadillo draws from Gloria Anzaldúa to disrupt Vasconcelos's model of hybridity that absorbs differences (Jewishness among them, we recall) in her praxis of reading Alcalá's novel and other works of Chicanx fiction. As Delgadillo has noted in her reading of Chicana fiction, including Alcalá's novel, Anzaldúa centres the figure of the mestizo in a way that does not eschew difference. That is, Anzaldúa's understanding of mestizaje allows for the particularities of Indigenous or Black identities and experiences to be present and thrive even within the hybridity of mestizaje. This fundamental aspect of Anzaldúa's work

52 Absorption Narratives

would also allow for Jewishness to thrive among crypto-Jews, such as Alcalá and her characters, disrupting the assimilationist impulse among cultural models of Jewishness writ large and in discussions of crypto-Jews in particular.

Alcalá's novel is typically considered a work of US Chicanx fiction – perfectly reasonable because Alcalá writes in English and was born in the US. However, my approach to Alcalá places *Spirits of the Ordinary* in the context of Mexican nationalism but as part of a broader, inter-American exploration of how Jewishness and racial alterity connect. Jonathan Freedman argues in *Klezmer America* that the novel "takes its narrative warrant from the plethora of fictions about Jewish Americans of the last century in order to address what the novel sees as a significant lacuna: the correlative inability to find a narrative frame for the question of Mexican – and hence ultimately Mexican-American identity" (233). Yet, when we read Alcalá's novel in the context of Mexican literature and history, we glean a fuller picture of Jewish Mexican identities that help to fill in what, in Freedman's terms, Alcalá perceives as a lacuna. For, as my reading of the novel in line with Vasconcelos shows, Jewishness has long been assumed – if very implicitly – to be a part of the amalgamated whole that makes up Mexican ethnonationalism. As such, to recentre Jewish experiences and identities and how they have been hidden in the national body requires refiguring a narrative of Mexican and Mexican American identities. This approach explores how this novel functions not just as US "ethnic literature" (ethnic here referring to both Jewish and Chicanx) but also in dialogue with Mexican Jewishness and Jewish literature of the Americas. Hence, my focus here is on how the novel fits into notions of Jewishness and Indigeneity within critical models of Mexican and Latin American literature.

The crypto-Jewish protagonist of *Spirits of the Ordinary*, Zacarías Caraval, spends his life dabbling in alchemy and searching for treasure. His wandering throughout Mexico and in the borderlands leads him to larger-than-life characters; his children also encounter similarly eccentric characters through whom we gain insight into religious and ethnic difference in Mexico. Zacarías's twin children meet a cross-dressing photographer, Corey, whom the narrator describes: "By concealing all but the essential line of a subject, be it the shadow of a nopal, a person, or a jug of water, Corey forced the eye to fill in the detail, brought the viewer into play as a willing or unwilling collaborator with the photographer in order to reveal to the eye what it was seeing" (165). By focusing on what Corey's photography conceals and reveals (and what it conceals by way of revealing and vice versa), Alcalá's novel shows an exchange between closeted Jewish identities, the concealment of

"There's No Jews on the Reservation" 53

cross-dressing, and ways of capturing and revealing hidden parts of identities. The novel thus evokes ongoing conversations about the benefits and challenges of analogizing queer identifications to Jewishness, the subject of the edited volume *Queer Theory and the Jewish Question*. In the volume, Janet Jakobsen reminds us in her provocative essay, "Queers Are Like Jews, Aren't They?" that "analogizing queers to Jews violates the categories that might otherwise separate them. This category is potentially a space of constraint or of possibility. ... To raise the Jewish question in relation to queer theory, then, is also to ask whether we can queer? queers" (86). Jakobsen's model of the relationship between queerness and Jewishness is chiastic, blurring the sides of the analogy to ask how the analogy changes the relationship of self to self. In Freedman's reading of *Spirits of the Ordinary*, "We can see ... why the Marrano presence is so important for Alcalá: it's a metonym for a wide variety of secret identities and hidden practices, forbidden and feared by Church and state alike" (237). Through focusing on the relationship between Corey's hidden identity and her photography, the novel implicitly asks how art – including fiction – might uncover hidden secrets; the novel questions the relationship between queer and Jewish identities due to their similar capacities to be hidden.

When at last Zacarías finds the mine for which he had been searching, he brings his hidden Jewish spirituality to bear on his own understanding of the Indigenous people whom he encounters there. Jewish mysticism is thus presented in a syncretic relationship with Indigenous spirituality. He comes to live among the Raramuri tribe, with whom he exchanges stories of their respective ancestral beliefs. Zacarías carves a figure eight into a stone wall, under which he regales the tribe with the stories he learned from his father: "He struggled to tell the story in el llanero, the common language used for trade in Northern Mexico, phrasing the complicated Hebrew ideas in his sparse Indian vocabulary. He did not know much Tarahumar. As he spoke, he heard muttered translations roll to the back of the room" (179–80). Critic María Alonso's reading of the novel foregrounds Alcalá's "linguistic syncretism," an element that comes into sharp relief through Zacarías's attempts to "phrase complicated Hebrew ideas in a sparse Indian vocabulary." Alonso's model of "linguistic syncretism" finds affinity with Cornejo Polar's position that Bakhtinian heteroglossia allows for thinking about hybridity so as to avoid the absorption of difference as a result of syncretism. The religious syncretism that characterizes Zacarías's encounters with the Raramuri is also present as the two exchange their individual spiritual beliefs. Notably, Zacarías carves a figure eight into the stone wall of the cave, evoking the number's significance in Hebrew of new beginnings.[6]

54 Absorption Narratives

After abandoning his family in search of the mines, under the figure eight that he carves in the stone, Zacarías begins anew, fostering a different type of spiritual framework predicated on the exchange between Raramuri and Jewish beliefs, and shortly thereafter becomes a healer. His journey of spiritual awakening is not only a recovery of his own crypto-Judaism. This exchange is marked by the convergence of spiritual and ethnic differences, both those within him and those between him and others. He tells the Raramuri about the four worlds in the Kabbalah and adds, "But I don't know what any of those laws mean *in this land*. They are very old, and from very far away" (180, my emphasis). Zacarías asks what kabbalistic beliefs mean not only in this ancestors' spiritual homeland but also in Mexico and, more specifically, among the Indigenous peoples along the borderlands. The character thus shows spiritual beliefs to morph and take on new meanings in different geographical spaces, leading him to feel confused because, in his particular case, there are no open observers of his beliefs in Mexico or along the borderlands. Zacarías's assertion here that he does not know what his beliefs mean "in this land" echo the legal document analysed by historian Ben Vinson and discussed in chapter 1 that stated that blood purity "in this kingdom" (what is present-day Mexico) meant not having a mixture of castes. Alcalá's novel brings crypto-Judaism into conversation with the loss of Indigenous land and identities in the geographical space of Mexico.

Zacarías finds commonality with the Raramuri on the basis of spirituality and geography. To his description of the four worlds, an Indigenous woman, Josefina, responds, "We too, believe in four worlds. We believe that God tried several other peoples before he made us ... we came from the land where the Apaches now live, to the north, where we descended from the sky. God gave us gifts of corn and potatoes in our ears, so that we could run fast, multiply and prosper. That is why we are called the Raramuri, the runners" (181). Zacarías and Josefina establish commonalities in their spiritual beliefs and, later, in the ways that they practise their religions. Josefina goes on, "We still have our sacred places, the caves and lakes where the creator spirit lives. These things, too, are secret. We must also pray in secret" to which Zacarías responds, "You are the ones who know and understand" (181). Zacarías enters into a syncretic exchange with Josefina on the basis of the secrecy in which both he as a crypto-Jew and she as a Raramuri are compelled to practise their religions. In this exchange, Josefina's assertion that they still have sacred places after being pushed into the mountains when the Europeans arrived creates a commonality and a contrast with Zacarías's circumstances as a crypto-Jew and part of the Sephardic diaspora. Displacement characterizes their respective religions and provides them a common referent in this place that is much closer to the homeland of the Raramuri, as we see through "we still have our sacred places, the caves and lakes where the creator spirit lives," but that is still not the ancestral homeland.

The exchange between Zacarías and Josefina highlights difference as well as similarity. I argue that the possibilities for identification sparked by this encounter, ultimately, underscore difference more than similarity. Likewise, as Dalia Kandiyoti notes in her recent book *The Converso's Return*, Alcalá "inserts a converso and crypto-Sephardi presence into our borderlands imaginary, going beyond the use of the figure of the crypto-Jew as grounds for understanding syncretism; she links the fates of Native Americans and Sephardi crypto-Jews as two groups who have been targeted for disappearance, to different extents and by different means" (107). The encounter between Zacarías and the Tarahumara also evokes questions of Jewish and Indigenous conditions on the basis of their respective connections to land, in line with Jonathan Boyarin and David Boyarin's claim that I discussed in chapter 1: "Traditional Jewish attachment to the Land, whether biblical or post-biblical ... provides a self-critique as well as a critique of identities based on notions of autochthon" (715). The Boyarins' position allows for a consideration of how Jewish attachment to the land both does and does not relate to Indigenous attachment to the land in such a way that, they maintain, allows for a self-critique. Similarly, Zacarías's encounter with the Tarahumara and his identification with them serve not as a form of mutual understanding but as a way for Zacarías better to understand himself. In this way, the model of crypto-Jewish engagement with Indigenous subjects is ultimately quite one-sided, although Alcalá's narrative certainly condemns Zacarías, as I show below. Similarly, Theresa Delgadillo notes in her reading of *Spirits of the Ordinary*, "The encounter at Casas Grandes puts varied spiritual traditions into conversation, creating the opportunity for exchange and spiritual renewal. These cross-cultural encounters among different peoples and worldviews – in a search for common ground that narrative events confirm is life altering for every participant – are temporarily, but not definitively, crushed" (155). Zacarías's attempt to establish a haven for intercultural exchange is not lasting, but Alcalá's presentation of this moment inspires hope that such exchanges can take place.

Zacarías's encounter with the Raramuri prompts him to become even more inwardly focused. After establishing these points in common with Raramuri religious beliefs and practices, Alcalá pivots to Zacarías's internal syncretism: his inward avowal of Jewish spiritual beliefs and his

56   Absorption Narratives

outward knowledge of Catholicism. The narrator tells, "Running out of family stories, Zacarías began to tell stories from the Bible. First those of the Old Testament he had learned from his secretive family, then those from the New Testament he had learned from the nuns at school" (181). Alcalá presents the kabbalistic beliefs that Zacarías has shared as "family stories" in contrast to those of the Old Testament "learned from his secretive family." Finally, Zacarías moves on to "those from the New Testament he had learned from the nuns at school" (181). He shares these stories, moving from the most personal, secretive, and familial to those told to him by the nuns, which he finds fascinating as stories but not part of his own belief system. Yet even the Bible is contrasted with his own "family stories" from the Kabbalah. Jewish mysticism is presented as the most intimate, closely held beliefs in Zacarías's world view. The novel suggests that the stories from the nuns are more different from the Kabbalah than the beliefs that Josefina shares with him. In this way, Alcalá further underscores a particular affinity between the crypto-Jewish character's beliefs and those of the Raramuri. The author also creates a syncretic model that allows for these various facets of spirituality to come into convergence with one another while surviving and flourishing on their own.

As a result of this exchange, Zacarías becomes a healer; people travel to see him in Casas Grandes. Despite the blending of religious aspects, however, Zacarías and Josefina are both able to retain and celebrate the particularities of their Jewish and Indigenous belief systems, thus resisting the assimilationist impulse of a model of Mexican racial identities, such as Vasconcelos's cosmic race. Yet, notably absent from the narration of Zacarías's time among the Raramuri are physical descriptions of the Indigenous characters. Alcalá refers to an Indian guide who leads Zacarías to Casas Grandes and to many of the people whom he encounters there. In his exchange with Josefina, she is described simply as "an old woman." The racial distinctions between Zacarías and Josefina that certainly inform their individual identities and their convergence here in Casas Grandes are elided, so that in this scene – and throughout the novel – characters' spiritual identifications and differences are emphasized while racial differences not mentioned at all. And yet these characters contrast with one another racially as much as (if not more than) in their spirituality. Perhaps it is for this reason that Zacarías's time as a healer is short-lived and ends in disaster, with a violent conflict between the military and the Indigenous inhabitants of Casas Grandes, where, it becomes catastrophically clear, Zacarías does not belong. The Indigenous people are brutalized in the encounter, while Zacarías, who escapes unscathed, is blamed for the conflict because he is a Jew. If,

"There's No Jews on the Reservation"   57

when it comes to spirituality, Zacarías's encounter with the Raramuri in Casas Grandes finds harmony through a syncretic mutual identification, the fact that the novel does not address racial and ethnic differences suggests a lack of resolution in this aspect.

Alcalá's novel fits within Latin American models of literary criticism due to the importance of syncretism as well as to Alcalá's use of magical realism commonly associated with Latin American fiction. Similarly, Jonathan Freedman's reading of *Spirits of the Ordinary* also notes Alcalá's "intense" research of both Mexican and Southwestern US history as part of a syncretic blend that makes up the novel: "The syncretism that characterizes the novel *Spirits of the Ordinary* is, like Zacarías's visionary experiences, deeply syncretic, a blend of Marquezian magical realism, Jewish mysticism, and intensely researched Mexican and Southwestern US history" (232). As Freedman suggests through "Marquezian" magical realism, *Spirits of the Ordinary* is a Latin American novel as well as a borderlands novel. In this way, the encounters that Alcalá models between Jewish and Indigenous characters speak to the particular liminality of the borderlands space as well as to inter-American syncretic spaces writ large.

Zacarías's geographical journey mirrors the crossings and hybridities that his spiritual journey encapsulates. Just as he journeys from Mexico City to the borderlands in the Chihuahua desert, he journeys from his own internal crypto-Jewishness out into contact with the Tarahumar, an exchange that takes on a supernatural spiritual meaning. And yet this supernatural endeavour is short-lived. Zacarías flees the mines when the soldiers arrive; the Tarahumara tell him that this isn't his fight. Yet the violence follows him back to his home in Mexico City. He is told that the conflict in Casas Grandes "isn't his struggle," yet he is also persecuted after the encounter begins because the military suspects "the Jew" of having instigated the conflict. He is simultaneously, on the one hand, not part of the conflict because he is not Indigenous and, on the other, suspected of being the ringleader of the conflict because he is Jewish. Moreover, his family's secret Jewish identity is no longer secret. Alcalá thus creates a narrative in which Jews and Indigenous characters are Othered in tacitly different ways. The Indigenous characters bear the brunt of the uprising, while Zacarías escapes unscathed.

After this encounter and the uprising in Casas Grandes, Zacarías briefly returns to his family, but leaves because his wife and family no longer need him and because he does not want those persecuting him to harm his family. After returning to his family following the conflict, he "became a phantom, a name carried by the wind, a set of letters that did not necessarily add up to a person" (232). His son Gabriel narrates

58 Absorption Narratives

the book's final chapter and, unlike Zacarías who "became a phantom" and crossed the border, Gabriel describes, "I left that night an exile, rejected by my own mother because of Evangelism" (238). Yet, both Zacarías and his son Gabriel find the spiritual belonging in the US that they sought in Mexico: Zacarías is received by an unknown stranger after he happens upon the stranger's garden that is identical to his own childhood garden, and the stranger tells him to come inside for it is Shabbos. Zacarías finally finds a place of spiritual belonging north of the border.

The narrator at the end who tells of his evangelism highlights the outsider status of those who observe religions other than Catholicism in Mexico, reminding readers of this shared category between Zacarías and the Tarahumara. Yet the novel also ends with Zacarías being welcomed into a garden – identical to his father's – for Shabbos. While perhaps Othered similarly to the Tarahumar through their shared spiritual difference from Catholics, he returns first to his family home and then to a Jewish space. He is able to discern what his religion might mean "in this land," but this happens away from the Indigenous people with whom he had previously come into contact.

Alcalá's depiction of Zacarías balances his persecution as a Jew with the problems that he causes both at home and among strangers. His mystical pursuits are shown always to leave him desirous of more knowledge, more jewels, and so on. And yet as readers we do empathize with Zacarías's grandiose curiosities in no small part because we understand his plight as a marginalized person who has been forced to conceal the most salient parts of his identity for his whole life. Nonetheless, his pursuits for fulfilment cause further harm to be visited on others who are also oppressed and who have been displaced from their land. The author thus explores crypto-Judaism in ways that account for the different forms of oppression faced by Jewish and Indigenous characters.

"There's No Jews on the Reservation": *The Master Butchers Singing Club*

On the other side of the US, at the US–Canada border, Pulitzer Prize–winning author Louise Erdrich's 2003 novel *The Master Butchers Singing Club* reimagines the German side of her family, a departure from her previous work that had focused on the Chippewa and Ojibwe parts of her heritage. To fictionalize her German grandfather, whose photograph is featured on the front of the hardcover version of the novel, Erdrich recounts the story of a German man, Fidelis Waldgovel, who

"There's No Jews on the Reservation"   59

immigrates to North Dakota after World War I with his pregnant wife, Eva. Their eldest son, Franz, is not the biological son of Fidelis but rather of Fidelis's close friend who died in combat and, as Eva reveals to her friend Delphine, was Jewish. After Eva dies, Delphine goes on to marry Fidelis, becoming stepmother to Franz and his younger half-brothers. Franz grows up to fall in love with a local young woman of very humble means, Mazarine Shimek, whose mother is indigent. At the end of the novel, the omniscient narrator reveals – through the focalization of the secondary character Step-and-a-Half, a Cree survivor of the Wounded Knee Massacre – that Delphine is, in fact, the biological child of Mrs. Shimek and that Step-and-a-Half rescued her as an abandoned baby and gave her to Roy Watzka to raise. Thus, Delphine and her stepson both have a genealogy that they themselves do not know; while Step-and-a-Half is not Delphine's mother, the Cree woman is an integral part of Delphine's origin story, and Franz's true Jewish ancestry remains a mystery to him throughout his entire life. Through secrecy and mistaken identities, Erdrich tells a story in which individual and collective ethnic identities coalesce around encounters with Others in shifting geographical spaces and in the wake of specific historical events.

Erdrich, in order to imagine her German heritage, incorporates a storyline of a clandestine Jew. The narrator never divulges whether Franz himself – who eventually dies after fighting for the US in World War II – knows that he is not Fidelis's biological son or that his biological father was a Jew. The author conjures a character similar to her German grandfather and envisions him as the father of a secret Jew. In this way, Erdrich's novel creates a genealogy of a German American family (similar to that of her own father) that incorporates tropes of crypto-Judaism in its depiction of German Ashkenazi characters. The novel brings together the traumatic memories of the Wounded Knee Massacre and World War II. In its inclusion of Jews who died in World War I (Eva's husband) and World War II (Franz), the novel tacitly links the genocide of Native Americans with the Holocaust. North Dakota thus becomes a contact zone for the encounters between Jewish, German Christian, and Native American characters in the interwar years. Jewish trauma from persecution in Germany and Native American trauma from the Wounded Knee massacre provide characters' backstories. As Natalie Eppelsheimer notes, "The atrocities depicted in *The Master Butchers Singing Club* span German, Native American, and Jewish history. Besides the two World Wars and the Holocaust, the novel talks about the US Army's massacre of Lakota in 1890, also known as the Massacre at Wounded Knee, which has received much less attention in history books" (67). The novel places Indigenous and Jewish trauma and

60   Absorption Narratives

memory into conversation with one another through a chiastic imagining of place and identity.

The Master Butchers Singing Club explores how the identities of Jews and Native Americans bear on their respective relationships to Europe and the Americas. Erdrich populates her novel with foil characters so as to imagine the interwar and postwar periods in the US as a contact zone in which Jewishness and Indigeneity are negotiated from a variety of perspectives and geographical spaces in what Michiko Kakutani terms a "Möbius strip of history" that tells of "the inevitable workings of an oddly symmetrical fate" (n.p.). The foil characters' chiastic relationships between German Jewishness and American Indigeneity craft a narrative in which (secret) Jewishness and hybridity between whiteness and Indigeneity are part and parcel of one another, a phenomenon that strongly evokes a racial paradigm of Latin America – crypto-Judaism – even as Erdrich's novel is set along the US–Canadian border.

Before marrying Fidelis, Delphine is in a relationship with and pretends to be married to closeted homosexual Ojibwe Cyprian, who also fought in World War I. The two meet when performing together in carnivals and return to her hometown, pretending to be married so as not to attract scandal, not because of Cyprian's sexual orientation but because they are cohabiting. The two attempt a relationship in earnest, but Cyprian is not honest with himself or with Delphine about his sexuality even after she sees him in a sexual encounter with another man. Cyprian at several points in the novel outs himself as Native American or is outed by other characters as Native American. Fidelis, for instance, is puzzled by Cyprian's comportment and, finally, realizes that he is a Native American: "It came to him. An Indian. Cyprian was an Indian. That's all it was, all along, that uneasy feeling. Somehow, he'd known and not known, the man was different. Thinking of Cyprian as an Indian now made things all right" (213). As readers already know at this point, Cyprian is a closeted homosexual, and Erdrich thus evokes a moment of dramatic irony through Fidelis's discovery that Cyprian is a Native American. He is thus doubly Othered as a Native American and as queer.

Cyprian's identity as queer and as a Native American allows him to foster affinity with a queer Jewish character. He leaves town after his relationship with Delphine becomes increasingly strained, returning years later with a Jewish man with whom he has been performing. When he returns and describes his new partner to Delphine, he tells her, "He made it over here from Lithuania and he's a Jew. I was a real curiosity to him at first. I took him home with me. ... Boy was he surprised" (317). When Delphine asks why, Cyprian responds, "There's no

"There's No Jews on the Reservation" 61

Jews on the reservation, I mean to speak of. I never knew one when I was growing up, any more than he'd know an Indian" (317). Erdrich uses the term "partner" in this exchange ambiguously to suggest that Vilhus is Cyprian's sexual partner in addition to his performing partner, more so because Vilhus has replaced Delphine as Cyprian's partner. When Cyprian tells her, "My partner's name is Vilhus Gast," the narrator states, "So that, thought Delphine, was that" (317), connoting that Cyprian and the new Jewish character to whom Delphine is being introduced are partners in multiple senses. Their partnership – in particular, Cyprian's own characterization of their points of identification – brings up the intersections between Jewishness, Indigeneity, and queer identifications. As Faulkner and Hecht have shown, Jewishness and queerness share a common "closetable" quality, particularly in this novel in which the only other Jewish character, Franz, does not know that he is the son of a Jewish man.

Cyprian and Vilhus's relationship is predicated in part on the "lost tribes" theory that is also part of the inspiration for Gerald Vizenor's *The Heirs of Columbus* (to be discussed in chapter 3).[7] Cyprian briefly mentions the lost tribes story to Delphine when he introduces Vilhus to her, suggesting that their shared experiences of wandering after being displaced led to an almost predestined re-encounter with one another in honour of their shared origin, despite a general lack of familiarity with one another as Jews and Native Americans. For Cyprian, this lack of familiarity is registered through a chiastic projection of their mutual unawareness. When Cyprian tells Delphine that Vilhus was surprised to meet him because "there's no Jews on the reservation," he posits an interchangeability between Jewish and Indigenous people based on their mutual lack of knowledge of the other. That is, he does not say, "there are no Native Americans in Lithuania" to explain why Vilhus was surprised to meet him, but rather suggests that Vilhus's surprise as a Jew meeting a Native American man is because Native Americans, such as Cyprian, are unfamiliar to Jews. He goes on to say, of Jews, "I never knew one when I was growing up, any more than he'd known an Indian. Except he did know about us and said he believed we were one of the lost tribes of Israel doomed to wander, too, like his people" (317). His use of the "except" breaks down the declaration of sameness between the Native American and Jewish characters by underscoring that Vilhus did have prior knowledge of Native Americans. From there, he returns to the sameness between the two by saying that Vilhus said that he believed that Jews and Native Americans were both lost tribes. In this sense, Erdrich draws on tropes of wandering that characterize both Jewish and Native American experiences. Vilhus and Cyprian do take to wandering

62   Absorption Narratives

together – specifically, as circus performers who put on a comical spectacle poking fun at Hitler. As Eppelsheimer notes, "It is also possible to read Cyprian's behavior as a way of demanding the American audiences' recognition of the racism in the country and the devastation brought on Native Americans" (72). This interpretation is particularly plausible insofar as the novel's ending reveals both the disintegration and trauma of the German American family due to World War II as well as Delphine's backstory trauma resulting from the Wounded Knee Massacre. The laughable spectacle that Vilhus and Cyprian create in their circus performance encapsulates the points of contact between the suffering of Jews under Nazism and the genocide of Native Americans.

That their shared queer identifications are coupled with Cyprian's closeted Native American identity recalls similar questions about the challenges of analogies between queer theory and Jewishness raised through the character of Corey in Alcalá's novel. Erdrich's novel complicates this analogy by asking whether Jews are analogous to queers in a way that is analogous to how Jews are analogous to Native Americans and to how Native Americans are analogous to queers. Moreover, it is telling that the only relationship that is viable for Cyprian as a queer Native American is with a queer Jewish character, the only outwardly Jewish character (Franz does not know of his own Jewish roots) and the first character to be outed as queer in the novel. Through her inclusion of a Lithuanian Jewish character, Erdrich furthers the metonymic relationship between Jewishness and Germanness by expanding German to Lithuanian by way of Jewishness. Erdrich also explored two-spirit identities and gender fluidity in relation to Native American identifications in her previous novel, *Last Report on the Miracles at Little No Horse*.

Erdrich rewrites her own family history and centres queer, Indigenous, and Jewish stories as she seeks to recover the story of her non-Jewish German grandfather. In this way, the author both reimagines her own family's story and rewrites twentieth-century US history centred on experiences that are often marginalized. As Natalie Eppelsheimer well notes, Erdrich's novel constitutes a counter-history to predominant narratives about World War II (52). Erdrich incorporates Franz's secret Jewishness partly as a way to develop the German American characters' complex relationship to Germany and to the US as a place of refuge in the interwar and World War II years. While Franz stays with Fidelis and Delphine, his younger brothers are taken back to Germany by their domineering aunt after their mother dies. When the Second World War begins, they fight for Germany and one of them dies. Franz, in contrast, becomes a pilot and fights for the US in the war, ultimately dying of complications from the injuries he sustained during the war.

"There's No Jews on the Reservation" 63

By pitting brothers on opposite sides in the war, the novel conveys the complexities and traumas of hybrid identities, phenomena made all the more prominent in the novel through Franz's Jewishness and his biological father's death during World War I. Franz's initial interest in flight is also tacitly ironic insofar as it is sparked by his admiration for Charles Lindbergh, whose anti-Semitic beliefs made his popularity difficult for Jews. Since Franz is unaware of his Jewishness, he does not perceive a tension, yet his admiration of Lindbergh nonetheless evokes a certain unease. Within the broader panorama of twenty-first–century US fiction, Erdrich's naming of Lindbergh evokes Philip Roth's 2004 novel *The Plot Against America* discussed in chapter 1.[8] In addition to the importance of the references to Charles Lindbergh for these reasons, Franz's interest in flight also serves as a point of identification between Franz and Eva, whom he takes on a flight in her final days of life in a moment that becomes a cherished memory for Franz and a singularly happy moment for Eva before she dies. Moreover, his interest in flight from a young age foreshadows his life-threatening injuries as a fighter pilot for the US in World War II, an element of the plot that I explore further below.

Delphine's friendship with Eva is depicted as a deeply intimate identification between the two women on the basis of their tragic family histories. In the difficult and gruelling day-to-day life of the small South Dakota town in the interwar years, the two women lend mutual support to one another as Delphine works with Eva in the butcher shop and minds her children.[9] Once Eva grows ill, Delphine cares for her in ways that further forge their bond, leading ultimately to Eva's confession to her: "Franz, he knows nothing about it. ... His father was not Fidelis. His father's name was Johannes Grunberg. A Jew" (138). As readers learn over the course of the novel, Delphine herself also has a more complicated parentage than what we and other characters in the novel had previously believed. And so Erdrich furthers both the secrecy and intimate relationships between others that is integral to Jewish–Native American encounters. That Franz dies not knowing his father was Jewish and with only Fidelis and Delphine knowing strongly evokes the trope of crypto-Judaism that has long undergirded cultural understandings of Jewishness in Latin America and the Latinx diaspora.

Erdrich's novel thus uses secret Jewishness as a synecdoche for Jewishness writ large and for Germanness. In so doing, the novel's depiction of the hybridity of culture and ethnicity that makes up Erdrich's own family incorporates crypto-Judaism. This depiction of crypto-Jewishness creates a model in which the marrano figure functions as metonymy insofar as, because of the place of Jewish Germanness in the

64 Absorption Narratives

US during the era of World War II, Erdrich's literary reimagining of a German immigrant to the US moves metonymically from German to Jewish and, specifically, crypto-Jewish. This figuring of the secret Jew dovetails with Erin Graff Zivin's "marrano-as-metonym" model in *Anarchaeologies*: "the melancholic sigh of the marrano subject, if not the historical crypto-Jew, then of the marrano-as-metonym, the spectral secret that haunts the Spanish imperial subject from its very inception" (*Anarchaeologies* 42). Obviously, Franz is not a Spanish imperial subject as is the Argentine author whose work Graff Zivin discusses in this context. Yet, in the contact zone created by the encounter of Indigenous and Jewish subjects in the Americas, the paradigm of racial mixture and hybridity that Erdrich's novel depicts closely resembles the forms of hybridity that would characterize crypto-Jewish presence in Iberian America. Moreover, Erdrich's use of the trope of crypto-Judaism – particularly in terms of the question of whether Franz himself ever knows of his own lineage – evokes Iberian American models of racial mixture and the role of crypto-Judaism therein. Put another way, the German Native American author explores the German components of her own identity and her family's belonging in the Americas (on the Canada–US border) in such a way that secret Jewishness is part of paradigms of racial mixture that evoke the inextricability of crypto-Judaism from preoccupations of caste and blood purity in Spanish America. Erdrich brings crypto-Judaism out of the geographical spaces with which it is usually associated (South America, Mesoamerica, the Caribbean, and the US Southwest) to tell a story in which individuals' own Indigenous and Jewish ancestry are unknown (and therefore secrets) to themselves.

In Erdrich's novel, the Jewish and Native American characters who come into contact with one another play a much smaller role than in the other novels I explore in this chapter. Yet, it is precisely this importance of these characters' encounters as a background story – specifically, the fact that Erdrich, as a way of exploring the German side of her own ancestry, sees it necessary to explore these moments of convergence – that makes this particular encounter so central to the novel and to my discussion here. While Franz and Cyprian are both secondary characters, they are central to Delphine's development as a protagonist and serve as important foil characters against which to read Delphine. Specifically, Erdrich divulges only at the novel's end that the woman whom Delphine had believed to be her mother and who had died was not her biological mother; rather, Delphine had been saved as an orphan by Step-and-a-Half. Delphine had been mothered by the same woman as Franz's young girlfriend, marginalized because she is the daughter of a poor single woman; Delphine and Franz's girlfriend

"There's No Jews on the Reservation"   65

eventually befriend one another, yet never learn that they are, in fact, half-sisters. For Erdrich, in order to explore German and Native American hybridity in twentieth-century US fiction, these chiastic foil characters – Delphine and Franz, both of whom are unaware of their true ancestry – see their life trajectories and identities determined by the course of history in ways that are particular to Jews and Native Americans. That is, Franz's severe injuries fighting against the Axis in World War II mean something particular for a German American character whose biological father – unbeknownst to him – was Jewish, just as Delphine's survival as a baby and her origin are tied to Step-and-a-Half, a survivor of the Wounded Knee Massacre. Tellingly, unlike the novels I explore in chapter 3, *The Master Butchers Singing Club*, despite its emphasis on characters' parentage and secret ancestries, does not explicitly tell origin stories of characters who are both Jewish and Native American. Through her crafting of chiastic characters who see their marginalization mirrored and complemented in other characters, the author preserves particular forms of marginalization even as she seeks to explore how these various experiences inform German American identities in the US, including her own.

The Master Butchers Singing Club is not the first of Erdrich's works to underscore Native American–Jewish encounters. Her 1991 novel *The Crown of Columbus*, co-authored with her then-partner Michael Dorris, imagines a fictional professor of Native American studies at Dartmouth who comes across evidence that Christopher Columbus was himself a crypto-Jew. As Casteel notes in her reading of *The Crown of Columbus* (in dialogue with Vizenor's *The Heirs of Columbus*, which I discuss in chapter 3), approaching Jewish–Native American relations from the perspective offered by these novels "turns the tables, considering Native American invocations of Jewish motifs in order to complicate current understandings of interethnic relations as governed by competitive memory" ("Sephardism and Marranism" 61).[10] Continuing this "table-turning" reading that Casteel offers of Erdrich's 1991 novel, I conclude that in *The Master Butchers Singing Club*, Erdrich offers a model of Jewish–Native American encounters that undoes competitive memory through a chiastic approach to the convergence between Germany and the US, between Jewish and Native American, in which the conceptual framework is that Vilhus is surprised to meet Cyprian because "there's no Jews on the reservation." Erdrich imagines the encounter between Jewish and Native American characters who serve as foil characters for her novel's protagonists and mirror the movement of memory throughout North America in the interwar period. These foil characters complement one another's specific experiences of Otherness

66 Absorption Narratives

and marginalization, resisting being "absorbed" into US hegemony so that they preserve the complexities and the forms of resistance that characterize their ancestries and identities. Erdrich thus creates a narrative that furthers Boyarin's endeavour not to "cancel out" the two sides of the analogy between Jews to Europe and Native Americans to the Americas. Recalling the importance that crypto-Jewishness has long had on racial paradigms in Latin American nations, Erdrich creates a fictional family history that takes account of the convergence between secret Jewish characters and Native American characters, thus bringing crypto-Jewishness into the fold of North American, post-Holocaust stories of collective memory and belonging. "There's no Jews on the reservation" is ironic on multiple levels. Not only is the logic that Cyprian applies to Vilhus immediately belied by his own addition of "except he did know about us," but Erdrich creates a fictional universe on the US–Canada border populated with secret Jews, not-secret Jews, and Indigenous people whose stories are bound up in racialized traumas.

"A Moreno Boy More-or-Less My Age": *Tomorrow We Never Did Talk About It*

Set between 1976 and 1981, Eduardo Halfon's 2011 *Tomorrow We Never Did Talk About It* ends with its ten-year-old narrator's father telling him that tomorrow he will explain the conflict that is forcing the family to leave Guatemala for Miami.[11] As the narrator informs us, however, he and his father did not discuss the conflict the next day. Nor would they ever. The ending punctuates a recurrent theme throughout the short novel: the silence, omission, and amnesia that inflect a child's perspective of a political conflict of which he knows very little. The only information his father does offer him regarding the conflict is to answer in the affirmative his question of whether the *guerrilleros* are *indios*. The narrator follows up by asking if the soldiers fighting them are not also *indios*, which his father also answers in the affirmative.[12] That the novel should end with a discussion about the ethnicity of each side of Guatemala's conflict preceding a mention of the father's silence about the conflict is telling, for the narrator's family of Jewish immigrants in Guatemala is positioned as outsiders to the conflict. His father's industrial success has afforded them a life that is comfortable and largely protected from Guatemala's mounting conflict. *Tomorrow We Never Did Talk About It* thus depicts Jews as being outside the conflict of the civil war going on at the time, belonging neither to the side of the *guerrilleros* nor to the *soldados* because, we understand here, they are not *indios*. Halfon thus ponders the place of Jews vis-à-vis Guatemala's tumultuous political landscape, positing Jews as marginalized to the political events that take place in the country while simultaneously grappling to identify with those directly affected by conflict.[13] Halfon's novel shows that Jews and Indigenous people experienced the Guatemalan civil war distinctly. More importantly, the novel suggests possibilities for bridging these ethnic groups' distinct relations to state violence.

Halfon questions what it means to experience the Guatemalan civil war as a Jewish child, and what role silence and memory play in that unique experience. The experience of a Jewish child is one in which he is marked by ethnic difference, yet young and vulnerable enough to be moved to affective identification with the racial or ethnic Other. Halfon has received such accolades as the José María de Pereda Prize for the Short Novel and the Guggenheim Fellowship. Moreover, the 2007 Hay Festival of Bogotá named him one of the thirty-nine best Latin American authors under age forty. His works have been widely translated and the translations have also received great praise. Recent critical understandings of twenty-first century Guatemala have focused overwhelmingly on Salvadoran novelist Horacio Castellanos Moya's *Insensatez*'s narration of Guatemala's civil war and its aftermath (Buiza "Rodrigo Rey Rosa"; Kokotovic 2009; Kroll-Bryce 2014; Sánchez Prado 2010; Venkatesh 2013) and Rodrigo Rey Rosa's novels (Buiza, "Trauma and the Poetics of Affect"; Cano 2012; Carini 2014), or both (Drews 2011; Gutiérrez Mouat 2013).

We may situate Halfon's production within critical accounts of recent Central American literature. Arturo Arias includes Halfon in a 2009 essay on recent trends in Central American literature in which he categorizes a recent contingent of authors in the following manner: "influenced directly or indirectly by globalizing tendencies and blending them in their very tropical way, young writers articulated a pastiche of myths and rites, whether with the purpose of conveying satires of cultural memory, or to demonstrate the absence of cultural memory" (145). Part of this latter category that Arias describes, *Tomorrow We Never Did Talk About It* evinces the absence of narratives regarding collective memory in its emphasis on silence and omissions. Elsewhere, Arias has noted a recent trend in Central American narrative that has sought to correct for intellectuals' previous inability to represent the Other, "a vital gesture toward the ethical encounters with otherness" (quoted in Buiza, "Trauma and the Poetics of Affect" 62). Halfon's novel dovetails with both of these trends through the work's attempt to create cultural memory through identification with ethnic Otherness. In *Tomorrow We Never Did Talk About It*, the silences of what was never discussed evince a lack of resolution with regard to the ethics of Otherness for

68 Absorption Narratives

this upper-class Jewish immigrant family's encounters with Guatemala's poor and Indigenous populations in the context of the mounting tension of armed conflict. Similarly, critical studies are lacking in the way of conceptualizing issues of memory among Jewish culture vis-à-vis recent history in Latin America. Most cultural criticism dedicated to memory and Jewish communities has focused on familial, less overtly political issues of tradition and intergenerational relations.[14]

Halfon's novel grapples throughout with Jews' relation to the political sphere. As my reading of *Tomorrow We Never Did Talk About It* shows, the narrator seeks to understand where his family belongs within the political turmoil of Guatemala in his childhood, which ultimately turns out to be the non-place of exile, similar to Perera's protagonist, who also does not identify with the political situation of Guatemala. Exile becomes the mode of politics that characterizes the Jewish experience. Before their exile, however, the narrator's family is already depicted as not participating in the country's politics. In his text "Dicho hacia el sur" ("Said Towards the South"), Halfon reflects on his four Jewish grandparents who immigrated to Guatemala, in his words, "shook off" their native countries like one might shake dust off their pants or hands, adding, "Maybe, enclosed in their respective Jewish communities, they never felt like part of those countries, those cultures, and therefore it was easy for them to shake them off" (124). Similarly, in *Tomorrow We Never Did Talk About It*, Halfon suggests Jews' exclusion from the broader community – and specifically the realm of active political participation – despite having enjoyed significant economic success.

In Halfon's novella, the experience of leaving the country is shown to be the mode through which his Jewish family experiences the political conflict, evoking vertiginous ideas of Jewish exile and diaspora. In this way, the novella also relates to Maurice Blanchot's essay "Being Jewish," in which Blanchot states, "The words exodus and exile indicate a positive relation with exteriority, whose exigency invites us not to be content with what is proper to us (that is, with our power to assimilate everything, to identify everything, to bring everything back to our I)" (127). For Blanchot, exile is the Jewish condition par excellence. Moreover, we may relate the exteriority that is part of being Jewish in Blanchot's estimation to the alterity depicted in the novel on the basis of ethnic identifications and in light of his impending departure. This exteriority to which Blanchot relates exile dovetails with critical considerations of the ethical encounter with Otherness that characterizes recent Central American literature. Yet, it is important to note that Halfon himself does not use the term "exile" in reference to his narrator in *Tomorrow We Never Did Talk About It* or in interviews or non-fiction

"There's No Jews on the Reservation"   69

writings about his experience leaving Guatemala. (He has noted that his father quibbles with his use of the verb "flee" to discuss the family's departure.) In the context of the family's outsider status based on their ethnic and racial identifications, however, the work evokes Yomaira Figueroa's distinction between exile and "destierro" that I discussed in chapter 1. Halfon's eschewal of the term "exile" relates to the narrator's complicated subject position vis-à-vis racial alterity and political violence.

Apropos of the narrator's exteriority to the conflict, we may return to his father's assertion that both the guerrilleros and the soldiers are indios. This categorization likely speaks to his father's own ignorance surrounding ethnic categories in Guatemala, for "indio" is an imprecise term. Halfon creates a paradigm of mutual misunderstanding between Jewish and Indigenous categories. Historian Greg Grandin concludes in *The Blood of Guatemala*, "The state's counterinsurgency ... was experienced in racial terms. ... Indians experienced the repression as Indians" (222). While, as Halfon posits, both sides of the conflict consist of Indigenous people, the victims of state violence nonetheless are abused and experience this abuse *as* Indigenous, whereby the body politic is coded as Indigenous. Both Halfon's narrator and his father's characterizations of ethnically Indigenous people do not take into account differences between indios and Ladinos, a term which may apply to mestizos or, more liberally, to anyone who does not identify as Indigenous. In this regard, *Tomorrow We Never Did Talk About It* suggests the question of whether Jewish Guatemalans may be considered Ladinos. Halfon reveals Jews to be misunderstood by and not fully integrated into Guatemalan hegemony, yet they are nonetheless distinctly different from Indigenous people, leading us as readers to wonder how Jews do or do not relate to the category of Ladino in a national context in which "Ladino" or "Indigenous" are often understood to be the only readily available categories for racial identification.

Halfon's novel appears during a moment at which historical memory is a central topic throughout Latin American and specifically Central American cultural productions. Of course, Perera's novel published in 1985 also focused on the political climate in Guatemala, though Jaime grew up in 1940s and 1950s Guatemala and did not experience the particular political climate of the 1970s as a child in Guatemala. Yet, the twenty-first century has seen a particular proliferation of novels that grapple not only with the memory of political events in the country but specifically with the modes of storytelling and transmission of those memories that have characterized collective memory in the nation.[15] Many of the thematic and stylistic elements of *Tomorrow We Never Did*

70 Absorption Narratives

Talk About It – namely the use of a child's perspective – are similar to recent fiction by Generation X authors from other regions of Latin America.

The impending condition of exile further complicates Halfon's fraught category as a Jewish Guatemalan author, an experience in which his narrator finds himself on the precipice at age ten towards the work's end.[16] While Perera recounts the increased violence of the early 1980s from the perspective of adults who were living outside the country at this time, Halfon's narrator also positions himself outside the political violence of the time in Guatemala despite still living there at the time. In this sense, the child narrator's looming exile comes to define the way in which the Guatemalan Jew experienced and was affected by Guatemalan state violence. Moreover, Halfon's somewhat unique position as an authorial voice who left Guatemala but was there during the conflict makes his intervention of particular value for considering Jewish political subjectivities vis-à-vis the racial Other in the context of Guatemala's civil war.

Tomorrow We Never Did Talk About It forms part of a sizeable contingent of recent Latin American fiction and film that has adopted a childhood perspective as a way of approaching the political context of recent history as well as exploring themes of memory. In these recent works of film and fiction, the childhood perspective often serves to emphasize the complexities of memory and the silences that have impeded the transmission of memory between generations as well as reconciliation with countries' recent political strife.[17] Moreover, a childhood perspective is often used to nuance the historical and political complexities regarding recent decades of political struggle throughout Latin America through generational confrontations between political actors and their children.[18] Halfon's novel thus contributes to a broader panorama of recent Latin American stories about childhood amidst conflict and chaos.

Within recent cultural productions of Central America, the childhood perspective of *Tomorrow We Never Did Talk About It* recalls the same perspective used in the Mexican–Salvadoran film *Voces inocentes/Innocent Voices* (dir. Luis Mandoki, 2004), the Guatemalan film *Neto's Silence* (dir. Luis Argueta 1994), and the Franco-Costa Rican film *El camino/The Way* (dir. Ishtar Yasín Gutiérrez 2007).[19] *Tomorrow We Never Did Talk About It* differs from *Voces inocentes* in the latter's overt depiction of graphic violence in which its child protagonists engage, a difference that is important to note here for my emphasis on the narrator's exclusion from the violence that plagues his country. Like my discussion of the film *Neto's Silence* and Perera's *Rites* earlier in this chapter, Halfon's novella speaks to class and race privilege in Guatemalan society.

"There's No Jews on the Reservation" 71

The novel's childhood perspective is at times particularly poignant due to the innocent child's lack of awareness of the differences between Jews and gentiles, and subsequent naivety regarding anti-Semitism.[20] The narrator references his family's Jewishness only tangentially, whereby we understand that the family's Jewish identity may be yet another topic that they will not discuss the next day, or ever. Nonetheless, the family's encounters with anti-Semitism and blatant ignorance towards Jewishness figure into the novel as parts of the narrator's coming-of-age process. Like the family's Jewish identification, acts of anti-Semitism are depicted very subtly, and in both instances may also be interpreted more as ignorance of Jewish culture than as anti-Semitism. The narrator recounts a scene at his grandparents' house in which some soldiers arrive unexpectedly and search parts of the house. While they are talking to his grandfather in another room, the narrator waits in the kitchen and watches as men with guns occupy the family home. At one point, one of them asks, "*¿Qué es esto?*" ("What is this?," my translation; *Tomorrow* 93) while tampering with the mezuzah in the doorframe, to which his aunt responds that it is a Jewish talisman with some Torah verses rolled up inside and that its purpose is to protect the house. The narrator observes as the soldier continues to tinker with the mezuzah, hitting it with his fist (93). Thus, the family – in this scene, paralyzed by the presence of soldiers in their home – is victim to the soldier's act of veritably attacking the family's mezuzah. Insofar as the family is also victim of the intimidation and violence of the military officials in this moment, Halfon offers a possible point in common between his Jewish characters and the victims of state violence who, as we know, consisted predominantly of Indigenous Guatemalans.

However, despite the threat of the soldiers' looming presence, we also see that the narrator's family is not on the side of the guerrillas. We learn that the family patriarch – the narrator's grandfather – had been kidnapped in 1967, before the narrator was born. While having a family lunch at a restaurant on a Sunday afternoon, the narrator tells us that his father whispered: "'*Esa señora allá, la del gabán rojo ... fue una de las guerrilleras que secuestró a mi papá*" ("'That woman there, in the red coat ... was one of the guerrilleras who kidnapped my father," my translation; 75–6). He goes on: "*Yo tenía casi nueve años y sabía algunos detalles del secuestro de mi abuelo: detalles sueltos, deshilvanados, irracionales*" ("I was almost nine years old and knew a few details about my grandfather's kidnapping: loose, unseamed, irrational details," my translation, 76). We learn that he was held for ransom and gave his kidnappers two gold-encrusted pens that he always carried with him; we thus surmise that he was kidnapped for economic reasons. The captors dubbed the

72 Absorption Narratives

kidnapping *"La Operación Tomate"* ("Operation Tomato") because his grandfather's skin was so light that it at times appeared pink. The narrator reflects that he had imagined the kidnappers very differently – telling us that he imagined them as dirty, stinky villainous men and not at all like the woman in the red coat. In this sense, we see that he has always known about violence, but now he sees that the realities of violence are more nuanced than he had previously thought.

Elsewhere, we see that the narrator's family has, by some characters' accounts, been victim of anti-Semitic violence. Once the family has decided to move to Miami, the narrator's grandmother asserts to him: *"Está bien que se vayan, mi vida ... Demasiadas balas en este país"* ("It's good that you're leaving, sweetie ... there are too many bullets in this country," my translation; *Tomorrow* 128). The narrator then reflects: *"me quedé pensando en el agujero que aún permanecía en la ventana del comedor de mis abuelos: un agujero circular y pequeño hecho por un balazo que disparó el vecino, decían, un señor ya mayor y algo borracho, decían, que odiaba a los judíos"* ("I thought about the hole that still remained in the window of my grandparents' dining room: a round small hole left by a bullet that had been shot by a neighbour, they said, an old drunk man, they said, who hated Jews," my translation; 128). Halfon's use here of "still remained" emphasizes that this violence had been visited upon the family in the past and that the bullets now pervading the country are, in a sense, nothing new for his family. His repetition of "they said," evokes the complexities of the transmission of memory and suggestively belies the veracity of the anecdote regarding the bullet hole's provenance. This conversation between the narrator and his grandmother immediately follows the sole direct narration of violence in the novel – a moment I will explain further – so we understand that the grandmother is referring to the mounting violence of the civil war. That the narrator should immediately recall the bullet hole resulting from a purportedly anti-Semitic act of violence towards his family again suggests parallels between the violence now going on in the civil war and anti-Semitic violence, thus signalling a possibility for identification between Jews and those whose lives were lost in Guatemala's civil war.

As we see through the mention of the bullet hole that "still remained," while violence is treated very obliquely in the work, it is always a looming presence. While Halfon recounts the devastating earthquake in the narrator's early childhood near its beginning, violence and destruction are largely absent from the rest of the text. However, the final chapter of the novella, homonymously titled "Tomorrow We Never Did Talk About It," is a vignette of the violence that

"There's No Jews on the Reservation"   73

came to characterize Guatemala in the late 1970s and early 1980s and that resulted in the narrator's family's emigration from Guatemala. The narrator recounts, "The first shots had sounded at ten o'clock in the morning. I didn't hear them. But I knew, from the gravity on my friends' faces, on Oscar's faces, that something important had happened" (118). The first and only narration of violence in the novel is presented obliquely and through absences: the absence of the narrator's witnessing aurally the gunshots, only shown by the presence of his schoolmates' facial registers that something had happened. The grammatical shifts from preterit "I didn't hear them" to the pluperfect "something important had" in the original Spanish text are noteworthy. Like in the shared title of both the last chapter of this monograph and the novella, the idea of postponement or of a past anticipation of an event that the narrator would never experience – first-hand violence or a substantive conversation about this violence – characterizes the narrator's relation to his childhood and to the political sphere of his home country. Moreover, the temporal shifts correspond to characteristic psychological responses to trauma through temporal shuttling between past and present.

Violence is central to the novel's plot as well as to recent Central American literature writ large. Arias points out that, in recent Central American literature, "the climate of violence continues to permeate everything, Nonetheless, it is no longer political violence, with a certain rational logic that makes it possible to explain who is against who. Now it is an irrational, violence of the soul, the senselessness of which permeates everything and everyone" (146). While the oblique references to violence that are included in *Tomorrow We Never Did Talk About It* are circumscribed to the context of the civil war in the early 1980s, the novel nonetheless implicitly deals with this profusion of violence insofar as the narrator, who is not Indigenous and therefore, as we see through his brief conversation with his father, does not belong to either of the known sides of the conflict and is largely sheltered from the violence, still comes into contact with violence and must reckon with its reality.

In light of the complexities of both his family's relatively few roots in Guatemala and his exile at a young age, Halfon's identification as Guatemalan is, as he has attested, quite fraught. Nonetheless, *Tomorrow We Never Did Talk About It* focuses – albeit somewhat obliquely at times – on a key moment of Guatemala's recent history that was also a watershed moment in the protagonist's coming-of-age process: the increased violence of the country's civil war in 1981 as a defining moment in his process of identity formation. In an interview given in 2010, the

74 Absorption Narratives

year before *Tomorrow We Never Did Talk About It* was published, Halfon stated the following:

> Guatemala for me is a big issue. I have a big problem with Guatemala. I left so young that I don't identify at all with the country, with the people. I see Guatemala as most people from the outside see it, as an outsider. So, the subject matter of Guatemala, socially, politically, the civil war that went on for forty years. The poverty, the violence of it, that is also one of those subjects that I'm tentative about. It'll get there. ("Writers On the Fly")

Written shortly after this interview, *Tomorrow We Never Did Talk About It*, his first novel set in Guatemala, may be understood as part of Halfon's working through his identification with the country. In keeping with his observation that he sees Guatemala "as most people from the outside see it," the novel is rife with moments that seem to be narrated from an exogenous viewpoint, despite being memories of a young child who was born in the country. These moments in which Halfon presents Guatemala, its people, and its political strife as exogenous may be attributed to his exile but are also often enveloped in differences in class, religion, and ethnicity.

As a way of exploring the identifications between people and the breakdown in transmission of memory – and as the novel's title suggests – silences play a central role throughout the novel. Ilan Stavans notes, in his afterword to the English version of the story "Tomorrow We Never Did Talk About It," that "this is the kind of tale in which what is said, what the narrator understands, and what the reader knows, is as important as what is kept out of sight, what falls into that nothingness we call silence" (loc. 267–9). The brevity of Halfon's work emphasizes both the innocence of the child's perspective and the problems of memory transmission typical of childhood narratives. The novel's first chapter, "*El baile de la marea*," is a snippet of the narrator and his father talking on the beach. The father abruptly tells the narrator that he drowned in the ocean when he was the narrator's age and offers no further details or explanations. In a sense, the novel's beginning chapter mirrors its ending in the narrator's reflection: "I wanted to ask my father things" (*Tomorrow* 16, my translation). The novel's first pages introduce the motif of truncated conversations or questions that the narrator struggles to formulate to his father, while the final section concludes that these conversations never took place.

Mostly, the silences and temporal jumps (the novel spans five years of the narrator's life yet is narrated over fewer than one hundred pages)

"There's No Jews on the Reservation"   75

lead readers to consider what the narrator cannot remember due to his young age at the time of the events. *Tomorrow We Never Did Talk About It* evokes Marianne Hirsch's notions of postmemory: "'Postmemory' describes the relationship that the 'generation after' bears to the personal, collective, and cultural trauma of those who came before – to experiences they 'remember' only by means of the stories, images, and behaviors among which they grew up" (3). Here, the lacunae of memory – evinced through the promise of conversations that would never take place as well as the elisions and silences in the novel's structure – dovetail with the narrator's family's lack of direct engagement with the conflict, a conflict that nonetheless prompts the family's exile and thus determines a great deal of the course of the narrator's life.

While childhood memories of political struggle have not been the immediate focus of much recent Central American literature, the topic has figured centrally in Southern Cone literature and literary analysis.[21] Similarly, Hilary Levinson analyses Roberto Brodsky's *Bosque quemado*'s depiction of material objects that "intervene in the novel's many distances, between Chile and exile, past and present, father and son, and image and text" (590) through the lens of Hirsch's postmemory.[22] As we observe through Levinson's emphasis on fissures and distance, *Tomorrow We Never Did Talk About It* forms part of a broader constellation of recent Latin American fiction that centres on the breakdowns in transmission of childhood memory in the context of exile and violence.

The second chapter is set in 1976, when the narrator is five years old, and recounts the February 4 earthquake that killed an estimated twenty-three thousand people and wounded another seventy-six thousand. The narrator awakes the morning of the earthquake to find the servants in his house crying. His uncle Benny asks him if he likes his house and explains to him that many people (an estimated one million) were left homeless after the earthquake. Benny, a volunteer firefighter, responds to this earthquake and takes the narrator along with him. They go to a part of town that he has never seen before and to which he refers as "<<*esa otra ciudad*>>'" ("that other city," guillemets original, my translation; 25), instilling in the protagonist an awareness of his good fortune and the differences between him and those Guatemalans who have less. He spends his day with the volunteer firemen distributing drinking water to local citizens without potable water. Later in the chapter he returns home and comments that the domestic staff have draped a cloth over his swing set so that they may sleep there instead of in the small room they share out of fear of another earthquake or fear of returning home to their decimated neighbourhoods. Thus, the

76 Absorption Narratives

novel begins with a depiction of a moment of national catastrophe that is shown to affect poorer sectors of the city disproportionately and to make class differences more evident to our very young narrator, who at this age is beginning to identify and empathize with those who are less fortunate than he. At the end of the day, however, he is safe at home and the woman who will sleep under his swing set is serving him hot chocolate and reassuring him that he is now safe from any further natural disasters.

In these cases of identification between the novel's narrator and people of lower social classes, ethnicity is an important factor. When he goes to "that other city" just after the earthquake with his uncle, the narrator observes: *"un niño moreno de más o menos mi edad lloraba solito sobre la banqueta"* ("a *moreno* boy around my own age sitting on a bench alone crying"; my translation; 26).[23] The description of this "niño" evinces both difference (moreno) and likeness (*más o menos mi edad*). At five years old, we understand that this is likely the first moment of identification between the narrator and a true Other. His observation that the child was crying *"solito"* suggests an empathetic identification through the retrospective narration decades later. We understand that the image of this crying, dark-skinned child has stuck with the narrator since his early childhood. While this character's ethnic categorization is ambiguous (i.e., we cannot categorize him as *indio, indígena, natural,* or *maya* on the basis of the information Halfon presents here), the narrator's use of "moreno" marks this child as not belonging to the category of Ladino.

Halfon's identification with this *niño moreno* as part of his narrator's consideration of his childhood in Guatemala suggests an identification between Jewish and Indigenous populations as an integral component of Guatemalan citizenship. Unlike this *niño moreno,* the narrator's grandfather is Lebanese, while the rest of his Jewish family in Guatemala, we surmise, is of Eastern European descent. The novel's final scene and the conversation that the narrator would never have with his father regarding the soldiers and guerrillas who were both *indios* evokes complex issues of the role of Jews in the context of political upheaval. Halfon's novel thus posits the complexities between ethnicity and active political participation. While the narrator does not discuss the earthquake or his experiences on that day later in the novella, his curiosity about the *indios* at the end of the novel recalls his identification at a very young age with the *"niño moreno"* crying after the earthquake at the beginning of the novel.

If, as Grandin suggests, the Indigenous victims of repression experienced state violence "as Indians," we may venture that Jews experienced

"There's No Jews on the Reservation"   77

state violence *as Jews* through the condition of exile. We may return to Blanchot's notion of exodus and exile in order to consider how Halfon's novel creates a crescendo throughout these five years of the narrator's life in which he becomes increasingly less innocent and more aware of the harsh realities of the world surrounding him. This crescendo culminates in exile and in silence. In the case of Halfon's narrator, who by his own account is neither a guerrilla nor a soldier because he is not an *indio*, the only place for him and for his family within the Guatemalan political sphere is to be found in the non-place of exile.

We wonder, then, what possibilities for identification as fellow Guatemalan citizens and as fellow humans Halfon is suggesting between Jews and the poorer, Indigenous characters – the young dark-skinned boy around his own age and the domestic staff in his home. In this regard, *Tomorrow We Never Did Talk About It* evokes questions of Otherness and state violence similar to those in Castellanos Moya's *Insensatez*, whose narrator also positions himself outside the political conflict in part because he is not Indigenous, yet ultimately comes to form significant affective identifications with the Indigenous victims of Guatemala's state violence. The crucial difference between these two works' narrators, however, is that Castellanos Moya's narrator (like Castellanos Moya himself) is not Guatemalan. It is therefore interesting to note the similarly exogenous position that Halfon's narrator occupies when recounting this time period. The sensation of distance and Otherness that characterize the narrator's relationship to his country and its traumatic past is due to his exile but also, we come to understand, to his family's Jewish and non-Indigenous ethnicity.

Conclusions

In these four novels – all of which are semi-autobiographical – Indigenous and Jewish subjects imagine their place in the Americas vis-à-vis one another. If indeed there are no Jews on the reservation – and no Indigenous people on the shtetl – these fictional depictions of Jewish–Indigenous encounters show that an awareness of the Other is nonetheless central to a sense of national belonging. For Joel Fleischman, Jews are "fellow people of color, victims of oppression," while for these authors, Jews are victims of oppression in different ways than Indigenous folks. Through Perera's and Halfon's shared emphases on their autofictional characters' exiles from Guatemala (Alcalá's questioning – through Zacarías's voice – of what the Kabbalah means "in this land" and Erdrich's depiction of Cyprian and Vilhus's wandering circus), the attachments of Jewish and Indigenous peoples to the land complement

78 Absorption Narratives

and disrupt one another in contradictory ways. In all of these stories, experiences of exile and displacement are presented as a condition that is capable of unifying Jewish and Indigenous characters, yet the particularities of Jewish and Indigenous presence in these shared spaces complicate empathetic identifications (with the exception of Cyprian and Vilhus). We might attribute these missed opportunities for identification to the paradigms of settler colonialism that signify that Jewish presence in Guatemala, the US–Mexico border, and the US–Canada border, though a function of the need to find refuge from pogroms and persecution, is nonetheless bound up in an imperialist, white supremacist agenda that allowed the immigration of light-skinned Jews to these places in the first place. The tendency of governmental leaders throughout the American hemisphere to allow entry to Jews as part of policies that sought (if implicitly) to increase the number of white people in their nations is the point of departure from which anthropologist Ruth Behar tells the story of her own family's history in Cuba and serves as a guiding framework for chapter 4 of this book. In the four works explored in this chapter, being Jewish and being Indigenous in the Americas means necessarily to account for the wandering, liminality, and secrecy that have characterized one's own group identity as well as to take account of the Other. Guatemala City, North Dakota, and the US–Mexico borderlands are depicted as spaces in which Jewish and Indigenous experiences converge to allow for explorations of what it means to belong to one of these groups in the specific time and space at hand as well as in the broader context of the histories of these respective groups throughout the Americas over the course of centuries. As we have observed in all of these works, Jew is not to Europe as Indigenous is to the Americas. Rather, any points of comparison come about only through an exploration of what codifies a person as Jewish or Indigenous in various geographies throughout the Americas in relation to historical events in both Europe and the Americas. Just as Jakobsen points out that asking whether Jews are analogous to queers is ultimately akin to asking whether we can queer queers, asking about Jewishness and Indigeneity in relation to one another similarly is a way to learn about one's own group as much as the other.

Worth noting here is the fact that Goldman and Halfon both draw on their autobiographical experiences as Sephardic Jews, while Alcalá and Erdrich both recount tales of secret Jews. Sephardism and secret Jewishness, in this sense, are shown to facilitate negotiations between Jewish and Indigenous identities. In keeping with paradigms of crypto-Judaism and racial mixture in the Americas. Without eschewing the differences between the groups, these literary imaginings of encounters

"There's No Jews on the Reservation"   79

between Jews and Indigenous peoples move past the model of competitive memory. These stories prompt us to think about what pogroms and the Holocaust mean for Indigenous peoples in the Americas and what genocide of Indigenous Americans means for Jews, bearing in mind that Jews and Indigenous peoples are absorbed differentially "in this land" – that is, in various locales throughout the Americas. These works create new cultural models for Jewishness and race, charting new, chiastic cartographies for race and identity by rejecting analogical thinking in favour of chiasmi that take Jewishness into account to consider Indigeneity and taking Indigeneity into account to consider Jewishness.

3 "What Is It We Absorb?": Fictional Genealogies of Hybridity between Jewishness and Indigeneity

As we saw in the previous chapter, paradigms of mixture and secrecy are present – and often predominant – even in literary accounts of encounters between Jewish and Indigenous characters in which hybrid (Jewish–Indigenous) ancestry is not explicitly present. Whereas in chapter 2 I discussed encounters between Jews and Indigenous characters as separate categories, in this chapter I focus on literary productions from throughout the Americas that depict characters who are both Indigenous (or mestizo, and their lineage thus is partially Indigenous) and Jewish. The novels discussed here foreground characters' genealogies to explore both the richness and the difficulties of Jewish–Indigenous hybridity, a thematic motif that has long been at the fore of literary and cultural thought in Latin America. Most notably, nineteenth-century Latin American fiction has been shown to hinge on love stories through which national identity is articulated. Drawing from Foucault's *History of Sexuality* and Benedict Anderson's *Imagined Communities*, Doris's *Foundational Fictions* charts how love stories – many of them between individuals of different races – served as a way of building nations in nineteenth-century Latin America following independence from Spain. More recently, Tuck and Yang's "Decolonization Is Not a Metaphor" focused on family relations in their emphasis on "adoption narratives" in which white authors seek to exculpate themselves from settler colonialism by imagining a white hero adopted by Native Americans. Worth noting here is that both Sommer's book and Tuck and Yang's article focus on James Fenimore Cooper (in Sommer's case, on how Latin American authors engaged with his writings), further linking the literary histories – and role of Indigeneity therein – of North and South America. In the novels discussed in this chapter, characters who have both Jewish and Indigenous ancestry resist assimilation in many ways; they also resist allegorical readings that

"What Is It We Absorb?" 81

would resolve the tensions and differences between these parts of their identities.

Flor de Mayo, one of the main characters of Francisco Goldman's 1992 novel *The Long Night of White Chickens*, most explicitly contests straightforward models of Jewish-mestiza hybridity. The character was born in Guatemala and is *mestiza* but grew up in the suburbs of Boston and was raised by a Jewish man alongside the novel's narrator, Roger, almost as his sister. Flor de Mayo reflects, "You know that famous definition of surrealism ... well what about a gringo Russian Jew and a Guatemalan *fufurufa* Catholic on a dissecting table?" (242). Flor suggests that her identity is as jarring a combination as the chance meeting of an umbrella and a sewing machine on a dissecting table (drawing from André Breton's first surrealist manifesto). Similar to the seemingly impossible presence of Jews in Indigenous spaces and Indigenous people in Jewish spaces in chapter 2 (seemingly impossible because of the belief that "there's no Jews on the reservation"), Goldman's novel imagines – through the voice of Flor – that Jewish–Indigenous identity is so unlikely as to be surreal. Flor adds to her surrealistic discussion of Roger's identity, "So OK, Guatemala, in what we like to think of as its deepest self, is Mayan. We, who aren't actually Indian, what is it we absorb? Not that supposed Indian lack of egocentrism, that community and cosmos first stuff, that's for sure" (242). Flor brings her own complicated mixture of Jewish and mestizo Guatemalan identity into conversation with the spiritual implications of Guatemalan Indigeneity for Guatemalans who do not identify as Indigenous. Maya spirituality, for Flor, is absorbed by those who "aren't actually Indian" in ways that remain mysterious. As the character's monologue suggests, hybrid identities between Jewish and Indigenous take on particular significance in relation to nationality and spirituality.

In this chapter, I focus on Indigenous–Jewish hybridity in four novels: Mordecai Richler's *Solomon Gursky Was Here*, Gerald Vizenor's *The Heirs of Columbus*, Francisco Goldman's *The Long Night of White Chickens*, and Michael Chabon's *The Yiddish Policemen's Union*. The four novels all depict characters whose genealogies contain a mixture of Jewish and Indigenous ancestors. Each novel questions Jewish and Indigenous belonging in their respective national contexts. While all four novels were written in English and published first in the US and Canada, Vizenor's consideration of the legacy of Christopher Columbus vis-à-vis Sephardic Maya and Goldman's geographical focus on Guatemala allow their explorations of Jewish–Indigenous hybridity to take account of Spanish American paradigms of culture and hybridity. Each of these fictional accounts of Jewish–Indigenous hybridity

82 Absorption Narratives

imagines this hybridity in a unique way: *Solomon Gursky Was Here* tells the multigenerational story of a Jewish family in which one of the patriarchs sired children with First Nations women he encountered throughout Canada; *The Heirs of Columbus* imagines Columbus as a Sephardic crypto-Jew who had sex with the Maya and tells the story of their progeny; *The Long Night of White Chickens* tells of Flor de Mayo's vexed identity as a part Indigenous Guatemalan woman raised as a Jew; and *The Yiddish Policemen's Union* recounts the story of Ber Shemets, the protagonist's partner and cousin who is the son of a zealous Jewish settler in Alaska and a Tlingit woman. These characters may be primary or secondary characters in the novels, but all play the important role of allowing the authors to question – from Jewish perspectives in the case of Richler, Goldman, and Chabon and from an Indigenous perspective in the case of Vizenor – the complexities of Jewish and Indigenous alterity in their respective national contexts and in the Americas writ large.

Following the question "What is it we absorb?," I read these four novels with a focus on how facets of Jewish–Indigenous hybridity are shown, at times, to absorb the particularities of the two categories and, at other times, to allow discrete facets of these identities to resist absorption and to flourish. My readings of these works underscore their respective authors' emphases on genealogy as a lens through which to explore identity and belonging. These novels focus on intergenerational struggles as a way of highlighting the complexities of multiracial identities vis-à-vis the national project and the centuries-long stories of Indigenous and Jewish presence in the Americas. Specifically, I consider how family lineage has pervaded Spanish American cultural production, such as the model of foundational fictions discussed in chapter 1. In the particular case of fiction that depicts characters with both Jewish and Indigenous lineages, such foundational fictions serve to highlight the fraught, often unequal relationships between various ethnicities that comprise individual identities in the present. These novels imagine possibilities for mixture that do not absorb or eschew the particularities of the discrete categories. Rather, Jewishness and Indigeneity are depicted to be often in conflict with one another even within a single individual, in line with Benítez Rojo's model of syncretism as a "signifier made of difference," discussed in chapter 1. These fictional texts parse the elements of Jewish and Indigenous identities that converge to comprise individual identities in ways that are explicitly connected to centuries of colonialism.

The genealogical emphases of these four novels take account of Jewishness and Indigeneity as categories that are marginalized in different ways. Moreover, the two identities are, for these novelists, different from one another in ways that often position the two in tension or even opposition to one another. For the Indigenous–Jewish characters in these works, these two aspects of their identities collide in ways that create internal and external conflicts. Throughout these texts, characters' parentage combining Jewish and Indigenous ancestors underscores the complicated histories of racialization throughout the Americas. If, as Ben Vinson noted in colonial Mexico, in *that* kingdom blood purity meant not having mixed blood (whereas in the Iberian Peninsula blood purity was predicated on not being Jewish or Muslim), in these novels, Indigeneity, Jewishness, and racial mixtures coexist in ways that simultaneously disrupt and reinforce one another.

In addition to their shared emphasis on family genealogies, these novels share an element of detective fiction.[1] Except for *Solomon Gursky Was Here*, each novel centres on an unsolved crime. For its part, *Solomon Gursky Was Here* has some characteristics of detective fiction insofar as it follows the investigation into the Gursky family history, including shameful family scandals. The crimes in these novels are bound up in complicated histories of race, specifically the convergence of Jewish and Indigenous characters in nations throughout the Americas. Most visibly in the case of Vizenor's novel – much of which takes place in courtrooms for hearings – the crimes and investigations into them have to do with questions of race and human rights violations. In all of these works, the mysteries of individual cases and family histories speak to broader, centuries-old histories of colonial power exerted along racial lines.

"Nothing More Than a Hyphen": *Solomon Gursky Was Here*

Jewish Canadian author Mordecai Richler's 1990 novel *Solomon Gursky Was Here* includes a family tree in its front matter, signalling the importance of family lineages even before the novel's first page. Over the course of the novel, one generation of the Gursky family is reduced, in the narrator's words, "to nothing more than a hyphen" (412). The narrator's information throughout is based on what character Moses Berger, erstwhile paramour of Solomon Gursky's daughter, Lucy, has been able to surmise over the course of decades of getting to know the family and seeking information about them. Ephraim, part of the third Franklin expedition, converted Indigenous people to Judaism. Generations later, his great-grandson, Henry, marries Nialie, a member of this group of Indigenous Jews. Their son, Isaac, cannibalizes Henry in order to survive after Henry dies in a snowmobiling accident. Aware

84   Absorption Narratives

that the family patriarch, Ephraim Gursky, born in London, was part of
the Franklin expedition, Moses is less successful in finding information
about Ephraim's son, Aaron, who fathered the novel's titular character,
Solomon, along with two other sons: Bernard and Morrie. Although he
lived to the age of ninety, there was little information about Aaron's life.
As the narrator notes, "So far as Moses could make out, Aaron had been
no more than a hyphen, joining the Gursky generation of Ephraim with
that of Bernard, Solomon, and Morrie. A shadowy presence inhibited
in the first place by his father's mockery and then by the turbulence
between his sons" (412). Aaron, half-brother to countless children born
from Ephraim's escapades with Indigenous women throughout his ex-
cursions, is but a hyphen. This hyphen signifies not only Aaron's function as a character who connects these generations but also the fraught
blending of Jewish and Indigenous cultures that his own generation of
Ephraim's sons embodies.[2] As a signifier, the hyphen is ambiguous: it
denotes likeness but also separation. Aaron's condition of being "no
more than a hyphen" tacitly questions cultural models of genealogies
that take discrete, individual categories of identification transmitted
from one generation to the next for granted as part of a hybrid identity.
The hyphen, in its dual, contradictory function of both joining and sep-
arating, problematizes the elements of Jewishness and Indigeneity that
are maintained and lost in the processes of hybridity that have come to
characterize the Gursky family over centuries. The hyphen that joins
generations absorbs difference. Richler's hyphen signals an intergenerational relationship in which the younger generation cannibalizes previous generations.

Solomon Gursky Was Here forms part, as David Koffman recently
noted, of a "steady trickle of literary interest in Indigenous people
and themes that runs through twentieth-century Canadian Jewish literature" ("The Unsettling of Canadian Jewish History" 92). Koffman
interprets this interest in line with Tuck and Yang's model in which
the settler "moves to innocence" (Tuck and Yang quoted in Koffman
94). Like the other novels discussed in this chapter, Jewish–Indigenous
hybridity forms part of the Gursky family genealogy in ways that both
complicate and seek to resolve Jewish anxieties about belonging in contemporary Canadian society. In turn, Richler continues a long tradition
of writing from the Americas that centres Indigeneity in ideas about national belonging and the concept of ethnic difference. For the Gurskys,
the outcome of the family's absorption of Indigenous culture is nothing
short of monstruous and catastrophic.

Richler's novels explore Jewish belonging (and not belonging) in
a region of Canada where national belonging is already fraught. The

"What Is It We Absorb?" 85

author's hometown of Montreal – also home to the Gursky family and the setting of much of the novel – has a complicated relationship to national identity. Not only does Richler's fiction grapple with Jewish and Indigenous belonging in Canada, but it also grapples with the place of the Québécois in Canada. Jews occupy a complicated space in Quebec in particular because of the importance of religion and lineage in French Canadian life. Richler's work illustrates the degree to which Jews in Montreal were, for nearly a century-and-a-half, what historian David Fraser has termed "honorary Protestants" due to the complex negotiations that took place between the Jewish community and local municipal agencies, because Protestants and Catholics were granted legal rights to denominational schools, whereas Jews were not. Richler's fictional representations of Jewish Montreal underscore such tensions as the Jewish School Question, a controversy that, as Fraser argues, was part of Jews' "collective understandings of what it meant to be Jewish and British subjects, and later Canadian citizens" (3). Jews were allowed to attend Protestant schools at the discretion of these schools, so that their access to education was "dependent on the absence or presence of Christian charity from the Protestant school authorities" (7). As Fraser illustrates with an example from Richler's breakthrough earlier novel, *The Apprenticeship of Duddy Kravitz*, these Protestant schools were often rife – both in the historical record and in the literary imagination – with blatant anti-Semitism. The Gursky family has a fraught relationship to Quebec, as Richler shows, for example, in the description of the elaborate seventy-fifth birthday party for Bernard Gursky: "a banquet in the ballroom of the Ritz-Carlton hotel, suitably bedecked for the occasion with Canadian, Québécois (this, in the name of prudence), and Israeli flags" (119). Whereas the Gursky family sees it prudent to outwardly avow allegiance to Quebec, their loyalty to Canada and Israel, respectively, are shown to be more sincere.

While much of *Solomon Gursky Was Here* takes place – like *The Apprenticeship of Duddy Kravitz* – in Montreal, many scenes set in the large city are still sprinkled with descriptions and conversations of the prairie and frontier. Richler describes, for example, a seventy-year-old man named Bert Smith, an Anglo-Saxon man who lives in "lowest" Westmount (an exaggeration of "lower" Westmount, an area of Montreal) in 1963. In a conversation with some of his neighbours, Smith extols his parents: "Theirs was the indomitable spirit that tamed the wilderness ... look at Saskatoon now. Or Regina" (*Solomon Gursky* 80). He goes on to ask, "Where would this country be today had it been left to your sort to pioneer the west?" (80). These young neighbours to whom Smith is speaking are described as both being white and Christian, so that, the

86 Absorption Narratives

passage suggests, a racist man such as Smith expects more of them – as if to live up to the legacy of his own parents who "tamed the wilderness." The project of "pioneering the wilderness" is thus shown to be understood by racist white Canadians as a WASP endeavour, as understood within the same mentality that discriminates against immigrants and racial Others in Montreal itself. As the narrator tells us from there, Smith "did not have to worry about Jews on the street that he lived on in lowest Westmount ... even so, there was no shortage of trash. Noisy Greek immigrants cultivating tomato plants in rock-hard back yards. Swarthy, fart-filled Italians. Forlorn French-Canadian factory girls" (80). He remarks to his landlady, "Happily we will not live long enough to see Canada become a mongrelized country" (80). Richler goes on from here to note that, in 1907, Canadian journalist John Dafoe "wrote an article aimed at enticing American immigrants to the prairie, assuring them that there was no chance of mongrel race or civilization taking hold in western Canada" (80). Thus, in Richler's narrative about Jewish belonging in both Montreal and in rural parts of the nation, anti-Semitism and anxieties about racial mixture are presented as threats to the country's white, Anglo-Saxon Protestant communities. And yet the novel also presents Jews as being settler colonists in their own right, although they are also the object of discrimination themselves.

As a way of reckoning with this condition of being out of place, Richler questions Jewishness in relation to the land and in relation to Indigenous people in Canada in *Solomon Gursky Was Here*. The novel is, at its core, a story about who belongs on which lands, when they belong (or used to belong) there, and why. To explore the topic, as Richler has done elsewhere, he turns to the figure of the Indigenous person. In this regard, *Solomon Gursky Was Here* is in keeping with *The Apprenticeship of Duddy Kravitz*. As a working-class Jew in Montreal's Mount Royal neighbourhood, Duddy constantly strives to earn enough money to buy his own plot of land in French Canada, because he has learned from his grandfather throughout his childhood and adolescent years that "a man without land is nobody" (*Apprenticeship* 49). As Casteel ("Jews among the Indians") notes, "Richler's Arctic Jewish epic is a logical extension of the gesture he had made thirty years prior when he put Jewish Montreal on the literary map in *The Apprenticeship of Duddy Kravitz*" (783). Duddy's urge to buy land exemplifies Koffman's model of Jewish settler colonialism that I discussed in chapter 1. In the novel's film adaptation, once Duddy finally buys land – the culmination of the titular "apprenticeship" – and shows it to his father and grandfather, his father exclaims, "Hey, it's Indian territory!" (*The Apprenticeship of Duddy Kravitz*, dir. Ted Kotcheff, 1974). In this way, owning land that

"What Is It We Absorb?" 87

was stolen from the Indigenous inhabitants is, for the Kravitz family, a *sine qua non* of belonging as a Jew in twentieth-century Canada. This phenomenon of replacing Indigenous people is more central to the narrative of *Solomon Gursky*. Specifically, Jewish absorption of Native lands and identities – a theme that Richler seeded in *The Apprenticeship of Duddy Kravitz* and expands here – characterizes the Gursky family lineage. A few years after publishing *The Apprenticeship of Duddy Kravitz*, Richler returned to the Indigenous figure in *The Incomparable Atuk* (1963). Notably, in that novel, unlike in *Solomon Gursky Was Here*, there is no genealogical hybridity between Indigenous and Jewish characters. Rather, the Indigenous figure serves solely as a relief of Jewish alterity. As Casteel notes, "*Atuk* is similarly preoccupied with interethnic contact between Jews and Inuit but focuses on the assimilation of the Indigene rather than the indigenization of the Jew and relies more heavily on caricature and farce. ... *Atuk* demonstrates the ambiguous status of Jewishness, which simultaneously occupies the dual and contradictory roles of marginalized Other and settler-invader" (Casteel, "Jews among the Indians" 785). If in *The Incomparable Atuk* and *The Apprenticeship of Duddy Kravitz* Richler explores Jewish alterity through Indigenous people and lands, in *Solomon Gursky Was Here*, Indigenous characters become absorbed into the Gursky family tree as a way of assuaging some of this difference. The genealogy of the Gursky family creates a story in which the family becomes Canadian by procreating with and/or marrying Indigenous women. Yet, the intergenerational tensions remind us that this absorption is a contentious, incomplete process.

These incomplete processes of mixing Jewish and Indigenous ancestry in Gursky's novel create a fictional genealogy that dovetails with national history, a model that has also been central to Latin American fiction dating back to the nineteenth century. I am not the first critic to consider *Solomon Gursky Was Here* in a framework informed by Latin American literary criticism. Indeed, of the relatively few critical articles that have been published about the novel, two invoke models of Latin American literature or draw comparisons between Richler's novel and canonical Latin American literature. Casteel reads *Solomon Gursky Was Here* within a context of Roberto González Echevarría's notion of "archival fictions" as well as Lois Parkinson Zamora's (1997) idea of "anxiety of origins." Casteel takes this latter term to refer to "the acute awareness of the absurd and disrupted character of origins in New World societies" ("Jews among the Indians" 789). For his part, Tamás Bényei compares *Solomon Gursky Was Here* to Gabriel García Márquez's *One Hundred Years of Solitude* on the basis that *Solomon Gursky Was Here* explicitly mentions that character Moses's lover reads García Márquez's

88 Absorption Narratives

novel in bed and because the novels share an emphasis on genealogy. Bényei (2003) notes, "In these narratives, it is precisely through the genealogical research or narrative logic that the notion of stable origin is challenged" (96). As Bényei states, in order to reflect on national history and identity, *Solomon Gursky Was Here* and *One Hundred Years of Solitude* recount multiple generations of a family's history in ways that challenge the notion of a single family's genealogical coherence. *One Hundred Years of Solitude* follows seven generations of the Buendía family as they marry and reproduce in the context of important moments in Colombian and Latin American history. Similar to Moses's role in *Solomon Gursky Was Here*, Melquíades, one of the few main characters in *One Hundred Years of Solitude* who is not part of the Buendía family, keeps track of time and is the probable narrator of the story.

To these existing readings of *Solomon Gursky Was Here* that make reference to Latin American fiction and literary criticism, I add Sommer's model of foundational fictions, specifically her provocative exploration of Jewish whiteness in *María* that I discussed in chapter 1. Like the novels that Sommer explores in *Foundational Fictions*, Richler's novel offers a fraught origin story of Jewish–Indigenous hybridity that underwrites national identity. Unlike in *María*, however, Nialie's character is herself both Jewish and Indigenous, whereas the Efraín character of whom Sommer writes is Jewish and passes as white (calling into question what was considered "white" in nineteenth-century contexts). In keeping with Sommer's model, the Gursky family origin story, even if on the surface it seems to be about overcoming racial, cultural, and religious differences, vexes and causes generations of unresolved tension. As Sommer notes throughout her analyses in *Foundational Fictions*, narratives of national belonging and convergence between distinct ethnic groups form the basis of national identity insofar as they are imperfect national romances. They are imperfect precisely because the very forms of hybridity that these novels celebrate absorb difference rather than maintain it. Similarly, *Solomon Gursky Was Here* conveys a narrative about a family's hybridity between Jewishness and First Nations in a vertiginously homogenizing way.

Solomon Gursky Was Here makes repeated gestures towards similarities of oppression among Indigenous peoples and Jews. For example, a character attempts to explain to another that the term "Eskimo" is offensive. He states, "An Eskimo or, more properly, an Inuit. Eskimo, don't you know, is an Indian word that means 'eater of raw meat'. It's pejorative ... like kike, to take a random example" (258–9). Yet, within the context of this novel, the analogy presented here is not a "random example." Rather, *Solomon Gursky Was Here* articulates a particular

"What Is It We Absorb?" 89

relationship between Jewishness and Indigeneity as a foundational hybridity that undergirds Canadian life. The character's use of simile here creates an analogy between the use of pejorative terms against Jews and those against Indigenous people. As Koffman notes, "Anglo-Protestant ideas that brought Jews and Indigenous peoples together have taken a wide variety of forms, and each case ought to be considered within its own context for what each imaginary reveals about the non-Jewish and non-Indigenous peoples who crafted it. Canadians from a range of cultural locations have tied Jews and Indigenous peoples together, and have done so since before Canada became a state" ("The Unsettling of Canadian Jewish History" 89). Put another way, "Eskimo" is pejorative "like kike" not because they are two random examples of ethnic slurs but because in the Canadian cultural imaginary, hegemonic ideas of ethnicity and belonging have posited Jews and Indigenous people as similar. The explanation of the similarity between "Eskimo" and "kike" on the basis of the meaning "eater of raw meat" also foreshadows Isaac's cannibalization of his father.

Elsewhere in the novel, Richler emmeshes the Jewish and First Nations groups by creating signifiers that could refer to either of them. Recreating a scene from the Franklin expedition, a character reflects on found objects: "These so-called symbols embroidered into the fabric are not Eskimo but Hebrew" (47–8). The president of the Arctic society attempts to disavow theories about the Jewish origins of artefacts, referring to them as a red herring.

> The so-called Jock Roberts *Yarmulke*, he said, was not a bona fide Franklin clue but a red herring. Or, he added, looking directly at Moses, more properly, perhaps, a schmaltz herring. It was inconceivable that it had ever belonged to any member of the Franklin expedition or even a Native. Most likely it had been the property of a Jew on board an American whaler. (49)

The same year, an expedition finds a prayer shawl that Moses identifies as a tallith. The confusion between Indigenous and Jewish objects speaks to the slippage between rhetorical devices used to signal ethnic identifications and their relation to place. That is, while the novel suggests that a Jewish object is mistaken as Indigenous because of a similar appearance, for the characters of the novel this similarity is forgone and the objects are confused, connoting attendant confusions between Indigenous and Jewish people. Throughout the lengthy account of the Gursky family, ambiguity between Indigenous and Jewish serves to reflect on and inscribe Jewish identity in Canadian history. Similarly, Casteel notes that the novel's retelling of the Franklin expedition makes

90   Absorption Narratives

Solomon Gursky Was Here, in Margaret Atwood's terms, "Richler's most 'Canadian' book ... a reclamation of his Native territory" (Casteel, "Jews among the Indians" 783). For Richler, the incorporation of Indigenous identities into Jewish family lineage serves as a way of claiming Canadian identity.

The Gursky family's story squarely inscribes Jewish–Indigenous lineage in the geographical space of Quebec. Ephraim established in Magog, Quebec, a sect of millenarians. Befitting the fact that Ephraim there converts First Peoples to Judaism, the name "Magog" evokes both the Magog tribe in the Bible and the nearby Memphremagog (an Abenaki name) Lake. It is not in the marginalized, far-flung locales of the Arctic where Ephraim sets up this group, but in a small town not terribly far from, and even farther south than, Montreal (almost in the US). The biblical meaning of the town's name evokes early Jewish eschatology. As Casteel has noted, "Ephraim exemplifies the chameleonic and performative qualities that have frequently (and negatively) been associated with Jewishness in the dominant culture" (Casteel, "Jews among the Indians" 790). It is in Magog that Ephraim begins his own tribe of Jewish Indigenous people. The setting of Magog, moreover, in rural Québec – as opposed to the rest of the novel's setting in Montreal, still part of the French-Canadian province yet less separatist than small towns in the region – evokes questions of nationalism and sovereignty.

The youngest generation of Gurskys, Isaac, is part Indigenous and part European. Importantly, he is Jewish in the matrilineal sense insofar as his mother is Jewish (although Nialie's own matrilineal Judaism does not extend beyond a few generations). Isaac chooses to study at a yeshiva in Crown Heights, New York, where Nialie is concerned that "the other boys wouldn't accept him as such a *shayner yid*. He would be picked on just because he's a different color" (102). In fact, he is expelled before graduating. Following the tragic snowmobiling accident, in which he is left alone and survives by eating his own father's flesh, the youngest generation literally absorbs the older generation, acting out centuries of fraught intergenerational conflicts in this Jewish–Indigenous family. While the other boys at the yeshivah do not "accept him as such a *shayner yid*" because he is Indigenous, his own family rejects him because of his cannibalism. Living in New York after the snowmobile incident, his aunt Lucy, who had once shown interest and affection towards him, rejects his phone call to get together in New York where they are both living, exclaiming to him, "I'm surprised you even have the nerve to call me, you disgusting little cannibal!" (534). Similarly, Moses Berger cannot bring himself to speak to Isaac, even if reaching out to him might make his genealogy of the Gursky family more complete.

He "pardoned himself for not contacting Isaac, an abomination to him" (551). Isaac embodies a shame that the older generations of his family cannot forgive; the intergenerational story thus ends on a note of irresolution in which the Indigenous-Jewish son is ostracized.

Solomon Gursky Was Here is a novel about cannibalized genealogies, and as with Sommer's and literary critic Carlos Jáuregui's critical models, both the cannibalism and the genealogy in the novel have everything to do with race and, specifically, with racial mixture. The coupling of genealogy with cannibalism as a way of exploring racial mixture as it informs national Canadian identity resonates with Jáuregui's model of *canibalía*, in which the figure of the cannibal – in its monstrosity and anomaly – serves as an organizing logic for coloniality in the New World. Cuban scholar Roberto Fernández Retamar famously argued in in his 1971 essay *Calibán* that the monstruous figure of Caliban is a more befitting figure for New World identity than Ariel, previously championed at the turn of the twentieth century by Uruguayan intellectual José Enrique Rodó, Jáuregui glosses Arielismo as "the privilege of the written word, the superior classification of the intellectual, the appeal to cultural essentialisms and tendency towards nationalist, classist, or ethnic syncretism" (39). In contrast, *calibanismo* celebrates racial alterity by celebrating the monstrous terms in which the bourgeoisie and white elite have seen Blackness and Indigeneity in the Americas. Calibanism resists ethnic syncretism through the maintenance of cultural difference – specifically, racial alterity. In *Solomon Gursky Was Here*, cannibalism serves a similar function: to disaggregate and to emphasize racial alterity that has been otherwise absorbed. The Jewish–Indigenous son cannibalizes his Jewish father as a way of surviving in the inhospitable winter of rural Canada and as a way of resisting a "tendency towards nationalist, classist, or ethnic syncretism" that Jáuregui notes. Yet, at the same time, cannibalism also serves the opposite purpose of having one generation literally absorb the next as part of a centuries-long chain of alternately hiding and unveiling that which is Jewish and that which is Indigenous in this family genealogy.

The theme of cannibalism in *Solomon Gursky Was Here* forms part of a broader motif of consumption. As is perhaps to be expected of a novel centred on a family of bootleggers that becomes a giant in the liquor industry, the novel repeatedly discusses alcohol. There are also many descriptions of gluttonous, lavish consumption of food. Most notable are the novel's several references to cannibalism. During Ephraim's expedition, Mr. Stanley – the surgeon aboard the ship at whose lectures Moses finds Ephraim was always present – notes of the shamans that they "have absolutely no understanding of the nature of delirium.

92 Absorption Narratives

When a patient becomes delirious, as in severe fevers, they take him to be mad, possessed of an irresistible desire for cannibalism" (433). The Jewish immigrant's first encounter with the Arctic and its inhabitants has to do with cannibalism, yet it is Ephraim's own great-great-grandson, Isaac, who is eventually forced to resort to cannibalism.

In a way that squarely inscribes the Gursky family into the narrative of national identity, Richler often emphasizes the importance of drinking for Canadian life. Through such references, the author depicts the Gursky family as providing what Moses refers to as the "soul" of Canada: "If Canada had a soul (a doubtful proposition, Moses thought), then it wasn't to be found in Batoche or the Plains of Abraham or Fort Walsh or Charlottetown or Parliament Hill, but in the Caboose and thousands of bars like it that knit the country together from Peggy's Cove, Nova Scotia, to the far side of Vancouver Island" (64). In this sweeping narrative of this family's history throughout generations – rife with sojourns to many of the places that the narrator names here – drinking is shown to "knit" the family and the nation together. The vice is also, of course, the source of the family's wealth, which is often depicted as bordering on the obscene. It is rumoured that the Gursky family is based on the real-life Bronfman family, the Jewish Montreal family who bought and ran the Seagram's company after becoming successful in bootlegging. The harmful effects of alcohol are emphasized throughout the novel, particularly through Moses's struggles with alcoholism. Moses's role in the novel emphasizes the excess of the Gursky family and its wealth.

Consumption, like cannibalism, functions to convey vicariousness in the novel. Moses chronicles the Gursky family story, in part, as if living vicariously through them. Such vicarious "absorption" characterizes the genealogy that Moses crafts (albeit through what he is able to discern of a "shadowy presence" here and there, as is the case of the "hyphen" generation). As Alastair Morrison notes, "If, as we read Richler's description, we feel a twinge of vicarious gratification, or, like the young observer, of jealousy, we are not simply debasing ourselves before some more abstemious authorial sensibility. In fact, the inevitability of our jealousy, our desire for gratification, is precisely what the book is about" (128). The reader lives vicariously through Moses's proximity to this lavish family. Yet the Gursky family also lives vicariously through Indigenous people, as we see through Solomon's desire to spread his seed among Indigenous women. The figure of the Indigenous person in Canada becomes a way for the family to become more Canadian – first through Solomon's desire for Indigenous women and, later, through the incorporation of Indigenous characters into the family lineage. In this way, Richler – a Jewish Canadian author – writes

"What Is It We Absorb?"   93

vicariously through these characters as a way of exploring his Jewish characters' Canadian identities. Yet, the Gursky family – and Moses himself – are by no means presented as admirable characters. Richler, through his scandalous – and even revolting – depiction of the eventualities of the Gursky family over generations, questions ideas about affinity between Indigenous people in Canada and Jewish Canadians by questioning what becomes absorbed or reduced to a mere hyphen over centuries.

"A Metaphor for Racial Memories": *The Heirs of Columbus*

Native American novelist and academic Gerald Vizenor's 1991 novel *The Heirs of Columbus* follows Columbus's "heirs" as they negotiate, dispute, and reclaim various aspects of their inheritance. The novel follows the trials and investigations surrounding the stealing and moving of Columbus's and Pocahontas's remains. Because the novel's postmodern, speculative style makes it virtually impossible to summarize the plot, I will not do so here. For purposes of my discussion, suffice it to say that, in Vizenor's rendition of the Conquest, Columbus is descended from Maya who first arrived in Europe (in a sense, "discovering" Europe as Columbus is believed to have "discovered" the Americas) and later set sail to the New World. This central conceit of the novel applies a chiastic logic to the historical and ongoing phenomenon of the Conquest by having the Maya discover Europe. In ascribing this past to Columbus, the novel also plays with the common legend that Columbus was himself a Sephardic Jew. In Vizenor's speculative retelling of the Conquest, Mayan and Sephardic identities converge in ways that, rather than merely contesting paradigms of coloniality, prompt readers to interrogate the ways in which the trauma of colonization continues to inform identities and power relations in the New World. The novel follows various crimes related to the remains of Pocahontas and Christopher Columbus in the Americas and in London, imagining tribal hearings. As Stephen D. Osborne puts it, "it is not the Great Discoverer who is on trial, but the grounds of judgment that underwrite the emplotment of his story as either romantic triumph or tragic catastrophe" (118). Vizenor interrogates modes of storytelling so as to recast epistemologies of European–Indigenous encounter and to rethink the origins of the entirety of the Americas' populations. To do so, Vizenor draws from legal and genetic paradigms, crafting a quintessentially genealogical novel. The fact that the remains of Pocahontas and Columbus are at the centre of the narrative brings together human rights, the law, and genealogy.

94 Absorption Narratives

Vizenor implicitly centres Spanish America in his narrative account of Indigenous rights through his focus on the figure of Christopher Columbus. That he should be descended from the Maya, and that his heirs now live in a space between the US and Canada, bridges the Americas through the logic of coloniality as well as the resistance to being colonized. As Michael Hardin notes, Vizenor's novel aligns in some ways with Mexican author Carlos Fuentes's *Cristóbal Nonato* ("Christopher Unborn") and Argentine novelist Abel Posse's *Los perros del paraíso* ("The Dogs of Paradise"): "Like Posse and Fuentes, Vizenor constructs Columbus in a manner which is nothing like the Columbus reconstructed by the historians ... or the Columbus of the nineteenth century poets" (31). Vizenor reimagines Columbus and the legacy of his actions in radically anti-colonial ways, most notably by upending the paradigms of genealogy created by Columbus's conquering the New World.

Vizenor's text, though *sui generis*, forms part of a broader literary history of the Americas centred on Jewish–Indigenous hybridity and the Conquest. Doris Sommer has also taken up the question of Indigenous hybridity in the wake of the Spanish Conquest in relation to Jewish hybridity. Sommer studied Cuzco-born author El Inca Garcilaso's rhetorical decision to position himself as a literary heir to León Hebreo. While not a literal genealogy in the same key as Vizenor's texts, Sommer's analysis nonetheless discusses textual Jewish–Indigenous lineages in the context of European presence in the Americas. Garcilaso's texts are famously concerned with lineage and mixture; furthering lines of enquiry into El Inca's emphasis on racial hybridity, Sommer focuses on the author's positioning of himself as heir to Hebreo as another important way in which El Inca contests the absorption of one culture by another as a foregone conclusion of the Spanish Conquest. In her reading of Garcilaso's self-fashioning, Sommer ("Mosaic and Mestizo") notes, "Garcilaso's work has sometimes been celebrated as an agenda for resolving cultural tensions, but his best readers notice that his tensions persist throughout the text, unabated" (282). As Sommer underscores, the author's emphasis on his own racial hybridity in relation to both Jewishness and the colonization of Spanish America allows tensions between cultures and races to thrive throughout the text. Sommer thus provides a framework for reading El Inca Garcilaso's self-positioning in a way that brings Jewishness to bear on forms of difference in the context of the Spanish Conquest, recalling Cornejo Polar's emphasis on syncretism through the "unabated" persistence of tensions.

In a similar conceptual framework, Vizenor, too, considers Jewishness and Indigeneity vis-à-vis Spanish imperialism in ways that invite

"What Is It We Absorb?" 95

readings of fiction and history alike with syncretism in mind as a guiding principle. Literary critic Karsten Fitz has studied *The Heirs of Columbus* in the context of syncretism and transculturation: "The syncretism of mixed blood is turned into a positive 'principle,' stressing the dynamic nature of culture in general and of Native American cultures in particular, radically defying closure, and vehemently turning against notions of national purity and/or rigidity" (257). In Fitz's reading of the novel, the figure of the trickster is a transcultural principle, a critical model that recalls Gates's *Signifying Monkey*. While the critic does not detail a working understanding or definition of either transculturation or syncretism, the understanding of crossbloods as syncretic dovetails with my own reading of Mayan–Sephardic hybridity in Vizenor's novel.

Much of the novel consists of the tribal hearings on the stealing and repatriation of the remains of Columbus, although the hearings also delve into other related crimes that, at their core, stem from the original crime of the European conquest of the Americas, albeit with the alternative twists and turns with which Vizenor vests this history. Through these scenes of the hearings, Vizenor creates a literary imagining of how human rights might be understood and claimed in an ideal setting. Andrew Uzendoski notes, "Vizenor suggests that human rights ideals will be fully realized globally only when international legal norms reflect the values of Indigenous epistemologies, and mandate the direct participation of Indigenous peoples" (22). Similarly, Osborne argues that *The Heirs of Columbus* "subjects Anglo-American law to satirical critique, but that law is not simply to be negated or resisted; it's to be toyed with, in a serious sense, to be 'signified on'" (116). The author crafts a tale of human rights deliberations that is, I argue, necessarily ludic because the forms of mixture and hybridity that comprise the characters he creates are so unintelligible to colonialist epistemologies that such a ludic play on words and play on reality is, however paradoxically, the only way of representing his characters authentically. The playful narrative is Vizenor's way of paying homage to the importance of the Native American trickster. Vizenor creates a space of legal hearings that allows individuals to speak their truths in ways that most fiction has not represented. The characterization of the novel as human rights fiction also begs for comparative analysis with Latin American literature as much as with North American fiction (the blurred lines between Canada and US national identifications being already complicated both through Vizenor's own tribal affiliation and through the novel's creation of the Indigenous state of Assinika on the US–Canada border). For example, as Ricardo Gutiérrez Mouat noted several years ago, a growing corpus

96   Absorption Narratives

of Latin American literature has "cited or rewritten" (43) human rights trials and truth and reconciliation commissions' reports. In US fiction, Louise Erdrich's novel *The Last Report on the Miracles at Little No Horse*, as its title suggests, reads as a fictionalization of a human rights commission report. Similar to these examples from throughout the Americas over the past few decades, Vizenor uses the novel as a medium through which to imagine an ideal mode of truth-telling and reclamation – in this case, of Indigenous rights vis-à-vis the lingering effects of colonization.

The novel's aspect of human rights fiction also relates to its qualities of detective fiction, insofar as human rights narratives and detective fiction share an emphasis on the relationship between a crime, a perpetrator, and a victim. Vizenor's text has some aspects of a detective novel insofar as characters seek to investigate and solve crimes. Vizenor's approach to detective fiction questions epistemological order in ways that further contest conventional worldviews. As Elizabeth Blair notes, the novel is more properly a "whodunwhat" than a "whodunnit" insofar as the "it" could be any of a number of possible crimes:

> Possible crimes include: the tax violations of Stone Columbus's high stakes bingo caravel; the theft of stones from the tavern on the mount; the conquistadors' burning of the tribal bear codex; the theft of New World gold; Spain's banishment of the Sephardic Jews; Columbus's enslavement of the Indians; his theft of New World names; Henry Rowe Schoolcraft's theft of the medicine pouches; their repatriation or theft back by the mixedblood shaman, Transom; Felipa Flowers's repatriation of tribal medicine pouches, ceremonial feathers, and bones; the theft of the remains of Columbus and Pocahontas. (157–8)

Through a narrative structure in which the crime itself is not directly named or resolved in a clear fashion, Vizenor calls into question both what we as readers know about the European conquest of the Americas and how we know it. In so doing, as Blair states, the author names various crimes against humanity that have taken place against Indigenous people and Sephardic Jews and that are part and parcel of the logic of imperialism and European presence throughout the Americas.

The novel's most literal exploration of genealogy takes place through a scientist's explanation of the genetic sequencing the team has devised to test Columbus's DNA. He explains, "The genome narratives are stories in the blood, a metaphor for racial memories, or the idea that we inherit the structures of language and genetic memories; however, our computer memories and simulations are not yet powerful enough to

"What Is It We Absorb?" 97

support what shamans and hand talkers have inherited and understood for thousands of years" (136). Through the speculative and science fiction aspects of the novel, Vizenor uses ideas of genetics and genealogy to subvert epistemological underpinnings of European–Indigenous encounters. Similarly, Bernadette Russo argues, "From the onset, *The Heirs of Columbus* ontologically challenges Eurocentrism through the creation of an alternative cultural memory. Within the borderless dimensions of science fiction, Gerald Vizenor's work comprises a richly woven tapestry of overt and subtle elements that serve to articulate and reclaim Anishinaabe identity and agency" (58). The projections and simulations used in the hearings and the codes of the genome narrative are an analogue for inherited racial memories.

In addition to the novel's conceit that Columbus is the descendant of Sephardic Jews and Maya, Vizenor also creates parallels between the novel's Sephardic characters and the Indigenous characters. Sephardic Jews are described as hand talkers in the novel. "You see, my relatives were hand talkers, Sephardic Jews" (148), explains Luckie White. Luckie, whose name has also been recorded in the synagogues as mazeltov, uses Sephardic Jews as an appositive to rename hand talkers. Through the grammar of her sentence, Luckie thus presents Sephardic Jews either as a subset of hand talkers or as if there is a one-to-one correlation between Sephardic Jews and hand talkers. Elsewhere, readers learn that Stone Columbus, the explorer's heir, "has indicated on talk radio, however, that he would, if he could, create a sovereign nation for Sephardic Jews, but he has no obvious plans to do so at Point Assinika" (157). The pursuit of a sovereign nation for Sephardic Jews posits a point of contact between Indigeneity and Jewishness.

Most existing analyses of Vizenor's novel have not focused much on the character of Treves, a Sephardic Londoner book antiquarian who becomes involved in Felipa Flowers's journey to re-inter Pocahontas's remains. However, I would argue that Treves, like the imagining of Columbus himself, allows Vizenor to explore more creatively the role of Jewishness in Indigenous–European encounters and the colonization of the Americas. The descendant of Sephardic Jews who have returned to England, he is a conduit through which knowledge of Indigeneity circulates between the New and Old Worlds. He also serves as a conduit for colourful puns through which Vizenor takes aim at other writers. Specifically, Treves discusses Arnold Krupat, a real-life literary scholar who specializes in Native American autobiography. Treves notes that Krupat's "discussion of 'racial memory' drew the sharpest marginal response" (Vizenor, *The Heirs of Columbus* 111). Treves goes on to relay novelist M. Scott Momaday's marginalia in Krupat's book on

98 Absorption Narratives

Momaday's writings: "The novelist noted, 'Krupat gives head to footnotes, how would he know about tribal memories?'" (111). As Rebecca Lush notes in her reading of the novel, "Treves argues that his book's value comes from allowing a reader to explore what Momaday might think about Krupat if he were to read his work. The guise of performance lends a sense of plausibility, but not authenticity, demonstrating another language game from the trickster. This absurd anecdote allows *The Heirs* to reference in particular Krupat's criticism of Momaday's blood memories" (11). That is, through allowing Treves the intermediary role of circulating texts and commenting on readers' responses to them, Vizenor is able to challenge the authority in interpretation that literary critics are often vested with. Specifically, Vizenor pokes fun at the Jewish scholar's interpretation of the Native American author's text, adding a further plot point through which to explore Jewish–Native American encounters in the novel. That Treves is himself Sephardic and not Native American vests his discussion of Momaday's responses to Krupat with a somewhat more objective distance from the subject matter, seeming to allow Momaday the last word while also – as a speaker within the novel – exemplifying once again the phenomenon of so-called Jewish redface, albeit not at the narrative level. Vizenor speaks here through a Sephardic character repeating the words of a Native American author responding to a Jewish scholar of Native American literature, creating a veritable hall of mirrors of utterances and identities.

Vizenor, a consummate author and academic, uses the speculative space of his own fictional world as a platform in which to contest other academics' interpretations of Native American fiction – specifically, to tear down Krupat. Fiction serves here to contemplate alternative epistemologies of racialization and hybridity in academic contexts. Treves's role as a bookseller who is privy to the marginalia of an author, such as Momaday, allows Vizenor to imagine an epistemological sovereignty on Momaday's part that allows both authors to resist Krupat's analysis. This playful and innovative reflection creates another register – alongside the genetic modelling and the tribal hearings – through which Native American autonomy is explored and celebrated against monolithic imperial forces.

Throughout *The Heirs of Columbus*, Vizenor recreates and scrutinizes a vast array of epistemologies of knowing Indigenous identities and memories – from genetic codes to human rights hearings to literary criticism. Ultimately, all of these ways of knowing lead to moments of aporia. The author's innovative and playful approach to storytelling creates a world in which none of these forms of knowledge is sufficient to understand the truths of colonization and imperialism – if for no other reason than that these truths themselves are, in Vizenor's universe, also fictions. The genome narratives are merely a metaphor for what the shamans and hand talkers have long understood.

"What Is It We Absorb?" *The Long Night of White Chickens*

The Long Night of White Chickens is narrated by Roger Graetz, an alter-ego of Francisco Goldman, whose mother is Guatemalan and whose father is from a Boston Jewish family. During his childhood years, the Graetz family brings a young woman, Flor de Mayo, to live with them, and the two live almost as siblings. Decades later, Roger returns to Guatemala to uncover the truth about Flor de Mayo's murder and to understand his own confused identity. Flor was murdered while running an orphanage in Guatemala City and accused – falsely, Roger believes – of selling babies illegally. The novel's 450 pages consist mostly of conversations between Roger and his childhood friend Moya along with remembered conversations between Roger and Flor and between Moya and Flor. These conversations ostensibly seek to discover the truth about Flor's life and death but ultimately reveal more about the complexities of both Roger's and Flor's Jewish and Guatemalan hybridity. Both characters, we learn, identify partly as Jewish and North American and partly as mestizo. These characters' hybridity is presented – in their own words – as bordering on the surreal because it is apparently a rare mixture. In his 2021 autofictional novel *Monkey Boy*, Goldman crafts a more autobiographical story about his childhood and his later forays into investigating Guatemalan state violence. Notably absent from this more autobiographical work is a character like Flor. Although there are multiple Guatemalan domestic workers in the text, none of them come to form part of the narrator's family as they do in *The Long Night of White Chickens*. In fact, in *Monkey Boy*, rather than having a surrogate sister, his narrator grapples with his relationship to his biological sister. Read retrospectively alongside *Monkey Boy*, Flor's murder in *The Long Night of White Chickens* allows the author to tell a story of political violence in Guatemala and of genealogical identity between Indigeneity and Jewishness through adoption rather than miscegenation. In this way, the tensions between these different facets of identities remain – and what is "absorbed" when they converge – thrive in particular ways in the novel's protagonists.

Flor serves as a relief and a proxy of sorts for Roger to work through his own vexed identity. Speaking of himself, he notes, "But even during happy times, never mind the cataclysmic, origins such as mine – Catholic, Jewish, Guatemala, USA – can't always exist comfortably

100   Absorption Narratives

inside just one person" (185). As Cornelia Gräbner notes in her reading of Goldman, Roger "is confused about his identity to a degree that encourages him to live vicariously through others" (55). Gräbner includes Goldman alongside Jennifer Harbury, a US author and human rights scholar who has no personal ties to Guatemala, situating both authors' perspectives as exogenous to the nation. Gräbner's reading of Goldman alongside a US-born author recalls Perera's claim that nothing he had seen elsewhere in the world prepared him for the violence he saw in Guatemala when he returned there and recalls Halfon's insistence that he sees Guatemala the way any outsider would. In this reading, the vicariousness with which the narrator approaches Flor's experiences furthers his outsider status to Guatemala, despite being as much a Guatemalan citizen as he is a US citizen and having lived part of his childhood there. The phenomenon of living vicariously through others relates directly to the idea of ventriloquism, also, in Glaser's terms, sparked by confusion surrounding one's own Jewish identity. If Goldman appropriates the voice of the Other, this appropriation is due more to the fact that the author writes his novel in English and publishes it in the US than to the fact of his own US–Guatemalan hybrid nationality. Roger seeks to understand himself through Flor, whose appearance he first describes to readers when seeing her corpse: "wide arching brows, the wide Asiatic cheeks, the haughty Maya princess nose, the feral brown skin with its tropical rainwater sheen" (40). The narrator interrupts himself as he takes account of Flor's corpse, *"My brown angel, qué pasó?"* as he recalls a story that she once told him about a boyfriend she had had who told her that, before meeting her, he had never thought that an angel could be brown. Elsewhere, Roger describes spying on Flor as a teenager while she would change her clothes: "I always thought that Flor looked just like Pocahontas" (172). When he sees her deceased corpse in Guatemala, he describes a "haughty Maya princess nose," whereas when recalling their adolescent years in New England he compares her to Pocahontas; his descriptions of her in relation to various Indigenous women change based on the location of Flor's body as he lays eyes on her – Maya in Guatemala and Pocahontas in the US. The imprecision of "Maya" as a catch-all category and his geographical error of the Powhatan Pocahontas in present-day Massachusetts notwithstanding, Goldman's comparisons recall Vizenor's focus on the remains of the Maya-descended Christopher Columbus and Pocahontas in his novel as a way of bringing a US Native American into dialogue with the legacy of Columbus and the Sephardim. The racial and geographical boundaries between Roger and Flor encapsulate the complexities of their shared yet different hybrid identities and their shared and

"What Is It We Absorb?" 101

individual geographical displacement across Guatemala and the US. He glorifies, exoticizes, and objectifies her as a way of reckoning with his own identity and place in both the US and Guatemala, such that her alterity takes on different functions but almost always positions her as the subject of his gaze. At other moments in the text, Flor Others Indigenous groups in Guatemala, so that the instances of Othering through observing and speaking through the Other become multilayered.

Because Goldman writes in English and the principal characters move between Guatemala and the US throughout the narrative, the novel seems more designated to US readers than to readers in Guatemala. This element of the novel evokes Walter Mignolo's concept of the "place of enunciation" (48), inexorably linked to imperialism and the relationship between the US and Latin America. Guillermo Irizarry draws on Judith Butler's *Frames of War* in his interpretation of *The Long Night of White Chickens* to argue that Flor's cadaver makes her life "intelligible *as a life*" (7). In Irizarry's reading, this intelligibility is predicated in part on the cadaver's ability to make Flor's life intelligible for readers in the Global North, "whose subjectivities are biased by an unequal order of global power" (7). For her part, critic Gabriela Yanes Gómez argues that Goldman may not be a "purely Guatemalan" author by virtue of his writing in English and living outside of Guatemala. Goldman writes from his own cosmopolitan experiences growing up mostly outside Guatemala, a condition that influences his writing. Given the implicit (and at times explicit, as we have seen) links between "cosmopolitan" and "Jewish," it becomes striking that critics such as Yanes Gómez and Gräbner write about Goldman as if he were not Guatemalan. I do not mean to say that these critics are anti-Semitic in their readings of him; rather, one wonders what these critics might have made – if anything – of Goldman's Jewish identity as it relates to their readings of his fraught relationship to Guatemala. The narrator of *The Long Night of White Chickens* also tells this story about Guatemala partly from the US. Thus, Goldman – similar to Halfon and Perera – depicts diaspora as a condition that situates an individual as outsider to their country of birth. Also like Perera's and Halfon's narratives, encounters with state violence that precede the narrator's departure from the country depict exile as the mode through which the Jewish character experiences national politics. Yet, unlike Perera's and Halfon's works, Goldman's creation of Flor de Mayo closes some of the distance between Jewish and mestizo characters in ways that refigure national belonging among Jewish Guatemalans and Indigenous Guatemalans.

Goldman vests his narrator with an awareness of the geographical and cultural differences between Guatemala and the US. Roger reflects,

102 Absorption Narratives

as he recalls a moment in which he literally sees Guatemala in a different light as Quiché vendors pack up their market stands in the late-afternoon light:

> If it hadn't been for that light ... maybe I would have thought, Poverty, soldiers, nuns and priests, torture, what else is new? Because if my months in Guatemala hadn't accustomed me to being at least aware of *that*, hadn't bred *that* silence inside of me. ... (Because who would want to listen to *me* go on about it down *here*? I used to talk about it much more when I was still *up there*. So that *down here*, when I find myself silently talking about it, I'm usually imagining someone listening *up there!*) (355–6)

Roger reflects, as he watches Indigenous vendors pack up their booths at the market, on what a stereotypical Northern gaze would capture of Guatemala. Yet, the nuances of the vendors' humanity that he is able to see in this moment – after returning from the lowlands to Guatemala City – reframe his thinking and compel him to tell his story in a different way.

Goldman's novel explores the difficulty of representing Guatemala without falling into stereotypical images, just as the author duly rejects facile categorizations of Jewish wandering and cosmopolitanism. Roger's experiences in Guatemala at times reproduce and, at others, problematize commonly held beliefs about the cosmopolitanism of Jewish experiences, an idea with which he grapples as the narrative itself shifts constantly between Guatemala and the US. Here again, this cosmopolitanism is simultaneously both a function of the privilege of being able to move around the world and an effect of not being welcomed in many places. We observe this being out of place from the novel's beginning. An early passage in *The Long Night of White Chickens* describes the library in the narrator's boyhood school in Guatemala. Among the shelves of books from the US, Roger recalls: "two short, segregated shelves designated 'Jewish' and 'Negro,' ... Maybe, as my mother said when I went home and told her about it, this was all just plain naïveté and Irish ignorance on Anne Hunt's part. After all, there weren't any 'Negroes' at the school to insult – Moya was probably the darkest kid there, but they had that and a world of things to insult about him" (27). Goldman's description of the school library crystallizes US ethnic categories and the ways in which Jews and African Americans are both Othered in a US context. The "Irish ignorance" is a reference to Anne Hunt, the school's rector, an Irish Catholic woman from Philadelphia. Even in Guatemala, where the Philadelphia-born rector and Roger would seem to have much more in common with one another than

"What Is It We Absorb?" 103

with Guatemalans who do not have US roots, the antipathy towards Irish immigrants and their descendants that was historically typical of many Bostonians still pervades. In *Monkey Boy*, Goldman reconsiders the bookshelf from the perspective of someone living in 2020, and notes that "Latino/Latina or Hispanic, or however Anne Hunt might have labeled it, wasn't on her map yet, and neither were Asian, Native American, etcetera. What would Ann Hunt's library look like now, if she were still alive and her mania for disaggregating and classification had never slackened?" (270).[3] As Goldman suggests in both texts, the message that this school library's organization conveyed to him as a child was that being "Jewish" or "Negro" meant, from the perspective of people like Ann Hunt, something different from "American," which consisted of white, non-Jewish US authors.

If being Jewish in Guatemala as a child makes Roger (and Goldman's autofictional narrator of *Monkey Boy*, Francisco Goldberg) feel less "American" as he casts his eyes on Ann Hunt's bookshelves, Goldman emphasizes throughout *Monkey Boy* that people in the US often treat Latinx Jews as if being Latinx and being Jewish were somehow incongruous. Francisco Goldberg has a comical moment in which a high school acquaintance "outs him" as Jewish in his adult years. A reporter writing about Francisco's first novel for the *Globe* says to him, "in her fax to us Lana Gatto alleges that you are not a Hispanic, err, or a Latino. She says that in high school your name was Frank and that you're Jewish" (97). The narrator comically retorts, "I admit it. I'm Jewish, and all these years I've been hiding my true identity behind the last name Goldberg" (98). Similar to critical responses to Goldman's work that interpret his cosmopolitan upbringing to connote that he is somehow less Guatemalan or not purely Guatemalan, in the US, Goldman's (semi-) autobiographical characters are treated as if they are not Latinx or not Guatemalan because of their Jewish identities.

The family's adoption of Flor is bound up in spiritual identifications. She "became the daughter of a tough old bird, of a moral as hell Boston Russian immigrant's son Jew (though only a sporadically practising Jew), and she fulfilled his every dream, every ambition he'd had for her, almost – Though don't ever imply that Flor was anything like an experiment to him" (49–50). Through Flor's recollections of her time in the convent orphanage as a child, Goldman recreates anti-Jewish attitudes among Indigenous Guatemalans similar to those that Perera's novel also details. After first stating that some of the nuns used Jews as a metaphor for evil, she elaborates, "Well, you know how it is there. Go up to an Indian town and tell them you're a Jew – not that I ever have, of course – and they look at you like you're out of your mind, or

104   Absorption Narratives

they look at you with terror, because they, some of them anyway, think that the last Jews walked the earth a thousand years ago and only come back as devils, with actual tails, no less" (170). Flor's observation that these towns would be surprised to see a Jew resonates with Erdrich's character Cyprian's assertion that his lover was surprised to meet him because there were no Jews on the reservation. Yet, unlike Cyprian, Flor assumes that Indigenous groups do know about Jews and actively discriminate against them. Indigenous characters are often equated by these authors with Catholicism, as Flor does here. Like Perera's novel and unlike the instances of possible anti-Semitism in Halfon's novella (which could be interpreted as ignorance more than wilful anti-Semitism), Flor vilifies Indigenous folks by equating them with vehement Catholicism and overtly anti-Semitic attitudes. Through such utterances, Flor perpetuates this assumption that Indigenous folks are necessarily anti-Semitic. She is Othered by Roger and Moya and Others Indigenous Guatemalans. Paradoxically, the Othering that takes place in this instance is one that equates the marginalized position of Indigenous people with the avowal of hegemonic Christian beliefs.

The novel's discussion of anti-Semitism in Guatemala anticipates some elements of Goldman's characterization of the country years later in *Monkey Boy*:

> My mother grew up in a country with a strong German Nazi presence. No other country in the Western Hemisphere was so infested. Once I was shown an archival copy of a US intelligence map from the late 1930s that counted the number of coffee plantations, or fincas, owned by German Nazis in Guatemala, each finca marked with a tiny black swastika, so many swastikas that the central portion of that map, all the way up to Mexico, looked covered by a thick swarm of flies. It's a good example, I think, of the peculiar uniqueness any small country can possess. (108–9)

While Goldman's autofictional narrator concludes that the abundance of Nazis in Guatemala says something about "any small country," the "peculiar uniqueness" in a country that, by his account, was more "infested" than any other nation in the Western Hemisphere underscores the extremes of anti-Semitism in Guatemala in particular; the interplay between the global and the particularly Guatemalan elements of anti-Semitism recall Zygmunt Bauman's ideas of the possibility and reality of the Holocaust. As *Monkey Boy* goes on to note, Francisco's parents were not allowed to marry in Guatemala because the archbishop did not deem it fit for a Guatemalan woman to marry a Jew, so his parents crossed the border into Mexico and married in a church in Mexico City.

As the narrator later notes, the same archbishop who did not approve of the mother marrying a Jew was also involved in the Church's complicity in Guatemalan state violence against Indigenous people. This aspect of the novel dovetails with Goldman's works of investigative journalism, most famously in his book *The Art of Political Murder*, recently adapted into a documentary by HBO. As *Monkey Boy* makes clear, instances of anti-Semitism and the support of Indigenous genocide readily coexisted. Nonetheless, as Flor's reflections remind us, Indigenous Guatemalans were often coaxed – through the power and influence of the Church – into avowing anti-Semitic beliefs. Again, the Maya are positioned uncomfortably vis-à-vis Jews because of broader paradigms of hegemony – namely, Christianity and whiteness – as we saw in the Canadian context of Richler's novel.

Where *The Long Night of White Chickens* most notably differs from the novels by Perera and Halfon is, first, in its depiction of characters' hybridity between Jewishness and mestizaje and, second, in its sustained dialogue that gives voice to a partly Indigenous character. Flor's lengthy contemplations of her own racial hybridity underscore the importance of racial ventriloquism. Like the instances of Jewish racial ventriloquism that Glaser studies in *Borrowed Voices*, Goldman and Roger alike – both Jewish, non-mestizo Guatemalans – speak as author and narrator through the voice of the character of Flor de Mayo, whom the narrator repeatedly describes as phenotypically Indigenous. Flor's musings – in the context of early 1990s literature about violence in Guatemala – resonate with testimonial accounts of political violence, most notably, the now very well-known *I, Rigoberta Menchú*. Menchú's testimonial account of her experiences were transcribed by the anthropologist Elisabeth Burgos who, like Goldman, wrote about Guatemala from outside Guatemala – in her case, Paris. Yet, unlike Menchú's, Flor's testimony does not detail the violence that she experienced but rather contemplates the convergence of racial and spiritual identifications that make up her own identity and Guatemala as a nation. After her death, Roger and Moya discuss Flor's "manifesto of her right to hold long monologues with herself" (179). Much of the novel consists of snippets of conversations that can be pieced back together to make up a more complete reflection on her identity. As Linda J. Craft notes, the conversations between Moya and Roger reconstruct Flor's story in a way that allows readers to get to know her complex soul (668). The testimonial aspects of the novel focus more on spiritual identifications than crime. The detective fiction aspects of the novel – insofar as Flor's murder is its narrative impetus – are similar to those of *The Heirs of Columbus*, in which present-day crimes are connected to the evils of the Conquest.

106 Absorption Narratives

In her own account, Flor's spiritual identifications border on the surreal. Roger describes her as "pretty schizophrenic about religion" (171), a characterization that recalls Gerald Vizenor's term *cultural schizophrenia*. An early review of *The Long Night of White Chickens* described it as a "powerful and often brilliant evocation of 'cultural schizophrenia'" (Carr "Book Reviews" 95). This model applies to both Flor and Roger himself. After Flor describes nuns who described Jews as evil and accuses Indigenous Guatemalans of being anti-Semitic, Roger describes her early years before living in the convent orphanage as "desert anarchy and near paganism" (*Long Night* 171), a desert that he says became surrounded by the seven years of Catholic teachings from the orphanage. The narrator discusses Flor's move from this "desert" to Catholicism and, to the surprise of the convent orphanage, to Judaism. As Flor recounts in a conversation with Moya, the Mother Superior at the convent orphanage told her that she could save Ira's soul. After she arrives in Massachusetts, however, she stops attending Mass because none of the priests there speak Spanish. Eventually, however, her affinity for Ira draws her to Judaism: "I loved Ira so much I was practically waiting for him to invite me to be Jewish" (170). Her own description of her religious identifications shifts based on where she is: first nonreligious, then Catholic in the convent, then Jewish in the US. Through this trajectory, Goldman figures Flor's spiritual orientations – and, notably, not the Graetz family's Judaism – as "wandering" through the many changes over the course of Flor's survival.

Flor's storyline dovetails with the adoption narrative that, Tuck and Yang argue, characterizes fictional accounts of Native Americans authored by white novelists. While Flor was first sent to the Boston suburb by Roger's grandmother to work as a maid for the family, the paternal affinity that Ira feels for her prompts him to adopt her and to raise her alongside Roger as if the two were siblings. This adoption takes on its own significance as a very literal form of absorption as she is legally, spiritually, and racially absorbed into the fold of the Graetz family. For Craft, Flor's spiritual fluctuations are part and parcel of the adoption narrative (672). Through her adoption, Flor becomes absorbed by the Jewish Graetz family and by mainstream (and white) upper middle-class suburban Boston life, such that this process is both patently spiritual and racialized. As Craft goes on to note in her interpretation of the description of Flor as "the pretty foreign girl who had started out as a nearly illiterate fourteen-year-old in the first grade" (347), the narrative eventually reaches a point at which it depicts Flor's origin as if she had never had any life before her arrival in the US. Roger's narrative absorbs her into his own family without realizing the complexities and

"What Is It We Absorb?" 107

nuances of the various identities and experiences that she continues to embody. Decades later, however, as he learns through her own words, she still wonders what it is that she herself has absorbed from Indigenous spirituality. These processes of absorption are never complete and continue to prompt both reflection and confusion.

Similar to Vizenor's focus on Jewish–Indigenous hybridity in the character of Christopher Columbus, Goldman's consideration of Indigeneity also reaches back to the Conquest and to religious thinking about the subjugation of Indigenous populations. Roger describes reading the writings of Fray Bartolomé de las Casas on the New York subway. He goes on to state that, after Flor's death, he stopped doing so; he adds, to further his contemplation of Las Casas, that his mother's father "had mestizo bloodlines going back to the Conquest" (189). Yet, as the narrative emphasizes through the almost constant references to Flor's phenotypically Indigenous characteristics, Roger understands himself to be ethnically distinct from Flor despite the fact that they are both mestizos. For her part, Flor understands herself as "not actually Indian." Through their discourse, these two characters recreate distinctions of racial hybridity that recall caste paintings from centuries prior. While, as Goldman makes clear in Monkey Boy, Roger's mother in The Long Night of White Chickens is very different from Goldberg's mother, Monkey Boy's narrator is also descended from an Afro-Guatemalan man. The novel includes a scene between Goldberg and his mother in which he shows her a photograph of her grandfather and points out that he appeared to be Black, a fact that she and her family denied throughout much of Goldberg's life.

Flor de Mayo is also depicted as being more accustomed to the US than to Guatemala as an adult, a compelling point of comparison between her and Roger. He recalls that she told him, when she returned to Guatemala City, "that Guatemala seemed even bigger to her than New York, harder to know, somehow but how could that be? Was it just war and terror and guerrilla and counterwar that made it seem bigger, made it throb invisibly out there, drawing all your sensations into it?" (122). While elsewhere Roger quotes from her letters or from conversations he remembers, in this moment he uses indirect speech to report what Flor says, furthering the shared experience both characters feel of being disoriented in Guatemala City. Both characters have spent considerable time in New York City, but neither is from there. That the city – home to the largest population of Jews outside of Israel – should serve as the reference point for Flor (who most recently lived there before moving to Guatemala City) and as a point of identification between Flor and Rogerio suggests a tension between US Jewish life and Guatemalan life.

108   Absorption Narratives

If his roots in the US vest Goldman and his (autobiographical) narrators with a sense of privilege, his ability to write compellingly in English – and thus reach a wide audience outside of Guatemala – also relates to a perceived duty to tell stories about political violence in Guatemala for English-speaking readerships. In an interview with Rodrigo Rey Rosa, Goldman contemplated the problem that Guatemala's violence presents to writers who feel compelled to share the experience of living through the country's violence with their readers. Goldman remarked to fellow Guatemalan author Rodrigo Rey Rosa in an interview:

> You let the reader see how it is to live in this atmosphere, so full of violence, death, and paranoia. You openly show a very ambivalent relationship to the country; you write constantly about the desire to escape. And you almost define the problem of being a writer in a situation like the one in Guatemala. You feel, first of all, that it's a radical experience that changes you; you're drowning in, and are being shaken by an incredible darkness. And you ask yourself: Why do I have to deal with this? What I'm seeing, is there anything universal about it? Do I have a duty to tell this story, should I leave, or do something else? ("Rodrigo Rey Rosa by Francisco Goldman" 2013)

In Goldman's own words, he has felt a sense of duty to convey the political violence and terror that characterized twentieth-century Guatemala to global (English-speaking) audiences. Through *The Long Night of White Chickens*, he accomplishes this objective through fiction, whereas in *The Art of Political Murder* he does so through long-form journalism. What unites these texts, regardless of genre, is that they bring the vexed dynamics of racial categories and national belonging into conversation with political violence and religious hegemony, insofar as *The Art of Political Murder* underscores the anti-Indigenous violence that characterized the political tumult in Guatemala. As we recall from chapter 2, Indigenous populations in Guatemala experienced the state violence in patently racialized terms. As Goldman shows, many Church officials in Guatemala were directly involved in this racialized state violence. These are the stories of racial hegemony and religious power that Goldman seeks to convey to his English-speaking audiences.

In addition to Goldman's contemplation of whether he has a duty to tell these stories to English-speaking audiences, the author also participates in salient conversations about racial politics and ethnic categories in the twenty-first–century US. Namely, the anxieties over "What is it we absorb" that Goldman voices through Flor and Roger in *The Long Night of White Chickens* linger and resurface in *Monkey Boy*, taking on the further complexities of present understandings of Latinidad in the US. When we read *The Long Night of White Chickens* from the perspective of the year 2021 and alongside *Monkey Boy*, the author's rationale for telling Flor's and Roger's stories in English for a US-based audience become clearer. As a Jewish Guatemalan American, Goldberg struggles to be accepted as Guatemalan or as a US citizen in either Guatemala or the US. He is perceived as too Jewish to be Latinx in the US while, as a child in Guatemala, he learned that "Jewish" was a separate category from "American." Well into his adult years, he experiences racial profiling as a Latinx man, including accounts of being erroneously profiled as a "Rican" and as a "Mexican." Goldman makes clear that any "cosmopolitan" identification by virtue of being Jewish also leads him to be patently Othered in both the US and Guatemala.

Goldman addresses syncretism more explicitly in *Monkey Boy* than in *The Long Night of White Chickens* by naming it as such. Francisco reflects, "The only time I've experienced what I believe were strong genuinely religious feelings was at the Catholic 'widows' Mass' in a sacred Maya town in the Central Highlands during the war. Possibly it was a syncretic Catholic Maya mass; the young priest was Maya and gave the Mass in K'iche" (275). As he goes on to state, such a syncretic mass would likely have had to be practised clandestinely during the war. He goes on to recall the "eloquent K'iche pronunciations that seem so suited for pronouncing sorrow, as some would say Hebrew is" (275). The narrator describes the syncretic Catholic Maya mass within the context of having to answer questions about having been baptized even though he is Jewish and his name is Goldberg, not unlike having to explain that he is both Jewish and Latinx. In this way, Goldman – if tacitly – brings together religious syncretism and Indigeneity (through his reflections on the Maya Catholic Mass) and his hybridity, which is also syncretic in its own way. While discussions of "absorption" do not appear in *Monkey Boy*, the line of Goldman's *oeuvre* through multiple decades would appear, indeed, to be an exploration of what becomes absorbed when Jewishness, Christianity, and Indigeneity converge. Moreover, the author repeatedly returns to the further mystery of how these various mixtures of race and ethnicity complicate the category of Latinidad in the US.

"Strange Times to Be a Jew": *The Yiddish Policemen's Union*

Throughout Michael Chabon's 2003 novel *The Yiddish Policemen's Union*, characters repeat the phrase "strange times to be a Jew." They are referring to the fact that their place of refuge – Sitka, Alaska, and its

110   Absorption Narratives

surroundings – has ceased to be the Zion it had previously been declared and is now being returned to the non-Yiddish, Native American Alaskans. To the same extent that the novel depicts "strange times to be a Jew," Chabon underscores also that Sitka, Alaska, is a strange *place* to be a Jew. Moreover, the novel's characters display what many would perceive as strange ways to be a Jew. *The Yiddish Policemen's Union* projects Jewish anxieties about belonging and rootlessness through an alternate history in which a Zion is established in Sitka, Alaska, after Israel loses the war and is denied statehood in 1948. Likewise, Alaska, in this alternate reality, is not granted US statehood but rather becomes a refuge for the Jews who had to leave Palestine. As a central part of this alternate reality, Chabon engages with Native American experiences, partly as an analogy for the Israel–Palestine conflict. Yet, the two sides of the analogy are not only parallel but intersect with one another through the racialized meanings that Jewish settler presence takes on. The novel's main character is the Yiddish-speaking Jewish Landsman, whose surname is overwhelmingly ironic given the sense of wandering and rootlessness that characterizes him. "Landsman" is also ironic in light of the tensions between the novel's Yiddish characters and Native Americans in Alaska, the latter of whom are characterized by their connections to the land. Over the course of the novel, the main characters attempt to solve the murder of a man named Mendel Shpilman in Sitka. With his partner, his first cousin Berko, Landsman comes to learn that his own uncle Hertz (Berko's father) murdered Shpilman, who was rumoured to be the next messiah but shirked this role because he was homosexual and did not see a way to reconcile his sexuality with being the messiah. In Hertz's own confession, he killed Shpilman "to put him out of his misery" (Chabon, *Yiddish Policemen's Union* 320). Through the family-centred police case and investigation, Chabon's novel brings genealogy to the fore of the fictional exploration of race and Jewishness in contemporary US culture.

Throughout *The Yiddish Policemen's Union*, Chabon employs the generic conventions of detective fiction as a way of exploring characters' connections to the land as mediated through their ethnic identifications. In addition to having characters perform "Jewish red face" at key moments throughout the novel, Chabon deploys the detective genre's typical "red herring," not unlike the "red schmaltz" in Richler's novel. The object that he deploys as a red herring is, in fact, none other than a red heifer. The red heifer, unequivocally connected with Judaism and Zionism, vests the novel with one of the quintessential conventions of detective fiction. At the same time, the complexity that the red heifer connotes for the coming of the Messiah at the advent of Zion takes on

"What Is It We Absorb?"   111

particular meaning here in the Jewish land of refuge in Sitka, Alaska. The red heifer distracts the detectives and the readers from the resolution of the crime (thus functioning as a red herring), just as the Jewish place of refuge established for Jews in and around Sitka is a detour from the Zionist idea of a Jewish homeland in the Holy Land. Moreover, Jewish presence in Sitka not only negatively affects the Jews who now inhabit Alaska but also further burdens the Native Americans who for generations had already lived in Alaska. Through this plot device, Chabon distills the fraught relationship between the idea of Zionism, the Alaskan territory, the "Yiddish" characters who have settled there, and the Native Americans in Alaska.

I am hardly the first critic to emphasize the importance of Chabon's use of detective fiction as a way of exploring Jewish experiences among the Native Americans in Alaska and, in turn, as a way of conceptualizing Jewish belonging in the US (although, in Chabon's imagined alternate history, Alaska remains a territory). Chabon's use of detective fiction also allows his exploration of Jewishness to be couched in something unmistakably "American." In Glaser's terms, "Chabon reinforces his commitment to cross-pollination by marrying a Jewish tale with Yiddish inflections and biblical undertones to a prototypically American set of linguistic and narrative rules: the staccato dialogue, the hyperbolic plot devices, and the layers of deception that characterize the midcentury detective novel" (loc. 3171–7). Similarly, for Sarah Phillips Casteel, "Even as if his characters are denied American citizenship and a sense of belonging ... Chabon lays claim to Americanness by telling his story through the language of a distinctively American genre: hard-boiled detective fiction" ("Jews among the Indians" 797). The conventions of detective fiction allow Chabon to explore the racial and ethnic dimensions of Jewish–Native American encounters in a way that engages with complex notions of hybridity in line with transculturation. Similarly, critic Carmen Birkle, borrowing from critic Mary Louise Pratt's transcultural model of the "contact zone," has explored the ethnic dimensions of Jewish American detective fiction. For Birkle, Pratt's model – often used to discuss Latin America – is useful for US Jewish fiction because "dominant and dominated cultures clash ideologically and sometimes physically. Assimilation through encounters with mainstream America, the loss of a specifically Jewish identity, and the need for and/or practice of the preservation of a Jewish culture, in both religious and nonreligious terms, is constantly negotiated in these texts" (54). Drawing from Birkle's model in which Jewish identities in the Americas are negotiated through detective fiction, I add that Chabon's work turns this notion on its head by placing the loss of Jewish

112   Absorption Narratives

identity into critical dialogue with Native American experiences. The plot device of the red heifer as a red herring furthers the novel's coupling of the detective genre and concepts of race through the biblical significance of purification. In light of the red heifer's significance for the building of the Third Temple, this figure also adds to the significance of Israel in this novel set in an Alaskan Zion following the Jews' loss of their homeland in 1948.

Chabon's contributions to detective fiction have been a central point of existing critical studies of the novel. In terms of the racialized elements of the novel, it is no coincidence that the novel's most phenotypically Native American main character is also the most observant Jew in the novel, Landsman's cousin and police partner, Berko. In a similar vein, existing studies of *The Yiddish Policemen's Union* have tended to focus more on the relationships between Jewish and Native American characters than on the phenomenon of hybridity between Jewish and Native American identities within a single individual character (specifically, Berko) in the novel. Through this character – and through his relationship to Landsman – Chabon brings together detective work, race, and family ties. From the first description of Berko, he is shown to embody hybridity in ways that underscore the complexity – the impossibility, even, in the reactions of some characters – of hybridity between Jewish and Native American identities. Specifically, Berko's Jewish and Native American traits are manifest in different registers. Whereas his Jewish characteristics are spiritual and behavioural, the narrative presents his Native American identity as more immutably embodied. The narrator informs readers that, when Berko first came to live with Landsman's immediate family at age thirteen (an adoption narrative similar to Flor's), he did not speak Yiddish and was not an observant Jew. At this time, Landsman's first encounter with his cousin, Berko is also presented as phenotypically Native American and distinct from Landsman's family. Landsman's mother even proclaims that she has no need for an Indian in her home, as if Berko were not her own nephew *because* he is Native American. Over time, however, Berko becomes the most observant member of Landsman's extended family. Yet his Native American and Jewish traits are depicted in constant tension with one another. Chabon introduces Berko to readers early on through the following description:

Now Ber Shemets, as he came in time to style himself, lives like a Jew, wears a skullcap and four-corner like a Jew. He reasons as a Jew, worships as a Jew, fathers and loves his wife and serves the public as a Jew. He spins theory with his hands, keeps kosher, and sports a penis cut (his father

"What Is It We Absorb?" 113

saw to it before abandoning the infant Bear) on the bias. But to look at, he's pure Tlingit. Tartar eyes, dense black hair, broad face built for joy but trained in the craft of sorrow. The Bears are a big people, and Berko stands two meters tall in his socks and weighs in at 110 kilograms. He has a big head, big feet, big belly, and big hands. (*The Yiddish Policemen's Union* 44–5)

The narrator's description of Berko's Jewish characteristics begins with behaviours and traits and transitions to the physical marker of his circumcision with the parenthetical disclaimer that his father "saw to it before abandoning the infant." Chabon thus marks Berko physically as Jewish and underscores the significance of circumcision for father-son connections in Judaism. His father's abandonment of him is in tension with circumcision.

It is the circumcision – the last description of Berko's Jewishness and his only embodied trait of Jewishness – from which the narrator pivots to talk about Berko's conventionally Native American phenotypical traits. Chabon's physical description of Berko emphasizes that the traits that he inherited from his mother are much more strongly manifest in his physical appearance than those from his father. Practices of Judaism, embodied Jewishness, and embodied Native American traits are thus presented in a metonymic relationship with one another, with the embodied Jewishness fulfilling a synecdochic function in relationship both to practices of Judaism (that is, the ritual bris that has now left an embodied marker of Jewishness) and to Berko's Native American body. His circumcision is a part of the whole body that is Native American, but it is presented as an imperfect synecdoche insofar as it is not representative of the whole. The description also suggests that Jewish genetic – at least phenotypical – characteristics are hidden. Similarly, Casteel notes, "Berko does not find easy acceptance among the Jews, as is suggested by the novel's emphasis on his Indian physicality, which is perpetually at odds with his Jewish dress" ("Jews among the Indians" 802). As Casteel emphasizes here through the tension between Native American physicality and Jewish dress, Jewishness in Berko's character seems less mutable than his Native American qualities. Berko's Jewishness is codified through dress and behaviour as opposed to embodied traits (except for the circumcision, the product of his father's adherence to ritual rather than a trait with which he was born). Also noteworthy in the narrator's description of Berko's Jewishness and his Native American characteristics is the use of simile in "like a Jew" and "as a Jew" in contrast to the much more literal "he's," "the Bears *are*" and "he has big hands" to describe his physical attributes. Jewishness, for Berko, is thus something that can be imitated or approximated but not

114   Absorption Narratives

fully embodied. Paradoxically, the mutability of Jewishness suggested by Chabon's description of Berko contrasts the Jewish characters' lack of assimilation throughout the novel.

In addition to the tensions between Jewish and Native American traits that Chabon presents in his description of Berko's appearance, the novel also suggests something "unclassifiable" about him in the way that he presents to other characters in the novel. A secondary character, Mrs. Kalushiner, "after careful consideration, can't fit Berko into her taxonomy of lowlifes" (*The Yiddish Policemen's Union* 69). Berko's appearance does not fit in with the "mouse-eyed shtinkers" (i.e., characters who appear phenotypically Yiddish) that Landsman routinely brings into this woman's house seeking leads on cases he is investigating. Mrs. Kalushiner notes that Berko could not be one of these "shtinkers," "not with that Indian puss" (69). She arrives at this conclusion "with all due respect to the beanie and the fringes" (69), renaming Berko's yarmulke and prayer shawl as a "beanie" and "fringes," as if to suggest that, from her perspective, these garments are no longer a yarmulke and a prayer shawl when sported by a man who looks like Berko.

If other characters and the narrator perceive contradictions in the way that Berko presents, these contradictions reflect the complexities of his origins as the son of a Native American woman and Yiddish man who is obsessed with Native American culture yet also seeks to exterminate the population – including the mother of his own son. Berko's father and Landsman's uncle, Hertz Shemets, is an expert on Tlingit art and artefacts, yet his Zionist radical fervour compels him to engage in terrorist acts. The narrator describes Shemets's study of Native American culture as a "beard for his COINTELPRO work" (Chabon, *The Yiddish Policemen's Union* 55), his terroristic activities to secure a Jewish homeland. Yet the narrator notes that, despite his avowed interest in Native American cultures as a "beard" for his COINTELPRO work, Shemets was also genuinely drawn to Native American ways of life. Through this storyline, Chabon (if inadvertently) signals a problem among Jews in the Americas: a fascination with Native American communities that shrouds exoticization and discrimination. Berko is the son of Shemets and a Tlingit woman, Laurie Jo, who was killed during Synagogue riots in which eleven Native Americans in Alaska were killed after a prayer house that Jews had built on disputed land was bombed. The backstory of Berko's mother evokes violence in disputed territories in Israel/Palestine and the Crown Heights riots of 1991. The fact that Laurie Jo is a Native American woman married to a Jewish man at odds with Native American communities brings the historical significance of the Crown Heights incident as a moment

"What Is It We Absorb?" 115

that defines race and Jewishness to the fore of the literary imaginary of Jewishness and Native Americans. The presence and settlement of Jews in and around Sitka following World War II necessarily evokes Israeli statehood. By extension, their contentious relationship with the Native Americans in Alaska is analogous to the tensions between Israelis and Palestinians. Yet the displacement of the Jewish state from a Zionist homeland in Israel to the remote region of Alaska means that the Yiddish speakers' longing for their homeland is also about Israel. In this sense, Zionism both is displaced to Alaska yet remains particular to Israel.

In the same introduction to Hertz's character, the narrator stipulates that his fascination with Native American culture is authentic, even if it is, in part, a cover for his actions against Native Americans. In this regard, the character suggests a Jewish investment in Native American culture that has a long history among European academics, especially anthropologists. For Casteel, "Hertz is a parody of the European Jewish émigré anthropologist or collector of Native art who recalls such historical figures as Franz Boas" ("Jews among the Indians" 42). Chabon's creation of this character and Casteel's interpretation of him speak to the particular interest that Jewish intellectuals have shown in Indigenous cultures and experiences. Specifically, there is a long history within anthropology of Jewish investment in Native American tribes that speaks to how Jews' and Native Americans' respective relationships to the land and to dominant understandings of centre and periphery inflect identities, belonging, and culture. To this point, anthropologist Jeffrey Feldman notes of Claude Lévi-Strauss: "he is both a citizen in the metropolis and an excluded other in the nation ... Strauss's Jewishness has taken shape through his movement between urban centers – Paris, New York, Jerusalem" (115). Lévi-Strauss himself avowed "the profound feeling of belonging to a national community, all the while knowing that in the midst of this community there are people who reject you" (quoted in "The Jewish Roots" 114). Similar to Lévi-Strauss's reflection here, Jewish preoccupation with Native American culture in *The Yiddish Policemen's Union* is couched within the marginalized and precarious moment in which the Yiddish characters are on the precipice of losing their territory. This vexed relationship of fascination and discrimination not only characterizes relationships between Jews and Native Americans but also is the origin – the foundational fiction – for characters such as Berko.

Hertz, through fathering Berko and his other actions, is a complicated character. We learn that "years ago his dining room table was a lively region, the only table in these divided islands at which Indians

116 Absorption Narratives

and Jews regularly sat down to eat good food without rancor" (Chabon, *The Yiddish Policemen's Union* 357). His contradictory relationship to Native American culture, at least in the past, facilitated community between Jews and Native Americans before leading to the death of the mother of his child. Chabon extends what Casteel terms his "parodical" depiction of Jewish fascination with Native American culture to make him a bona fide Jewish terrorist, a damning indictment of Jewish interest in Native American experiences. Jewish intellectuals' imaginings of Indigeneity also bring up broader questions about Jewish investment in racial alterity in relation to their own Jewishness.

Just as Berko is introduced to readers in terms of his conflictual physically Native American yet behaviourally Jewish descriptions, he casts off his Jewish identity following these same terms. When he discovers that his father had a hand in the violent acts against Native Americans in the St. Cyril Riots, his immediate reaction is to disavow his father and his religion: "'I tried my whole life,' he says finally, 'I mean, fuck, look at me!' He snatches the skullcap from the back of his head and holds it up, contemplating it with a sudden horror as if it's the flesh of his scalp" (Chabon, *The Yiddish Policemen's Union* 368). His exclamation of "I mean, fuck, look at me" seems to underscore the visual incongruity that many note in the large, phenotypically Native American man adorned in Jewish garb of the yarmulke and tallit. His Jewish markers of Jewish identification are garb that he can don and remove that are patently in tension with his immutable Native American features. Berko's disavowal of his Jewish identification in response to learning about his father's involvement in his mother's death underscores the uncomfortable relationship in which these different parts of his identity exist together inside of him. Moreover, that learning of his father's violent actions against Native Americans prompts this disavowal of his spiritual identification with Jewishness brings up the fraught points of contact between ethnicity, spirituality, and geopolitics in the context of Jewish–Native American relations.

The novel underscores the incongruity of Berko's hybrid identity as a function of fraught intergenerational relationships. Immediately after Berko proclaims to Landsman, "Look at me!," Berko explicitly presents his Jewish identification not as a religion but in terms of a father-son relationship. Removing his tallit, he admonishes his father, "Every damn day of my life, I get up in the morning and put this shit on and pretend to be something I'm not. Something I'll never be. For *you*" (369). When Hertz responds that he never insisted that his son observe the Jewish religion, Berko retorts, "It has nothing to do with *religion* ... it has everything to do, God damn it, with *fathers*" (369–70). As in the

"What Is It We Absorb?"   117

description of Berko's circumcision, Chabon presents the character's Jewish identification in relationship to Hertz and as something that Berko performs. When he learns the truth about his father's involvement in his mother's death, he rejects not only his father but his Judaism. Here, the father-son relationship is a rupture, not a binding tie. The precarity of this relationship comes into clearer relief as the narrator follows Berko's exclamation with, "It comes through the mother, of course, one's being or not being a Jew. But Berko knows that. He's known that since the day he moved to Sitka. He sees it every time he looks into a mirror" (369). The narrator's emphasis here that Berko has known that his "not being a Jew" has come from his mother not since birth, but since moving to Sitka, underscores the outsider status that Berko takes on among the Yiddish community of Sitka. Hertz's response here – to shoot himself – further underscores this severed relationship. Moreover, the narrator's reminder that "it comes through the mother" underscores the severed tie between Berko and his now deceased mother. The irony of Berko's attempts to be more Jewish and his inability to do so because his mother was Native American and non-Jewish becomes tragically stark in this scene as we learn of his own father's role in his mother's death. Like in Richler's novel, the Jewish–Native American son of a Jewish man has a catastrophically contentious relationship with his father. Berko, we learn, has been dutifully devoted to Jewish practices in an effort to please his father, to the point that he defines himself as pretending to be something he is not.

Conclusions

Throughout these four texts, Jewishness and Indigeneity converge in ways that emphasize the difficulty and uncomfortableness of racial and spiritual hybridity. If these characters embody certain Indigenous or Jewish traits, elements of one often seem to bely the other part of their identities and show Jewishness and Indigeneity sitting uncomfortably with one another.

The novels' shared elements of detective fiction speak to characters' needs to resolve mysteries of complex genealogies. As Vizenor's novel makes clear, however, there is no single, coherent genome narrative that can make up for what remains unknown and hidden to these characters about their own identities. And yet, Vizenor's novel is more optimistic about possibilities for healing from racialized trauma than the other authors discussed in this chapter. Through the use of red herrings, red heifers, and red schmaltz, these authors tell stories in detective form as a way of exploring the hidden parts of individual and group identities.

118 Absorption Narratives

Moreover, these complicated, mysterious parts of individual identities are bound up in broader concerns of national and regional belonging. Roger Graetz reminds readers that, even during peaceful moments, Jewish, Guatemalan, Catholic, and US identifications rarely coexist peacefully within one person. As Goldman shows through his exploration of political violence in Guatemala, and as we see through the other novels discussed in this chapter, moments of national and collective crisis – the return of the Yiddish territory to the US in Chabon, the various crimes in Vizenor, and the lingering effects of settler colonialism in Richler – force characters who embody both Jewish and Indigenous identities into further crises of identity.

Only one of the works discussed in this chapter, *The Heirs of Columbus*, emphasizes Sephardic identities, which is striking in comparison to chapter 1 and given the racial mixture and secret Jewishness that have characterized the history of Sephardic communities for centuries. For Vizenor, Sephardim encapsulate the phenomenon of racial mixture in the Americas following the European conquest. In contrast, Richler, Chabon, and Goldman seem to imagine Jewish–Indigenous hybridity from their lived experiences as Ashkenazi Jews (and with mestizo ancestry, in Goldman's case).

Still, the paradigm of secret Jewishness seems to be a spectral presence throughout these three works. We observe the shame and secrecy that plague the youngest Gursky generation, the "surreal" combination that Flor de Mayo understands her identity to be, and Berko's self-described, similarly unbelievable clash of identities. These novels show the convergence of Jewishness and Indigeneity colliding in ways that compel characters to dissemble or to grapple with the complexities of their hybrid genealogies within broader paradigms of racial difference and colonial power. In this sense, the novels share a great deal in common with and exemplify the trials and contestations at the heart of Vizenor's courtroom novel. Much like the nineteenth-century foundational fictions that Sommer has explored, these novels foreground genealogies that incorporate centuries of fraught racial convergence.

4 Accidents of Racism: Passing and Absorbing Blackness into Jewishness

As discussed in the chapter 3 reading of Hertz Shemets's character, anthropology and ethnography have served as a locus through which Jewish scholars have explored specific fascination with Indigenous peoples. Furthering that conversation, in this chapter I take into account narratives in which explorers, translators, and humanities professors at times reproduce and at times challenge the organizing logics through which racial categories are articulated and maintained. Specifically, the texts I discuss here speak to the convergence of Black and Jewish individuals throughout the Americas. In this chapter, all three texts are authored by Jewish-identified authors. As a point of entry, the chapter begins with a reading of Ukraine-born Jewish Brazilian author Clarice Lispector's 1960 short story "The Smallest Woman in the World." Whereas Chabon's *The Yiddish Policemen's Union* recounted a Jewish character who was simultaneously fascinated by and hateful towards Native American culture, Lispector's story offers an example from a Jewish storyteller of a European explorer who "discovers" an Indigenous African person. While Lispector's story is very different (in terms of genre, publication date, and theme) from Philip Roth's *The Human Stain* and Achy Obejas's *Days of Awe*, the three texts have in common an exploration of the ways in which Jewish and Black positionalities collide in academic spaces. In these works, Jewish subjects find themselves in spaces in the Americas in which Jewishness is intertwined in various ways with Blackness. For these authors, Jewishness and Blackness are both uprooted in their own ways, recalling Figueroa's insistence on the need to conceptualize destierro beyond its colonialist underpinnings. In what follows, I argue that the uprooting of Black and Jewish characters in these three works of fiction offers models of resistance against colonialism and patriarchy.

120   Absorption Narratives

"The Smallest Woman in the World"

Clarice Lispector's 1960 short story "The Smallest Woman in the World" tells the story of "Little Flower" (as she is named by Marcel Pretre, the Frenchman who "discovers" her), a member of a particular race of the tiniest people in the world in a fictional rendering of anthropological "discoveries." Lispector, born in Ukraine to a Jewish family and raised in Brazil from the time she was an infant, challenges notions of margins and peripheries along racialized lines by having a French explorer "discover" and name the woman whose image is then reproduced in life-sized colour in newspapers distributed in the metropole. The story of "Little Flower" recalls the nineteenth-century case of Sara Baartman, the so-called Hottentot Venus, who was brought from Africa and displayed throughout Europe and whose body was used to form the basis of much racialized thinking in Europe from the early nineteenth century onward. Focusing first on Pretre's response to coming across "Little Flower," the narrative recreates a Eurocentric view of Indigenous African people insofar as, as Rafael Climent-Espino has noted, "the reader views the reality of these tribes (Bantus, Likoualas) through the view and description of the explorer" (339). Yet, Pretre is not the main narrator of the text – rather, an omniscient third-person narrator voices other characters' thoughts, jumping back and forth between Africa and the unnamed urban space that is most likely Lispector's own city, Rio de Janeiro, in keeping with the rest of the stories in the collection. Despite the use of an omniscient, third-person narrator, the text is characterized by a degree of narrative focus on the character of Pretre in a way, I submit, that questions the presumed neutrality of an omniscient narrator and, in turn, the standpoint of the author and her readers. This narrative structure raises questions about the racialized thinking that informs the encounter between a European explorer and a pygmy character. Such narrative ambiguity is necessarily influenced by Lispector's own subjectivity as a European-born Jewish Brazilian author writing a fictional account of the varied responses to the image of an Indigenous African person in bourgeois urban households.

Lispector is often discussed as a Jewish author, yet explicit references to Jewishness seldom appear in her works. In a sense, Jewishness is often absorbed in Lispector's own storytelling. Yet, as an increasing corpus of scholarship has studied in recent decades, Lispector's texts nonetheless lend themselves to explorations of Jewish themes as well as of Jewish approaches to writing. Critic Naomi Lindstrom's discussion of Lispector is couched in a framework of "absorption." Lindstrom notes that previously existing critical studies of the Brazilian author "claim to

Accidents of Racism 121

have found in her fiction evidence of the Jewish culture that Lispector *absorbed* in her family of origin, but subsequently downplayed" (83, my emphasis). As Lindstrom shows, reading for "Judaic traces" in Lispector's work is critical both to understandings of Lispector's works in and of themselves and of Latin American Jewish culture. In the case of this particular story, I would add that how Jewish subjects imagine encounters between white European and Black African characters has everything to do with how Jewishness and racial alterity are registered in fiction.

The biblical allusions in the story are abundantly clear from its beginning, which strongly evokes Genesis and the Garden of Eden. Much has been made of the moment at which Pretre "names" the smallest woman in the world. Lispector's narration characterizes Pretre's decision to name her: "Feeling an immediate necessity for order and for giving names to what exists, he called her Little Flower" (501). Not only does Lispector evoke the Bible here, but she also tacitly characterizes Pretre's act of naming as a "necessity for order," underscoring taxonomist impulses as colonialist, patriarchal, and Eurocentric. For Claire Williams (1998), this naming has the effect of "framing her within his discourse and linking her directly to nature by using an affectionate but patronizing diminutive, as if classifying a botanical specimen. The act of naming is a direct reference to Adam's assertion of primacy and authority in the book of Genesis" (171). Naomi Lindstrom has discussed the significance of biblical references in Lispector's works writ large. Similarly, Climent-Espino submits that "naming implies a control over discourse, a hegemony over what is named, not only is it controlling the signifier, but also the signified" (341), specifically apropos of Pretre's "sudden need to restore order." Lispector never offers readers another name for Little Flower, such that Pretre's is the only signifier associated with this character. As Williams underscores, the name he chooses for her emphasizes gender and size. The name also equates the character with the earth in a way that, I submit, is patently racialized. That is, his naming of her in a way that links her to the place where she is found dovetails with vertiginously essentializing and fetishizing tropes of Indigenous and Black identities in connection to the land.

If, for Pretre, this character becomes known as Little Flower, then much like a rarefied flower from a research exploration in Africa, this character's likeness becomes circulated and commodified among urban dwellers in an urban space that remains unnamed in the story. Whereas Little Flower is named by Pretre, the city in which her image is circulated does not ever have a name in the text. As Lispector recounts newspaper readers' responses to the photo of her, the text underscores urban

122   Absorption Narratives

middle- and upper-class people's fetishizing and exoticizing reactions to the world's smallest woman. Yet, these responses are also patently humanizing in provocative ways. Yudith Rosenbaum's reading of the story notes, "The desire of possession, racial preconceptions, the exploration of foreign work and so many other crude, savage manifestations show that two orders confront one another: one, the domestic, marked by cultural habits, whose nobility is shown to falsify its real nature, the other of barbarism that throbs underneath the social veneer" (153, my translation). The two registers are in constant tension with one another as Little Flower travels – through the circulation of her image – between the two realms. Michael Colvin relates this dynamic between centre and periphery to the narrative structure of the story, which he deems cannibalistic: "The narrator's ambulatory perspective, shifting seven times, complicates the embedding technique by constantly questioning the notion of center" (84). The narrative levels of the text – which I will discuss further – replicate separate spheres of reality and the consumption of information about alterity within urban, middle-class spaces.

Finally, towards the end of the story, the narrative returns to "the rare thing" itself, "Little Flower," who is described as "enjoying the ineffable sensation of not having been eaten yet" (505). This description is, of course, ironic in the sense that her likeness has been consumed – at least in the narrative structure of the story at this point, even if the narration is returning to the moment before the photo is taken and distributed – by the camera, the newspaper, and the viewers of the newspaper throughout the city. At the intradiegetic level, Little Flower is devoured by Pretre and the newspaper readers who react to seeing her photo reproduced. On an extratextual level, this character is devoured by Lispector as a Jewish Brazilian writer who – from Brazilian urban spaces – writes of this exotic character. Lispector's use of the term "eaten" here ("devorado" in the original Portuguese) recalls my focus in chapter 3 on cannibalism as a particular form of absorption.

Lispector's narrative hinges on the reactions and perspectives of Pretre and those who consume the image of the small woman in the newspaper. A woman responds that she is a "coisa rara" and the narrative immediately returns to Pretre and Little Flower in Africa, stating, "And the rare thing itself?" as if responding to the woman in the story as well as to readers' curiosity as to the whereabouts of the little woman herself. The fact that readers, the character in the metropole, and the narrator are all thus similarly interpellated in the story creates a particular effect of Jewish ventriloquism that we have not yet seen in *Absorption Narratives*. Specifically, Lispector creates a space in between the subjectivities of the smallest woman, Pretre, the readers of the newspaper, and the narrator. Yet, in this moment, Lispector also seems to conflate the latter two in a way that positions her readers similarly to the readers of the newspaper image. The story never explicitly references any aspect of Jewishness. Nonetheless, Lispector's intricate positioning of Pretre's character in relation to both the smallest woman in the world and to her own narrator – and, by extension, to her readers – creates an interplay between subjects and narrators that necessarily evokes questions of Lispector's own positionality as a European-born Jew who lived her entire life in Brazilian urban spaces.

The fact that the names of the cities and nations in which the image of Little Flower is reproduced and circulated never appear emphasizes the importance of the relationship between centre and periphery in discussions about alterity. That is, the country in which Pretre "discovers" Little Flower is described only as being in Africa, and readers are privy to no information about the places in which her image is circulated save for references of "homes" and "apartment buildings" and the quotidian items in them, such as rulers, hairpins, and armchairs. In one of these households, the mother speaks to the father "José," which suggests that the country in which the families are reading the newspaper is a Spanish- or Portuguese-speaking country. Moreover, the rest of the stories in the collection are set within urban, middle-class family households in Rio de Janeiro. The unnamed country in which families see and discuss the small woman's image is likely Brazil – given that the name she ascribes to the character José is a common Portuguese name and, unlike her naming of Pretre and her description of Africa, there is no indicator that the country in which the image is reproduced is *not* Brazil. Yet, the fact that she does not give the country a name introduces ambiguity in the relationship between Europe, Africa, and the space in which the image of Little Flower is reproduced. Thus, the interplays between margin and periphery become even more complicated insofar as Brazilian self-understanding as a racial melting pot undergirded widespread beliefs about national identity in the mid-twentieth century. Specifically, sociologist Gilberto Freyre's notion of *democracia racial* – racial democracy – an idea that has been increasingly contested but that nonetheless has had enormous staying power in notions of national identity, remained more-or-less prominent in Brazilian society during the time when Lispector penned this story. Historian George Reid Andrews has outlined that Freyre's ideas about racial democracy were inspired, in part, by his exposure to the Jim Crow South as a student in Texas in the 1910s and 1920s and that the model of racial democracy is not entirely dissimilar to predominant cultural attitudes about race in the US in the 1980s

124 Absorption Narratives

and 1990s. In the 1950s and 1960s, racial democracy was increasingly scrutinized within academic circles, in Harold Winant's terms, "deriving its momentum from worldwide horror at the Holocaust and Nazi racism, and influenced by the Brazilian racial democracy paradigm as formulated by Freyre" (229). In chapter 5, I will discuss further what happened with the idea of racial democracy in Brazil over the next decades. But what is important for my discussion here of Lispector's story is that her narrative goes against the idea of amalgamated racial blending that largely characterized popular beliefs about race at the time by showing how racial difference is perceived within urban, middle-class family settings.

Elsewhere, Lispector's story discusses possession of the small woman's reproduced image in ways that evoke the Atlantic slave trade. "To tell the truth, who hasn't wanted to own a human being just for himself?" (504), the narrator of "The Smallest Woman in the World" asks after recounting that one of the people who saw the woman's image in the newspaper wanted to possess her. The narrative ambiguity throughout the story both damns the bourgeois reception of this character's image and empathizes with these middle-class characters. As Adriano de Paula Rabelo's reading of the story's "social and anthropological discomfort" concludes, "Rather than induce the reader into an easy indignation with the exclusion and segregation in which a significant number of people among us live, in Lispector's work social problems are always interlaced with existential questions" (88). Leaving room for – perhaps troubling – narrative and ethical ambiguities alike, the text invites readers to consider how they see themselves reflected in the various characters' responses to the image of the woman whom Pretre finds. Likewise, the text asks readers in turn to contemplate the omniscient narrator's – and Lispector's own – position as a writer who is representing racial alterity and imagining the ways in which readers react to difference.

Yet, while the text invokes the history of the slave trade through the responses to an Indigenous African woman's image in the newspapers, the text eschews the real presence of African descendants in Brazil. In this way, Lispector's text evokes the problem within "racial democracy" that racial discrimination – specifically, the fetishization and commodification of Blackness – was often seen as a problem of other countries rather than of Brazil itself. Through the characters' responses of longing for possession of the smallest woman in the world, the text reveals bourgeois reactions to racial alterity in Brazil to be predicated on dehumanizing hierarchies and colonialist circulations of possession and fetishization.

Throughout the characters' responses to the images of the smallest woman in the world, fetishization of Black bodies is a recurrent theme. Similar to Perera's discussion of how his non-Jewish, light-skinned teacher fetishizes the dark-skinned mestizo character, Lispector's story, too, constitutes a narrative written by a Jewish author who gives an account of how white and light-skinned characters fetishize Black and Brown bodies. Through the characters' reactions to the image, Lispector's text adds a layer of narrative that is situated between Pretre's Eurocentric gaze and that of the readers – who, to be sure, may also be Eurocentric and colonizing. At any rate, this in-between narrative space recalls Lispector's own positionality as a European-born woman raised in Brazil who is writing a fictional story about an African woman and the exoticizing responses to her image.

At different points in the story, Pretre describes the smallest woman in the world through similes that compare her to a monkey. He tells the newspapers that she is "black as a monkey" (501). Lispector's story ventriloquizes the white European explorer to use his voice to describe the Black character through a dehumanizing simile. His act of naming her "Little Flower," which is also narrated through his dialogue, metaphorizes the Black woman by equating her with nature in an essentialist, exoticizing manner. The simile of "dark as a monkey" or "dark like a monkey" (another feasible translation of the original Portuguese "escura como un macaco") evokes more directly racist tropes of Western colonizers equating Blackness with primates, whereas "Little Flower" functions on a more seemingly benign – still racist, sexist, and exoticizing – register deployed through metaphor.

While Little Flower is not literally eaten, her likeness and, in a sense, her identity, are devoured by those who read the newspaper and dream of what they might do with her image. While, undoubtedly, the story of what happens to the smallest woman in the world and to her image is certainly exoticizing and paternalistic, Lispector does suggest that "love is to like the strange color of a man who isn't Black" (506). Here, the narrative pivots to depict the small woman's fascination with Pretre, described here as being of a "strange color." Significantly, his "strange color" is couched within a description of what "love" means for the Little Flower character. For her, it means to like the strange colour. A fascination with European whiteness equates to love in Lispector's articulation of this character. As Lispector states elsewhere in the text, love is also the feeling of not having been eaten. Through associative property, loving Pretre for liking his strange colour is metonymically linked to resisting being devoured. In this case, being devoured relates very literally to cannibalism, not unlike my

126 Absorption Narratives

discussion of Richler's novel in chapter 3. Once again, cannibalism – here, the imminent threat of being eaten that Little Flower feels – is intricately linked to colonialism and the absorption of racial difference. Through linking the love that the character feels as a result of liking Pretre's skin colour to the love that she feels because she has not been cannibalized, Lispector seems to invert the tropes of cannibalism and absorption of difference that long undergirded Latin American literary paradigms. The Ukrainian-born Jewish Brazilian author disentangles myths of racial mixture and so-called racial democracy by underscoring the desires for possession and consumption that the image of Little Flower evokes throughout middle-class urban households in Brazil. Thus, the author suggestively questions how forms of racial and ethnic difference function in twentieth-century Brazilian society in ways that, without directly or explicitly naming racism, underscore the fraught reality of the idea of racial democracy in Brazil. "The Smallest Woman in the World" resists the idea of absorption of racial difference that was, at that time, deeply engrained in Brazilian society and that, as I will show in chapter 5's discussion of Cao Hamburger's film, would come increasingly under scrutiny. Through deploying the character of Pretre as an anthropological scapegoat, Lispector questions the Eurocentrism and investment in whiteness that pervaded the idea of racial democracy through imagining how society might respond to the image of a character like Little Flower.

The Jewish Brazilian author tacitly grapples with how Blackness has been encountered, observed, and represented. In so doing, Lispector speaks to Jewish–Black dynamics both within Brazil and elsewhere. Understandings of race – and specifically of Blackness – in Brazil have shifted during the six decades since Lispector's story first appeared in ways that have altered how Jewishness converges with Blackness. Nonetheless, Lispector's story remains relevant for what it may yet contribute to critical understandings of Jewish perspectives on race. Namely, Lispector's use of an unnamed, omniscient narrator aspires to eschew her own Jewishness – her gender and her nationality are also unnamed – throughout the story, suggesting a paradigm in which the alterity of the Jewish author is effaced in order to craft a narrative about racial alterity. Yet, as we have seen, traces of Jewishness are nonetheless present in the text. Readers come to see their own complicity in the circulation of Little Flower's likeness and become interpellated in Lispector's world, thus necessarily calling into question how Jewishness figures into the acts of coloniality that characterize the text as well as how Jewish voices such as Lispector's might contest coloniality.

Lily White Ass: *The Human Stain*

The Human Stain succeeds Philip Roth's previous novels *American Pastoral* and *I Married a Communist* to complete the loose trilogy of 1990s novels narrated by Nathan Zuckerman, likely an alter-ego of Roth himself. The trilogy stands out among Roth's work as a novelistic endeavour to foreground the role of Jewish communities in twentieth-century US history. Throughout the trilogy, Roth emphasizes Jewish involvement in communist and radical politics. Farther removed in its plot from the previous two, *The Human Stain* focuses on how race factors into Jewish belonging in the US. As Zuckerman contemplates at the novel's end, "Was [Coleman Silk] merely being another American and, in the great frontier tradition, accepting the democratic invitation to throw your origins overboard if to do so contributes to the pursuit of happiness?" (334). Zuckerman's claim of "merely being another American" speaks to both Jewish and Black absorption into the paradigms of assimilation. The specific naming of the "frontier tradition" evokes Koffman's model of Jewish settler colonialism and participation in manifest destiny, a model in which Coleman can participate only on the condition of disavowing his Blackness and passing as Jewish and white. In this way, Roth anticipates the idea of the "American absorption project" of which he would write in his next novel, *The Plot Against America*, as I referenced in chapter 1.[1]

Silk is a character through whom Roth explores how Jewishness comes into contact with Blackness within academia; Silk is not a Black character in his own right.[2] For Glaser, *The Human Stain* is a novel in which "the archetypical Jewish author manifests his vexed relationship to race and canonicity by articulating the concerns of the endangered Jewish intellectual and proponent of universal humanism through the mouth of an African American passing for a Jewish professor" (loc. 2246). In other words, Roth contemplates – and perhaps even laments – the extent to which Jews have largely come to be accepted unquestioningly as part of whiteness. In the face of this loss, Roth imagines and ventriloquizes a Black character who passes as Jewish in order to benefit from the upward social mobility that post–World War II society in the US has afforded to Jews but not to Black folks. *The Human Stain* offers a timely – both for 2000 and through a diachronic reading from 2023 – commentary on the politics of race on college campuses.

Jews in the Americas in the early twentieth century came to understand themselves as part of the nations to which they immigrated through a complicated matrix of political events determined, in large part, by World War II and its aftermath. The trajectory that Roth creates

128 Absorption Narratives

for protagonist Coleman Silk is similar. Coleman enters the Navy in World War II as a light-skinned Black man and emerges from his service a Jew, unbeknownst to him. In a sense, World War II makes him Jewish. The similarities between Jewish and Black people that Coleman embodies – namely, his wiry curly hair and his penchant for boxing – allow him to pass as Jewish. Once he realizes the social mobility and acceptance afforded to him by passing as Jewish, he begins to do so more actively, but not without painfully forgoing his relationship to his mother. Coleman Silk is absorbed into a narrative of whiteness – specifically, Jewish whiteness – in postwar US culture. Paradoxically, the character's passing and his ability to deny his race reveal the extent to which twentieth-century lives in the US were, in fact, determined by racial identifications. Dean Franco argues that "Roth's literature, especially *The Human Stain*, actively deconstructs the very idea of racial classification by pitting competing models of race against each other; by parodying the idea of racial "essence"; and by skewering the logic that inheres in racism and anti-Semitism ... in our contemporary liberal and liberated society, our social being is nonetheless plotted by racial typing" (89). Coleman Silk's absorption into white Jewish culture – and, by extension, into white culture – serves precisely to underscore the degree to which Blackness cannot be assimilated into white US culture in the same way that Jewishness came to be assimilated into whiteness over the course of the twentieth century.

Silk not only is compelled to disavow his Blackness but also becomes interpellated through speech acts that, since he is read as white, take on particular meanings – namely, white supremacy. As Jennifer Glaser notes, Silk "is marked in ways he does not realize, ways that leave large swaths of the world and his own interiority illegible to him" (loc 1471). In this way, Roth's portrayal of Coleman Silk exemplifies Du Boisian "double consciousness," which Du Bois famously described: "It is a peculiar sensation, this double-consciousness, this sense of always looking at one's self through the eyes of others, of measuring one's soul by the tape of a world that looks on in amused contempt and pity" (*The Souls of Black Folk*).[3] Through Coleman Silk's story, Roth brings to the surface what cannot be absorbed and what cannot be effaced in one's avowal of identity.

For Roth, Jewish investment in Blackness allows for an exploration of race and identity politics in the late 1990s. The novel begins with Zuckerman's musings on the Clinton-Lewinsky scandal and late 1990s sexual sensibilities. Within the setting of the fictional Athena College, where Coleman Silk is a renowned professor of classics, the novel explores race, class, and sexuality as they come to bear on Jewish and

Black identities in the age of "political correctness." Coleman Silk sparks a controversy and resigns over a scandal he inadvertently causes by using the term "spooks" to mean ghosts but which is interpreted to refer to Black students using the term as a racial slur. Inspired by a similar event involving a sociology professor at Princeton in the 1980s, the controversy begins when Silk asks, well into the semester, if any of the students in his course know the two students who have been absent all term, asking "Are they spooks?" By his own account, Silk is using "spooks" as a term for ghosts, but some students present in the class relay to them that the professor asked this and, as African American students, they are upset that the professor used a term that has historically been used as a racial slur against Black folks. Unwittingly, Silk utters a phrase that exemplifies Brodkin's characterization that Jews were able to become accepted as white in the twentieth-century US by avowing white supremacist ideas. He is later persecuted by a young colleague, Delphine Roux, who is scandalized by his comments and also by his sexual relationship with a custodial worker, Faunia Farley, after the death of his wife, Iris, who dies of a heart attack shortly after his ouster from Athena and whose death Coleman therefore blames on the college administration for persecuting him.

Silk is described as an "attractive package of a man even at his age, the small-nosed Jewish type with the facial heft in the jaw, one of those crimped-haired Jews of a light yellowish skin pigmentation who possess something of the ambiguous aura of the pale blacks who are sometimes taken for white" (15–16). The "ambiguous aura" that Zuckerman describes in Silk is precisely what allows him to pass as Jewish rather than Black over the course of his adult life. Zuckerman's perception of Silk anticipates the story with which Melanie Kaye/Kantrowitz opens her book *The Color of Jews* of her own early childhood perception of a light-skinned African American. The author tells a story of her Jewish mother in 1950s Flatbush boasting of her eight-year-old daughter's "colorblindness" when the child spoke often of her ballet instructor yet never mentioned he was Black. Kaye/Kantrowitz reflects, "The truth is I don't notice not because I am color blind – who by age seven is? – but because I come from a Jewish family and neighborhood with wide varieties of skin color in which ... a light-skinned black man does not stand out as different" (2). Roth takes a similar example of a light-skinned Black man who does not stand out as different from Jews as one of the central conceits in *The Human Stain* – passing as Jewish and white. That is, in Roth's fictional universe, an ethnically ambiguous man such as Coleman Silk is easily perceived by Jews as Jewish.

130   Absorption Narratives

Roth suggests a certain interchangeability between anti-Black racism and anti-Semitism in the novel. Before Zuckerman learns that Coleman is in fact Black, Coleman tells him that in the Navy he was mistaken for a Black man. The character equates his oppression as a Black man early in life with his later plight as a man living as a Jew. Silk goes so far as to claim that he is a victim of Black anti-Semitism: "Thrown out of Athena ... for being a *white Jew* of the sort those ignorant bastards call the enemy. ... What is the major source of black suffering on this planet? They know the answer without having to come to class. ... Who is responsible? The same evil Old Testament monsters responsible for the suffering of the Germans" (16, my emphasis). His assertion that he has been targeted as a "white Jew" speaks to the phenomenon of Jewish whiteness that became increasingly pervasive over the course of the twentieth century and of which Brodkin writes. Specifically, it suggests that white Jewishness is a specific sort of Jewishness, starkly belying a simple correlation between Jewishness and whiteness. Yet, at the same time, Silk also conjures the phenomenon of Jewish avowal of white supremacy and overt anti-Black attitudes that has allowed many Jews to be accepted as white. Roth shows that, by Silk's own account, he has long since ceased being a Black man and become a white Jew. Here, the layers of ventriloquism become somewhat vexed. To recapitulate, in this instance, white Jewish author Philip Roth is speaking through his alter ego narrator Nathan Zuckerman who is quoting Coleman Silk, a man who was born African American and has been living as a Jew for decades. Here, this voice – layered and imagined across races and cultures – is speaking as a Jewish voice against Black anti-Semitism, an exchange of utterances that is obviously more than a little fraught. And yet, there is also a way in which Roth is articulating something close to an anti-racist stance through his ability to empathize with Coleman's difficulty in being accepted as a more authentic version of himself despite having established himself as a respected academic.

Roth absorbs Blackness into Jewish identities both through his own writing of the novel and through Nathan Zuckerman's retelling of Coleman's story. Zuckerman, like in the rest of the novels in which a narrative alter-ego of Roth appears, learns about and recounts Coleman's life story, but in this case, that life story is the outing of Zuckerman's friend and neighbour as a Black man who has been passing at Jewish. The narrator appropriates the character's identity as well as his well-kept secret. Luminita Dragulescu discusses the novel in terms of "narrative passing," an attempt that, as the critic shows, is "inherently insufficient" (99). Passing is only made visible when it fails, as Glaser notes: "Passing, which disavows visible difference in favor of a

Accidents of Racism   131

willed sameness, undermines the stakes of multiculturalism as it was practised at the time Roth was writing *The Human Stain*. In particular, it plays with multiculturalism's central argument: that recognition by another is the precondition of identity" (loc. 2410). If, in the late 1990s, recognition by the other was the predominant racial paradigm within a society that sought to foster multiculturalism, some twenty years on, the racial trauma of the very variety that Dragulescu notes in her study of the novel has become more central to academic conversations on race and belonging in spaces such as the fictional Athena College. Because of this emphasis, I would venture that *The Human Stain* would fail miserably as a twenty-first–century campus novel. The central conceit of the reaction among what Fox News pundits today would label the "woke mob" to Coleman's seemingly innocent use of the term "spooks" makes a strawman argument out of political correctness rather than recognize the realness of the pain that the use of a term such as "spooks" would prompt – whether in 2023 or in 2000 – when used to refer to Black students. What does withstand the test of time (two decades, at any rate) is Roth's exploration of the complexities of Blackness and the lifelong struggles of having one's identity legislated from without.

Elsewhere in the novel, Silk does reproduce self-hating, racialized language. In dealing with the fallout of the incident with college administrators, he reaches a breaking point at which he tells the Dean, "I never again want to hear that self-admiring face of yours or see your smug fucking lily-white face" (81). The Dean, Primus, is left bemused by the situation and wonders to his wife afterward, "'Lily-white? Why 'lily-white'?" (81). Primus's confusion here is one of the few clues to Coleman's true racial identity. Later in the novel, readers come to learn that Coleman's brother, Walt, told him after Coleman told their mother that he would be marrying Iris (and had decided to pass as white): "Don't you *ever* try to see her. No contact. No calls. Nothing. Never. Hear me? ... *Never*. Don't you dare ever show your lily-white face around that house again" (145). In this moment, Coleman Silk was severed from his Black family and began to live as a white Jewish man. The fact that he should, decades later, repeat to his white boss what his brother said to him suggests both a self-loathing and an absorption of his brother's disparaging comments. Here, racial trauma – specifically, the trauma of feeling compelled to disavow one's own Blackness and even one's own family – does resonate with race relations in a more contemporary framework.

Some critics have named Anatole Broyard as the inspiration for Coleman Silk's character (Kaplan 2005; Parrish 2004). Yet, Roth insisted that this interpretation was wrong in a rather humorous, open fight against

Wikipedia that he waged through a letter to the *New Yorker*. In his open letter to the *New Yorker*, penned so that it could properly serve as a secondary source, Roth underscores the "spooks" incident involving Melvin Tumin, a sociology professor at Princeton, in 1985. The author insisted that the incident of a professor who asks whether students whom he has not met and whose race he does not know are "spooks" "is the initiating incident of *The Human Stain*: "It is the core of the book. There is no novel. There is no Coleman Silk without it. Every last thing we learn about Coleman Silk over the course of the three hundred and sixty-one pages begins with an unwarranted persecution for having uttered 'spooks' aloud in a college classroom" ("Open Letter"). Roth goes on to use the term "witch hunt" to describe both Tumin's and Silk's experiences following the incident – in keeping with 1990s thinking on "political correctness" and with twenty-first–century laments of the "woke mob." As Roth makes clear, the narrative impetus for the story is the incident of uttering "spooks," which unleashes a story that is predicated on the racial trauma of passing and the disavowal of one's identity.

Seemingly unbeknownst to Roth, this story does resonate uncannily with the life story of Anatole Broyard, who began to pass as white while in the Navy during World War II. Yet, Roth notes in his open letter, "I had no idea what it was like for Anatole Broyard to flee from his blackness because I knew nothing about Anatole Broyard's blackness, or, for that matter, his whiteness" ("Open Letter").[4] Roth's characterization here of Broyard's "blackness, or, for that matter, his whiteness" dovetails with Henry Louis Gates's discussion of "choices" of passing in the case of Broyard in *Thirteen Ways of Looking at a Black Man*. After he first characterizes passing as a "sin against authenticity," Gates notes, "When those of mixed ancestry – and the majority of blacks are of mixed ancestry – disappear into the white majority, they are traditionally accused of running from their 'blackness.' Yet why isn't the alternative a matter of running from their 'whiteness'?" (*Thirteen Ways* 207). In stories such as Broyard's and Coleman's – in the case of the latter, most markedly through his girlfriend's distraught reaction to realizing that he is Black and his own despair as a result – running from one's whiteness is not a viable choice. Gates's words evoke Brodkin's paradigm of Jewish avowal of white supremacy as a way of coming to belong in the twentieth-century US. Similar to Gates's question of why there is not a matter of running from one's whiteness, Daniel Itzkovitz posits in "Passing Like Me" that "the Jewish movement into 'whiteness' must be understood in terms of an alternative formulation as well, one in which Jewishness was popularly conceptualized as existing problematically 'outside' of whiteness'" (40). In other words, the "options" for passing

Accidents of Racism   133

need to be problematized insofar as being viable alternative choices that are afforded to individuals.

Coleman Silk's avowal of whiteness as a way of coming to pass – unlike Broyard, who did *not* claim to be Jewish – presupposes Jewish avowal of whiteness. Zuckerman, he tells us at the novel's end as he contemplates Coleman's grave after discussing Black history with Ernestine, feels "seized by" Silk's story. Parrish interprets Zuckerman's being "seized by" Coleman as an example of the hold that Ralph Ellison's literary production held over Roth. In Parrish's reading, Blackness in literature thus absorbs Jewishness. Yet, I would argue that it is not Blackness that absorbs Jewishness in Roth's novel but rather whiteness that absorbs both Zuckerman and Silk – the very whiteness that, by the late twentieth century, allowed Jews to be accepted as (mostly unquestionably) white while continuing to avow their Jewishness yet that does not allow Black folks to be accepted as light-skinned, multiracial members of society.

In *The Human Stain*, Roth explores whether the metonymic function with which Jewishness has come to be vested over the course of twentieth-century US history creates a category capacious enough to include Blackness. As Jonathan Freedman notes in *Klezmer America*, Jewishness went from being a synecdoche of ethnicity in the US to becoming a metonymy for other minority groups. *The Human Stain* explores the capaciousness of Jewishness as a category through questioning whether Coleman might pass as Jewish. Paradoxically, it is Coleman's unwitting avowal of white supremacy – the ultimate marker of Jewish whiteness in Brodkin's schema – that unleashes Nathan's fascination with his life and, finally, Nathan's discovery that he has been passing as a Jewish white man. Similarly, Zuckerman strongly implies that Coleman's passing as a white Jew is inexorably linked to the scandal prompted by his use of the term "spooks." The narrator wonders, in his conversation with Ernestine, whether there is in fact a connection between Coleman's passing as white and his ouster from Athena. He observes that the deceased man's sister "preferred not to contemplate the specific details of his destruction. Nor did she wish to inquire into any biographical connection between the injunction to revolt that had severed him from his family ... and the furious determination ... with which he had disassociated himself from Athena. ... Not that I was sure there was any connection, any circuitry looping the one decision to the other" (332). Within the schema that Brodkin creates of avowal of white supremacist attitudes as part of Jewish passing as white, the novel leaves open the question of whether Coleman Silk would have been able to pass as a Jew if not as a white Jew.

134 Absorption Narratives

Even more forceful a critique of academic stances on racial politics than those voiced by Coleman are those that Zuckerman and Roth recount in the voice of Coleman's sister.[5] Zuckerman and Roth speak through Ernestine as they spoke through Coleman earlier in the novel. Yet, because Ernestine has been estranged from her brother due to her disapproval of his choice to escape his own Blackness, her quibbles with "political correctness" arguably carry more weight than her brother's disavowal of racial justice discourse because she clearly has different racial sensibilities than her brother. Roth strategically places in Ernestine's mouth the words that most strongly damn campus cultures – from Black history month to her own brother's use of the term "spooks." After Zuckerman informs her of the incident that caused Coleman to leave Athena, his sister responds, "Sounds from what you've told me that anything is possible in a college today. Sounds like the people there forgot what it is to teach. Sounds like what they do is something closer to buffoonery" (328). Jonathan Freedman characterizes Ernestine's speech here as Roth's "most scathing attack on academic p.c" (171). Yet, Ernestine explicitly recriminates her brother in explaining why their brother Walt would have no interest in knowing that Coleman has died: "As white a college as there was in New England, and that's where Coleman made his career. As white a subject as there was in the curriculum, and that's what Coleman chose to teach" (336). Ernestine's condemnation of classics as "as white a subject as there was in the curriculum" anticipates present-day debates and processes of reckoning over whiteness in that field. Ernestine thus seems simultaneously to disparage her brother's escape from their shared Blackness and the campus's embrace of "political correctness."

I would venture that Roth's creation of Ernestine verges on the implausible. If Roth's creation of a Black man who has chosen to escape Blackness through his avowal of a white Jewish identity to the point of unwittingly avowing white supremacy makes sense, the fact that his sister should simultaneously bemoan both, on the one hand, her brother's decision to teach in such a white institution and, on the other, the campus's response to effective – if not intended – white supremacy, lacks some verisimilitude. For Freedman, Ernestine "seems to have been rendered into a stick figure rather than a character, a mouthpiece for her author's opinions rather than a representation of a complex human being who holds a bundle of contradictory ideas that exist in taut and complex relation to the rest of her life, like her brother Coleman or the narrator Nathan" (172). Ernestine contradicts her earlier critique of the whiteness of the instutition in her later critique of the students' vulnerability. She laments that "Reading the classics is too difficult, therefore it's the classics that are to blame. Today the student asserts his incapacity is a privilege. I can't learn it, so there is something wrong with it" (330–1). In addition to the contradictions between Ernestine's utterances, Roth voices a critique of campus cultures that eschews the pain that would certainly arise from Black students' learning that they have been referenced aloud by a professor using a term that has historically been used as a racialized derogatory term. On the other hand, Ernestine's beliefs regarding racial politics are clearly positioned between those of her two brothers, Coleman and Walter, who chided Coleman after learning that he was passing as white for the damage that it was causing to their mother. Ernestine informs Nathan that Walter will not care to hear about Coleman's death or of the scandal that led to his leaving Athena. She is an intermediary character with respect to Coleman's and Walter's more polarized stances on racial politics.

The Human Stain certainly offers a provocative glimpse into race and politics at a small liberal arts college in the late 1990s. Furthermore, the novel contemplates the construction of race through its characters' actions and their conversations about these actions. As Glaser notes, "By focusing on teachers ... Roth presses us to consider the epistemology and institutionalization of race – how we know ourselves racially through the teachers and texts that instruct us" (loc. 2491). With a focus on how Jewish immigrants to the US and Afro-descendant families in the US are racialized in twentieth-century culture, Roth taps into conversations about the construction of race throughout the Americas on the basis of paradigms of slavery and Jewish immigration to the Western hemisphere to escape persecution. Specifically, *The Human Stain* posits a cultural model in which Blackness and whiteness converge through mechanisms of religious identifications in ways that strongly evoke paradigms of syncretism.

Through his exploration of Jewishness vis-à-vis Blackness, Roth signals a racial category that, as my discussion of his novel in line with Itzkovitz's and Gates's respective considerations of passing shows, evokes questions of possibilities for avowing whiteness beyond the compulsory disavowal of Black or multiracial identity. In this way, *The Human Stain* questions the Black–white binary model of racial identifications in the US through suggesting a model of affinity between racial ambiguity and Jewishness. Similar to Behar's description of her family's survival in Cuba as an "accident of racism," Silk's accidental racism – if an isolated speech act – unleashes a chain of events that reveals his survival in white academic spaces also to be accidents of racism in their own right. Yet, such accidents of racism, we see, are not accidents at all; rather, they are functions of investment in whiteness throughout the

136   Absorption Narratives

Americas that operate along lines of colorism and that compel light-skinned Jews and gentiles alike to avow white supremacy (even if unwittingly) in order to survive and thrive in the Americas.

An Accident of Timing and Geography: *Days of Awe*

Similar to Perera's lament that his father never answered the question of "why Guatemala," *Days of Awe*'s narrator, Alejandra San José, describes her birth as an accident of timing and geography, a characterization that also recalls Behar's "accident of racism." The "accident" of Alejandra's family's presence in Cuba was so strong a coincidence that she was born in Havana on January 1, 1959, the first day of Castro's government. Behar's and Obejas's respective understandings of their accidental Cubanness evoke a tacit tension between Jewish exile, on the one hand, and Black experiences of being unwanted, ousted, and erased from the national body politic in Cuba. That is, where Behar acknowledges her family's presence in Cuba as an accident of racism insofar as their presence was a circumstance of the government's desire for more white and fewer Black people, for Obejas's narrator her family's presence in Cuba was an accident in that it was but one of many stops along the journey that her Sephardic family took in its centuries of exile. Moreover, throughout the novel, Obejas brings together the legacy of the Holocaust – through characters who fled persecution to escape to Cuba or the US and through a brief reference to the *St. Louis* affair – with an exploration of how Blackness and racial mixture characterize spirituality in Cuba. Similar to Glaser's reading of *The Human Stain* as a novel that emphasizes academic endeavours as a way of inviting readers to reconsider how race is constructed and understood, *Days of Awe* uses the activity of translation – both the narrator's work in medical and legal interpretation and her father's occupation as a literary translator – as a lens on race and ethnicity. To this point, Maya Socolovsky has argued, "the text ... counters a critical reading that would focus solely on its ethnic content or its historical aspect by blurring and complicating the very notion of history and historical narrative. In its own troubling of the history and authority of history and language, the text asks its readers to deconstruct its own presences and to turn it inside out, into a phantom of itself" (227–8). Expanding on Socolovsky's call to read *Days of Awe* as a phantom of itself, as a relief rather than a mimesis of racial and ethnic identifications, I read the novel as a textual exploration of how racial categories are formed in contact with one another and how these categories are translated across generations and across geographical contexts. Translation serves as a form of absorption through which difference moves and is erased across languages, contexts, and races.

The semi-autobiographical narrator realizes as an adult that her Cuban family has crypto-Jewish roots that her parents never disclosed to her. As part of a family of refugees from Castro's Cuba, protagonist-narrator Alejandra San José becomes determined to learn about her family history as a result of work-related trips to Cuba and of lesbian relationships. Throughout the novel, Obejas intermingles lesbian sexuality with crypto-Jewishness, both "closetable identities" (as discussed in chapter 1) and both, in Obejas's estimation, facets of identities and experiences that are not only concealable but that also often remain out of reach to oneself. As Alejandra comes to learn over the course of her journey into her family history, the ways in which her ancestors identified with ethno-religious hybridities were many. Moreover, the ways in which her family members come to negotiate and understand their own identities, and the various mechanisms through which they disclose and veil these identities, are individual. Through Obejas's narrative, hybridity and syncretism come into contact and are constantly problematized by external pressures to assimilate as well as by identity categories of sexuality and political orientations. Moreover, throughout the novel, the family's Sephardic identity is presented as both analogous to and mutually informed by categories of racial alterity. In *Days of Awe*, racial chameleonism is present mostly through clandestine Jewish rituals and through santería.

From the novel's beginning, Obejas shows syncretism and racial hybridity as inexorable from one another; they are the organizing principle of Alejandra's very existence, as the narrator's description of her birth makes clear. She describes that each of her parents prayed in their own way as the doctors fought to keep her alive as a newborn. As Dara Goldman argues, "As the doctors treat Ale's condition ... her mother performs the rituals of Afro-Cuban santería while her father quietly prays in Hebrew. In this way, Ale is the child of disparate and contradictory legacies; in order to survive, she must somehow reconcile this amalgam of competing systems" (63). From the novel's earliest pages, it is clear that this reconciliation process takes place through writing and translation. Obejas questions what her narrator terms the "inevitability" of characters' Jewishness as well as other racial categories that bear on their identities.

Days of Awe, like *The Human Stain*, explores not only how race is constructed and contested but also how academic and literary understandings of race are in flux and dispute. Specifically, both novels underscore the complexities of passing and of crypto-identities to

138 Absorption Narratives

consider epistemologies of race and identities. I am not the first scholar to study *Days of Awe* and *The Human Stain* in the same monograph. Freedman's *Klezmer America* moves from a chapter on Roth's novel to one on *Days of Awe* and *Spirits of the Ordinary*. To introduce the latter chapter, Freedman notes, "The dominant metaphors US literary critics employ to delineate the notion of hidden or secret identities are those of passing, derived from African American history and reanimated in African American cultural criticism, and the language of the closet, derived from the lesbian and gay male experience and put into discursive play by critics in queer studies" (213). From there, Freedman discusses the importance of cultural models of crypto-Jewishness and marrano identity. As Coleman Silk's story shows us, akin to the marrano model in which one's own identity is often a secret even to oneself, the effective functions of racial identities (i.e., the damning effects of unbeknownst white supremacy) are, in a sense, similarly secret to the protagonist himself. Whereas Freedman juxtaposes his discussion of *The Human Stain* and that of *Days of Awe* in side-by-side chapters, because of this point of comparison that Freedman notes and, moreover, because of the (often latent) importance of Blackness and Afro-Cuban culture in *Days of Awe*, I argue for the importance of a comparative reading of the two novels due to their shared emphases on academic understandings of crypto-identities and the role of Blackness therein.

One of the main innovations of Obejas's novel is its treatment of exile and diaspora. Rather than emphasize or privilege the Jewish experiences of exile to the exclusion of other racialized forms of exile, the author focuses on the untranslatability of "destierro," a concept that applies both to Jewish exile and to Indigenous and Black experiences of dispossession being uprooted from their lands. She states: "In English, *destierro* always converts to exile. But it is not quite the same thing. Exile is *exilio*, a state of asylum. But *destierro* is something else entirely: it's banishment, with all its accompanying and impotent anguish. Literally, it means to be uprooted, to be violently torn from the earth" (309). Obejas offers this clarification of the untranslatability of *destierro* within the context of a novel whose narrator's survival as an infant is indebted to her parents' prayers in Hebrew and to Afro-Cuban saints. In this regard, *Days of Awe* bridges some of the conceptual schisms between Jewish exile and Indigenous relations to the land with which the Boyarins take issue and that I addressed in chapter 1. Similarly, Yomaira Figueroa's brilliant discussion of *destierro* – mentioned in chapter 1 – draws from Obejas's discussion of the term to focus on the concept as "a precarious condition for Black and Indigenous peoples" in order to "turn away from its bourgeois underpinnings and instead

Accidents of Racism   139

understand it as a vector of dispossession constitutive of colonial modernity" (223). For Figueroa, *destierro* is a conceptual lens through which to think through decolonial praxis. In the novel, Obejas presents *destierro* as a word that is untranslatable. Reading Obejas's discussion of (largely autobiographical) Sephardic experiences through Figueroa's focus on *destierro*, we see that Obejas herself posits this move from the "bourgeois, colonial" underpinnings of *destierro* as exile to *destierro* as being "violently torn from the earth." This is in line with a move from bourgeois, colonial understandings of Jewishness to a more capacious understanding of Jewish experiences in the Americas in dialogue with and mutually co-constitutive of Black and Indigenous experiences in the Americas. The novel explores Sephardic experiences of exile and diaspora – from the days of the expulsion to her family's own exile from Castroist Cuba – to be inextricable from broader conversations on race, ethnicity, and belonging. All the while, Obejas never loses sight of the complicated, shifting dynamics of privilege and vulnerability that are at play in these interethnic negotiations. Nonetheless, much of the existing criticism of *Days of Awe* has eschewed the centrality of race in Obejas's exploration of Cuban American and Sephardic experiences both in Cuba and in the US. To this point, the novel also incorporates discussions of *Latinidad* in the US, a topic I explore further in chapter 5.

While existing critical discussions of the novel have focused on the intersections of Latinidad and Jewishness, one of the greatest contributions that Obejas makes to cultural understandings of identities in the Americas is through *Days of Awe*'s focus on Blackness and Indigeneity as they relate to national identities in Cuba. In addition to coupling santería with Castro's government and her own birth in the novel's first pages, Alejandra also tells of her great-grandfather Ytzak, who "liked to say that he was more Cuban than the Indian chief Hatuey" (120). The novel presents this characterization of Alejandra's great-grandfather within the context of describing her grandparents as "more assimilationists than Clandestine Jews" (119–20) and goes on immediately to talk about Ytzak's passing as Catholic in some places in Cuba yet being an open Jew when in Havana. Thus, for Alejandra's great-grandfather, to be Cuban means to be "more" Cuban than Hatuey, which for Ytzak means hiding his Jewishness at times. Yet, as Alejandra also notes of her great-grandfather's refrain, each time he pronounced this self-description, he was "apparently forgetting that Hatuey was born in Hispaniola, modern-day Haiti" (120). Ytzak thus inadvertently posits being taíno as the *sine qua non* of Cuban identity to the extent that one's actual Cuban nationality was ultimately irrelevant. Alejandra's ancestor's claim also reminds readers that Cuba did not exist as such

140   Absorption Narratives

during the time of the Conquest while at the same time he tries to be "more Cuban" than an Indigenous man. Thus, Obejas creates competition surrounding national identity between Indigenous and Jewish figures. Yet Ytzak also absorbs both Indigenous identity and the legacy of resistance against colonization that Hatuey exemplifies as a way of understanding himself to be Cuban.

By including this reference to Hatuey, Obejas creates a narrative in which her characters grapple with Cuban national identity as Jews in relation to Indigeneity. *Days of Awe* is not the only work of literature to do so. Yiddish author Oskar Pinis wrote the 1931 *Hatuey*, an epic poem about the legendary figure. As Rachel Rubinstein has noted, "Invoking Hatuey could thus gesture towards revolutionary, nationalist, and Afro-Cuban modernist mythologies, thus illustrating both his ubiquity and his malleability as a signifier" (n.p.). More recently, an opera adaptation, *Hatuey: Memory of Fire*, has been performed in a number of cities, including Montclair, New Jersey, where a review in the *New York Times* of the 2018 performance included the concession, "Yes, it felt odd to see a predominantly Black and Latino cast perform in Yiddish" (da Fonseca-Wilheim, n.p.). The review underscores another form of racial ventriloquism insofar as it notes the surprise of seeing Black and Latinx actors perform in Yiddish.

As the narrator makes clear, Ytzak's strategy to be "more Cuban than Hatuey" means at times hiding his Jewish identity in order to pass as white or, more specifically, as not Black in Cuba, although sometimes he reveals his Jewish identity. Ytzak lived his entire life hiding his Jewish identity in Oriente and practising joyously when in Havana. As Obejas underscores, his survival was always precarious and predicated on colourism (akin to the "accidents of racism" that Behar notes in her film):

> [Ytzak] and the handful of other crypto-Jews he knew in Santiago all went about their lives pretending, fearful. Unlike their neighbors, they occupied a kind of netherworld: White enough, even the darker Sephardim, to separate themselves from the misery of the Africans, but never sure how long their passing would last, or what their fates would be if their lies were uncovered. Never officially allowed in the Spanish colonies, their misery came from both within and without: Essentially illegal, formally nonexistent, survival required compromising the most basic aspect of their souls – to survive as Jews they had to pretend to be otherwise. (121)

Throughout the novel, Alejandra's discussion of her family's hidden past in Cuba is contextualized with the colourist racial paradigms of Cuba that allowed her ancestors to live and thrive in the nation because

Accidents of Racism   141

they were "white enough to separate themselves from the misery of the Africans." The description that they "occupied a kind of netherworld" speaks to a similar function of racial ambiguity that arises in Black–white racial paradigms, similar to my earlier discussion in this chapter of *The Human Stain*. Yet, this very character of Ytzak positions himself as "more Cuban than Hatuey," such that the racial paradigms against which he defines himself and his family as crypto-Jews in Cuba account for both Blackness and Indigeneity as categories that serve as a relief for Jewish Sephardic difference. Elsewhere in the novel, Moisés's granddaughter, Deborah, asks Alejandra whether she thinks that the Menachs are "judeo-Indigenous or crypto-Jews" (335). Alejandra's response is to insist that one could be both. The (false) dichotomy between judeo-Indigenous and crypto-Jewish is paradoxical because it dichotomizes two things that are already inherently hybrid and often (though not always) co-constitutive of one another. For Kandiyoti, in this conversation between Moisés and Deborah, "Jewish and Marxist messianism blends with an idealized *mestizaje* that willfully denies extinction (of Indians and Conversos/Jews) by asserting it remains 'in the blood' and the continuity rather than the disappearance of indigeneity" (*The Converso's Return* 112). The debate between "crypto-Jews or judeo-Indigenous" also recalls Ben Vinson's analysis in which being crypto-Jewish in Iberia was a similar affront to imperial notions of blood purity as caste mixture in the New World.

Alejandra's negotiation of her identity reaches its culmination, in part, through the arc of her tumultuous relationship with her lesbian lover, artist Leni. Her encounters with Leni encapsulate the racial, sexual, and spiritual aspects of her own identity with which Alejandra grapples. In the earliest descriptions of this new character, the narrator describes: "What I can't tell her, even to this day – what I can barely admit to myself – is how much I secretly envy the inevitability of her Jewishness" (182).[6] This "inevitability" that Alejandra envies and admires contrasts starkly with her own Jewish identity that, to this point, remains a secret even to her. Obejas's mention of envying the inevitability of Jewishness recalls Alistar Morrison's reading of *Solomon Gursky Was Here* in its emphasis on the "inevitability of jealousy" that the Gurskys are shown to feel for the Indigenous people who legitimately belong to the land. We also recall Grabner's reading that Goldman's narrator lives vicariously through Flor de Mayo. Moreover, Obejas's model of Jewishness as either inevitable or a hidden, "closetable" identity recalls the complexities of passing in *The Human Stain*. For Alejandra, the question of what she is fleeing from or towards by existing as a gentile or as a Jew is bound up in fraught paradigms of

142   Absorption Narratives

power and hegemony that compel individuals towards assimilation. Moreover, the protagonist's (growing) self-understanding as a Cuban Jew is informed by racial paradigms of mixture in Cuba that are inclusive of – yet do not often acknowledge – Blackness. Alejandra's use here of "inevitability" anticipates a later moment when she refers to the "inevitability" of their intimacy once she and Leni are no longer in a sexual relationship, again drawing a parallel between Jewishness and sexuality.

While Alejandra is Cuban and crypto-Jewish in contrast to Leni's Ashkenazi Jewishness, Alejandra recognizes that she appears whiter than Leni and therefore, unlike Leni, benefits from functions of white privilege. Nonetheless, she couches their relationship with one another as a function of a shared recognition of the privileges from which they each benefit despite their different marginalized statuses. Alejandra reflects, "What Leni and I really shared was a certain shame about belonging to oppressed minorities that had their own paradoxical privileges in the world" (179). She reflects that, despite seeming unmistakably Latina in her command of Spanish or her dancing skills, "I could also – with my white Cuban skin, my perfect English – enter any retail store with the assurance that I could wander the aisles at liberty, sure to be perceived as the descendant of an Italian dancer or, perhaps, a French winemaker, if I had any ethnicity at all" (179). Yet, Leni's Jewishness is more "inevitable," and therefore less chameleonic. The narrator contrasts her ability to assimilate with Leni's, noting, "Ironically, Leni … who insists there's no Jewish 'race' … had a much harder time finding that no-ethnic-fly-zone" (179). Obejas depicts this difference in how the two characters present as a central element to the negotiations between their identities that is fundamental to Alejandra's self-understanding as she learns of her Sephardic roots. Here and throughout the novel, racial and ethnic differences are revealed to organize Jewish (both Sephardic and Ashkenazi) experiences in and beyond Cuba.

Rather than discuss race and ethnicity, most existing criticism of the novel has focused on translation and bisexual desire in the novel. Yet, the latter two are inexorable from race and ethnicity. Sexual, racial, and spiritual identities become subject to various forms of translation throughout the novel. Alejandra works as an interpreter for legal and medical cases, an occupation that draws on her lived experience as a bilingual Cuban-born American. As she emphasizes throughout, her father has a fraught relationship with her profession because he is a literary translator. Despite the fact that they both work as translators, their occupations serve more to divide them than to unite them.

Accidents of Racism   143

For Enrique, translation is something sacred, akin to his clandestine Jewish rituals. Moreover, the art of translation connects him to Spain, the land from which his Sephardic family was ousted generations earlier. His fraught connection to the Iberian Peninsula is also presented throughout the novel as part and parcel of his Jewish (and Sephardic) identity. As Alejandra observes, "For my father, who saw his parents scurry to hide the menorah and candles whenever a stranger showed up, being a Jew was something tangible: It was the void between Cuba and Spain, between him and everybody else" (119). Through her characterization of crypto-Judaism as the "void between Cuba and Spain," Obejas suggests the condition of secret Jewishness as the organizing paradigm of coloniality. As a Cuban living in the US, the Spanish language both divides and connects Enrique to his country of birth as well as to the land from which his ancestors emigrated.

Throughout the novel, Enrique focuses on the place of Sephardism vis-à-vis Spanish (and, by extension, Hispanic) identities in ways that dovetail with mestizaje. Specifically, he often avoids acknowledging his own Jewishness by talking about Jewish blood as part of Spanish ancestry. Alejandra notes that her father had a tendency to evade the question of whether he was a Jew by responding, "All people of Spanish descent have some Jewish blood in them, of course" (32). Enrique thus describes the relationship of Jewishness to Spanish descent in a manner akin to Vasconcelos's notion of "hidden striae" that I discussed in chapter 1. Yet, whereas Vasconcelos seeks to absorb Jewishness into Spanish descent as part of his model of "cosmic" mixture, Enrique's flattening of his own difference is an effort to avow sameness within Cuba and in the Cuban diaspora. As our narrator goes on to add, in these exchanges in which her father would claim that all people of Spanish descent "of course" have Jewish blood, if the person asking followed up by asking whether he practised Judaism, he would retort, "Who doesn't? Don't all the great religions owe something to Judaism?" (37). In this comment, Enrique again emphasizes the ways in which Judaism forms part of other categories. His emphasis here on Judaism rather than "Jewish blood" underscores not the transmission of ethnic Jewishness but the importance of Judaism for other religious beliefs, signalling the importance of syncretism in Judaism's presence in the Americas. Yet later, once Alejandra finally asks her father whether they are Jewish, "So we're Jewish, at least part Jewish?" he responds, "We're Spaniards, we're Catholic, we're like everybody else in Cuba" (115). The sequencing of the parts of his response – his redirection from Jewish to Spaniards, followed by "Catholic" and then "like everybody else in Cuba" first tacitly equates "Jewish" with "Spaniard," in keeping

144 Absorption Narratives

with his earlier utterance. His addition of "like everybody else in Cuba" suggests either a strong assimilationist impulse on his part, or his own desire to inscribe Jewish identity – despite his efforts to dissemble and veil his own practices – within social understandings of what it means to be Cuban.

Despite her fraught relationship with her father, Alejandra has inherited faithfully his perspective on the place of Jewishness within Cuban identity. She explains to readers towards the novel's beginning, "My father's a Jew, a real Jew, but it's complicated. It's a long story, technically a little more than five hundred years old. It is, in many ways, a select history, even though its effects are global" (32). The narrator's move between "a select history" and "global" effects frames her search for her family's Sephardic roots as a quest for something that is hidden in plain sight and impossible to disentangle from other sociocultural forces that have threatened to absorb Sephardic identity. Throughout Obejas's novel, the particularities of Jewish identity are absorbed into non-Jewish culture in ways that almost always call attention to the lasting presence of Jewishness.

Obejas's story of Sephardic Cubans emphasizes exile and wandering not only as key elements of Jewish experiences, but as a veritably essential part of Jewish identity. Alejandra remarks, "exile and diaspora are like genetic markers for Jews, as normal as hair or teeth" (34–5). Such affirmations are vertiginously essentializing, and certainly call for further reckoning and scrutinization when placed, as they are in the case of Obejas's novel, in dialogue with Indigenous and Black identities and experiences, as Figueroa's discussion of destierro in the novel does. In the case of Castro's Cuba, exile is by no means a phenomenon circumscribed to the political subjectivities of Jewish communities (although Jews as a group certainly had a fraught relationship with Castro's government). Most Cuban Americans depicted in the novel abhor Castro and are waiting anxiously for his regime to end. As the Soviet Union is about to fall, for instance, Alejandra recounts a humorous encounter with her local Cuban bodega owner, Santiago, who relishes in what he sees as Fidel's inevitable demise following the collapse of the Soviet Union. He proclaims, "You know how much money he takes from those Russians? A million dollars a day! He can't survive! He'll come down" (170). In this bodega filled with a Cuban owner and other Cuban clients, a diasporic Cuban community coalesces to speculate on Cuba's future without the Soviets' support of Fidel. Tellingly, this moment is one of the few in the text at which Alejandra depicts a unified solidarity among Cuban Americans.

Accidents of Racism   145

Yet this same moment of the Soviet collapse affects Enrique not only as an exiled Cuban but also because of his closeted Jewish identity (which, at this point in the novel, he still has not discussed with Alejandra). In fact, it is this moment that prompts Alejandra's difficult confrontation with her father. First, as she is leaving the Cuban-run bodega, Santiago offers Alejandra a sack of groceries to offer to her father "as a gift. In honor of a free Germany" (171), which she initially protests, anticipating the fraught geopolitical significance for her father of what a "free Germany" means. Enrique becomes distraught as he watches the news coverage, insisting that the newscasters should talk about what is happening in Cuba also as the television shows images of neo-Nazis sporting bald heads and swastikas. When her father becomes outraged over these "German punks," Alejandra challenges him, "A little racial memory, Papi? A little trouble with the family secret?" (173). Although she protests the shopowner's offer of free groceries to her father "in honor of a free Germany," she is visibly upset that her father refuses to acknowledge that he is troubled by the images because of his own Jewish identification. This exchange is also meaningful for the binary that it presents between Enrique's insistence that the television reporters talk about Cuba and his distress over the image of the neo-Nazis.

Only at the end of the novel do readers glean the particularities of Enrique's relationship to the Holocaust *as* a Cuban Jew. That is, the narrator learns and recounts her father's own heartbreakingly difficult experience with the *St. Louis* affair. Alejandra, in a conversation with Moisés, discovers that, while the ship was docked in Havana, Enrique fell in love with a woman onboard whom he saw from land. When the *St. Louis* left Havana – a moment Moisés describes as "When the ship finally pulled up finally pulled up its anchor, a great wail came from the ocean liner as well as the shore" (350) – Enrique became despondent and felt betrayed by the world and by his grandfather for having connected him with his Jewish identity. Alejandra asks, "How could [his grandfather] have thought that being a Jew could possibly be a good thing? If he loved [Enrique] so much, how could he have exposed him to so much hatred and pain?" (351). The tragedy and anti-Semitism of the *St. Louis* affair, which Obejas goes on to describe as a moment that solidified anti-Jewish attitudes in Cuba and emboldened the Nazi regime back in Germany, compel Enrique to practise his Judaism in private.

This scene in the novel evokes Zygmunt Bauman's model of the place of Holocaust memory in *The Holocaust and Modernity* in which the reality and the possibility of the Holocaust are interrelated yet distinct. Enrique, as a Jew, is troubled by the events in Germany in the 1990s

146   Absorption Narratives

because of the lingering effects of the Holocaust's reality in ways that, as Alejandra's comment shows, are unique to Jews. Moreover, Alejandra's accusation of her father's "racialized memory" speaks to the racialization of both Sephardic Jews and of Jews writ large. The only time she references race in the presence of her father – a Cuban Sephardic Jew living in the US – is prompted by images of Germany on the television. Again, the novel's constant reminders of the interplay between elements of Jewish experience that are particular to Jewish communities and those that are extrapolated to non-Jewish come to the fore.

Moreover, Obejas's multifaceted depictions of characters' political subjectivities also disarticulate a monolithic depiction of Jews as staunchly anti-Castro, a narrative that long pervaded (and stereotyped) Cuban Jewish immigrants in the US. Jewish support of Castro is evident most strongly in the novel through Moisés's fervent loyalty to Castro, even if he often questions the leader's decision. The narrator describes, "Certainly Fidel, who wasn't baptized until he was about five years old, might have been mistaken for a Jew in those early years, but he'd surely shrugged it off. To be a Jew meant nothing to him, except perhaps the possibility of a clamorous fight" (119). Again, the idea of an "inevitability" of Jewishness – as if one is Jewish unless baptized as a Christian (as Castro was at the age of five) – surfaces to remind readers of the pervasiveness and ambiguity of crypto-Jewishness.

It is only as an adult that Alejandra ever defines herself as a Jew. She not only discloses this identity through her narration to readers, but also loudly counters proselytizers who ask her if she's found Jesus by replying, "I'm a Jew" (272). In an almost visceral reaction to the overwhelming questioning of zealots, she seems to surprise herself through this exclamation. Obejas juxtaposes this encounter with Christian proselytizers with another moment, several years later, when her father is released from the hospital to go home to die. After sharing this exclamation, she reflects, "It was for my father, for Luis and Sima, for Leah and Ytzak – and for me. In that moment, under siege in a sterile airport, I avenged the injustices of five hundred years ago, even if for only an instant, even if only in my own small way" (273). Obejas shares Alejandra's only outward avowal of Jewishness in the context of her father's impending death, an utterance Alejandra understands as an homage to her father, his parents, and his grandparents. The author thus suggests a certain "inevitability" in her own narrator's Jewishness, a quality that she envied in Leni. That is, her outward exclamation to strangers that she is Jewish is, as the narrator underscores, an immediate reaction prompted by feeling "under siege." Her identification as Jewish, which she has never previously acknowledged out loud, surfaces here in an instant in which she sees herself as different from the people asking her if she has found Jesus. That she should link this experience to the moment when she learns of her father's impending death underscores the degree to which she has internalized her father's secret Jewishness.

For Alejandra and her father, translation – in both its academic and non-academic variants – serves as an analogue for the intergenerational transmission of Jewish identity and memory. Ethnicity and translation are intimately linked throughout the novel. Enrique feels a connection to his native language after moving to the US because of his work as literary translator. As part of the one-and-a-half generation, Alejandra (also called Ale) is in contact with other Latinx characters in her work as a legal interpreter. In addition to the linguistic connections that her work as an interpreter afford her with her place of birth and her family's heritage, she also points specifically to the racial significance of her work as an interpreter. For Freedman, "Unlike less successful translators, Enrique is dislocated from the first – at once part and not part of the Catholic Cuban culture from which he comes – and uses the dislocation of his crypto-Jewishness as the ground of his profession (in all senses of that charged word)" (248). However, if Ale's proficiency in Spanish brings her closer to the people for whom she interprets, her light-skinned appearance has the effect of making her feel more distant from them. Surprisingly, it is through Leni, the non-Latinx Jewish character, that Ale feels more connected to her own Latinidad and the "darkness" therein. She notes, "With Leni, I was closer than ever to all the dark peoples for whom I interpreted and to whom I represented a system and established order that I never felt a part of. With her, I relished in my own darkness" (179). Not only does Leni's inability to find "that ethnic no-fly zone" prompt Ale to reflect on her own Jewishness (i.e., the "inevitability" that Ale envies), but their relationship makes the narrator feel more connected with her own Latinidad.

Insofar as Ale's "relishing in her own darkness" makes her feel closer to the people for whom she interprets, translation takes on a racialized significance in Obejas's novel. Just as her mother prays to the Virgen de Caridad de Cobre while her father secretly prays in Hebrew during her tumultuous birth, the racial and ethnic implications of santería and crypto-Judaism form parts of Ale's identity of which she herself is unaware for much of the novel. These categories, which had previously been hidden or absorbed in her own self-identification, become more apparent to her as she grapples with her relationship with her father, a relationship characterized simultaneously by mutual understanding and misunderstanding. Both characters are crypto-Jewish Cuban immigrants to the US whose work consists of translating

148   Absorption Narratives

between English and Spanish. Yet, the secrets and their different perspectives on these facets of their own identities more often impede mutual understanding than facilitate it. Ale often translates her father's words and story into her own understanding to make sense of who he is and the parts of her own identity that she has inherited from him. In this intergenerational exchange of understanding and misunderstanding, Ale challenges her father by ascribing to him such psychological functions as "racialized memory," putting words to what her father has silenced in himself.

Conclusions

These three works all centre on "racialized memory" in their own ways. Lispector imagines a Black woman who is put on display for the world and never explicitly names Jewishness. In contrast, Roth and Obejas foreground the porosity between Blackness and Jewishness while also highlighting contention and difference between the two categories. These works offer a précis of how twentieth-century politics and history have defined and problematized understandings of race throughout the Americas.

Whereas, in Roth's novel, Coleman can identify either as Black or Jewish against a landscape of Black–white race relations, Obejas populates her novel with characters who identify and present in complicated ways. Alejandra's ancestor sought to be "more Cuban than Hatuey" and, in the present, she envies Leni's "inevitable" Jewishness and feels closer to the dark-skinned Latinxs for whom she interprets. Even in her discussion of race in the US, Obejas's frame of reference for race and difference – informed by Cuban, Caribbean, and Latin American models – orients her story in markedly different ways than Roth's account of Black–Jewish convergence in the US. If her survival as an infant had to do with her mother's prayers to Afro-Cuban deities and her father's secret Jewishness, her adult life remains oriented within similarly multifaceted understandings of ethnicity and spirituality.

Through their emphases on academic understandings of race and ethnicity – whether through anthropological "discoveries" (Lispector), a campus setting (Roth), or the occupation of translation/interpretation (Obejas), these authors all interrogate the limits and possibilities of Black–Jewish convergences within broader panoramas of racialization and racial categories in their respective nations and throughout the Americas. These Jewish-identified authors question how Blackness and Jewishness have traditionally been understood and reimagine convergence between the two. In so doing, they question how race itself

Accidents of Racism 149

is understood and contested. Moreover, they question who is understood as an expert on race and how knowledge of race is produced and maintained. Throughout these texts, language and translation serve to interrogate the epistemologies of race and ethnicity that have been the organizing principle of societies in the Americas since the Conquest and the beginning of the Atlantic slave trade. Language is used by these texts' main characters to maintain and, alternately, to contest forms of power and hegemony that have upheld imperial forms of knowledge and power. In so doing, they foreground the ways in which Black–Jewish interactions might contest these imperial forms.

5 Creole Dreams: Blackness and Jewishness in Urban Spaces throughout the Americas

If Lispector imagined the response among dwellers of a large, modern city to the image of an African Indigenous person "discovered" by an explorer, urban spaces in cities throughout the Americas (including Brazil) have often come to be defined by the racial demographics that inhabit them and the shifts among these demographics over time. Focusing on the convergence of Chicanx, Jewish, and Black residents of Los Angeles, Dean Franco recently noted that in these spaces "the desire for everyone to have equal access *beyond race* – remains a dream for some, even as groups working in the name of Jewishness address structural racism and racial inequity" (25). As Franco rightly notes here, and as I argue throughout this chapter and the following, the daily lives and encounters between Jews and their non-white neighbours in cities across the Western hemisphere underscore, paradoxically, both a Jewish investment in passing as white and a Jewish investment in anti-racism. If Franco focuses on the metaphor and metonymy of "the border and the line," Michael Chabon's protagonist Archy Stallings in *Telegraph Avenue* articulates his "Creole dream" that, in his mind, "means you stop drawing those lines." Taking into account how "groups working in the name of Jewishness address structural racism" as well as how groups working in the name of Jewishness perpetuate structural racism, this chapter takes account of fictional depictions – a work of documentary theatre, a fictional film, and a novel – of boundaries between Black and Jewish neighbours in the US and Brazil.

In his groundbreaking recent book *How to Be an Antiracist*, Ibram X. Kendi notes that to be anti-racist means necessarily not to speak of "ghettos" and "Black neighbourhoods," noting his own erstwhile belief that choosing to live in a poor Black neighbourhood would give him a more "authentic" Black experience. Yet, Kendi tacitly relates this idea of "authenticity" of Black neighbourhoods to Black responses to the

Creole Dreams 151

O.J. Simpson trial – specifically, comedian Chris Rock's 1996 HBO comedy special *Bring the Pain*, in which the comedian moves from mocking white reactions to the O.J. Simpson verdict to stating that Black people in the US were having their "own civil war" (between "Black people" and "n***ers."). Rock draws a distinction between what he perceives as dignified and undignified Black people, a racist distinction that Kendi associates with his own thinking about Black neighbourhoods and authenticity. As I will elaborate further at the end of this chapter, Michael Chabon was directly inspired by his own reaction to the Simpson verdict to write his novel *Telegraph Avenue*, which focuses on how white Jewish and Black characters converge in Berkeley/Oakland. More broadly, bearing in mind Kendi's reflections, a focus on how Black and white characters cohabitate in urban spaces, we see, is key to both racist and anti-racist thinking.

In cities throughout the Americas, convergences and divergences between Black and Jewish characters distill centuries of tensions and complicated points of identification. In the US and Brazil alike, Black citizens' relationship to the nation stems from their ancestors' arrivals on slave ships, whereas most of their Jewish neighbours trace their families' presence in the same spaces to their ancestors' search for refuge from pogroms and, later, the Holocaust. Yet, for Baldwin, the distinction between slavery and the Holocaust is that the nations of the Americas offered refuge to Jews whereas they actively enslaved Black folks. Belonging and citizenship for Black and Jewish people in the Americas are still affected by these disparate histories, which Rothberg terms "competitive memory." While competitive memory presents an impasse, considerations of how anti-Black racism and anti-Semitism operate similarly – that is, on the bases of subjugation and exploitation – may move towards combatting each of them discretely, according to W.E.B. Du Bois.[1] Du Bois finds parallels and overlaps between Black and Jewish experiences without eschewing the differences between the two groups. I trace how these three works of fiction engage with double consciousness in their voicing of Black and Jewish experiences in various urban spaces.

These cities' diachronic histories reflect race relations and the possibilities for coalitions between Black and Jewish communities over time. What all three of these works share is a connection to a specific neighbourhood that is characterized by past traumas related to Blackness and Jewishness. And yet, all of these authors underscore that these spaces are also necessarily characterized by encounters with folks from different racial groups and are part of a broader, inter-American relationship between specific ethnic groups and the spaces they inhabit.

152 Absorption Narratives

For the authors I discuss below, this history has led to particular relationships – alternately, of fascination, attraction, and repulsion – that characterize the convergence of Black and Jewish individuals in these specific spaces. Organized in chronological order of when the works in question were released, this chapter also moves from the most contentious imaginings of Black–Jewish relations to the most optimistic. Throughout the works I discuss here, specific neighbourhoods – Crown Heights, Bom Retiro, and Telegraph Avenue – set the stage for a vexed convergence of Black and Jewish characters.

In these works – in which Black authors speak through the voices of Jewish characters or vice versa – we observe both the phenomenon that Glaser notes of "Jewish literary blackface" and an inversion of this model. The first chapter of Glaser's *Borrowed Voices* considers the controversy sparked by Hannah Arendt's essay "Reflections on Little Rock." In the 1959 article, Arendt weighed in on conversations on school integration in the US in an essay whose rhetorical ethos she based on the fact that she, as a Jew, took her solidarity with any oppressed group for granted and hoped that the readers did, too. Glaser (2016) notes, "It is precisely the Jew's unique purchase on suffering, Arendt suggested, that affords Jewish intellectuals such as herself the right to function as mouthpieces for the concerns of 'oppressed or underprivileged peoples,' particularly African Americans, without sanction" (loc. 443). In Glaser's reading of Arendt and in the works I consider here, Jewish preoccupation with Black suffering is part and parcel of the politics of speaking for the racial Other. I bring the phenomenon of racial ventriloquism into conversation with Du Bois's double consciousness, in which the Black subject is always doubly conscious of the self and the ways in which the self is perceived by others. While speaking through Jewish characters allows Smith to voice this double consciousness, Hamburger and Chabon verge on appropriation.

Voicing Competitive Memory: *Fires in the Mirror*

On August 19, 1991, Rabbi Menachem Mendel Schneerson's motorcade struck another car in Crown Heights, Brooklyn, and veered onto a sidewalk where children were playing, hitting and killing seven-year-old Guyanese American Gavin Cato and seriously injuring his cousin, seven-year-old Angela Cato. This prompted contentious encounters between the neighbourhood's Black and Jewish residents. The episode inspired playwright and actress Anna Deavere Smith to pen her ambitious one-woman play *Fires in the Mirror*. For Smith, the only way to tell the story of the conflict was by listening to and speaking through others' voices. Based on hours of interviews she conducted with the people she portrays, the play brings together characters who are quintessentially integral to Black social movements in the US – Angela Davis, the Reverend Al Sharpton – and leaders in Jewish US history, such as Letty Cottin Pogrebin. These well-known US characters' monologues are interspersed with those of Guyanese, Australian, and European characters. Revived to critical acclaim at New York City's Signature Theater in 2019, *Fires in the Mirror* offers an extraordinary contribution to woefully needed cultural understandings of how race in the US is unique within the Americas and the world yet is also bound up in broader transnational phenomena of race and belonging.

Smith captures these nuances through the way she writes characters' words as a playwright and through the way she acts them out. *Fires in the Mirror* is part of a more expansive corpus of plays that Smith has written (and in many of which she herself has performed) that she terms "verbatim theater," the inverse of Glaser's critical model in which Jewish authors speak through Black characters. The playwright insists on the importance of speaking interviewees' words word-for-word and using the same intonation that they used in their original utterances. A review of the 2019 version of the play notes that "though the piece unfolded as a series of monologues, there was an implicit dialogue between Smith and her subjects" ("Review: Reflections That Sear" n.p.). Yet, as Janelle Reinelt noted after comparing the video of *Fires in the Mirror* and the published text, Smith "does not quite perform 'verbatim' theatre. She does vary the occasional word, or engage in some repetition. … I point this out not to detract from Smith's enormous accomplishment, but to underscore the critical rhetoric with which she has been constructed to be a bearer of truth, accuracy, and validity" (611). While I discuss the work's place within a broader panorama of documentary, verbatim, and testimonial theatre at greater length when I discuss the performances of it, what is important about Reinelt's discussion here of veracity is its relationship to Smith's repetition word-for-word of what her interviewees say.

Smith ventriloquizes Jewish voices and Black voices. In his book *Cities of the Dead: Circum-Atlantic Performance*, Joseph Roach considers mimicry and performance in the context of Paul Gilroy's notion of the Black Atlantic in the context of what he calls "surrogation," which I also would liken to racial ventriloquism. Roach draws from Erik Lott's work on minstrel shows and cites Homi Bhabha: "'Mimicry,' writes Homi K. Bhabha, 'is at once resemblance and menace' (86). This is so because, even as parody, performances propose possible candidates for succession. They raise the possibility of the replacement of the authors

154 Absorption Narratives

of the representations by those whom they imagined into existence as their definitive opposites" (6). Roach focuses on the intercultural composition that characterizes cultural productions from the Atlantic world through his discussion of performance. For Roach, this intercultural hybridity is part and parcel of understanding what theatre has to tell us about the relationship between history and memory. For Smith, Black–Jewish relationships are necessarily part of such hybridity. Her verbatim style of theatre, like Roach's discussion of mimicry, allows the playwright and performer to facilitate a conversation between two diametrically opposed groups.

The ventriloqual aspects of *Fires in the Mirror* share similarities with testimonial theatre and testimonial writing more broadly. As I also discuss in my reading of *Telegraph Avenue*, the ventriloquism in which Smith engages does constitute speaking for the other, but it is fundamentally predicated on *listening* to the other. Richard Schechner's review of the play underscores Smith's "deep listening" throughout the play, an act that is predicated on empathy. I liken Schechner's emphasis on deep listening in Smith's play to recently deceased philosopher María Lugones's model of "faithful witnessing," which Lugones maintains is key to coalition-building among people who are differently and multiply repressed. Likewise, Smith speaks through her characters in a way that listens to them so as to create solidarity against hegemonic forms of oppression while attending to the salient differences between herself and the characters she voices as well as those among her characters.

In her own words, Smith has long been aware of the ways in which people of different races do or do not commingle. Specifically, since her childhood she has observed how Jewish individuals interact with non-Jews and racial others. Her 2018 *New York Times* piece "The First Time a White Person Wrote 'Love' to Me" describes her junior high and high school experiences. She begins by noting that, rather than attend the new junior high school in her neighbourhood of Baltimore, she was sent to a predominantly Jewish junior high school because, in her words, her mother, like many other educated Black citizens of Baltimore in the 1960s, believed that it was best to send their children to predominantly Jewish schools because they believed that Jews valued education. Smith reflects, "I assessed the following as best an 11-year-old could: Integrated schools taught, in surgical detail, where you did not belong. White Christians and Jews stayed apart. We Negro kids divided along class lines: where we went to church, by neighborhood and by our mating habits" (n.p.). As Smith recalls from her own childhood, integration served more to foster a sense of where one did not belong

Creole Dreams   155

than where one did. As Smith goes on to note, she and Ruthie, a Jewish girl whom she befriended in this school, remained close throughout their adolescence. She describes Ruthie as the Jewish daughter of a violinist in the Baltimore Symphony and that, from her perspective as an adolescent, "Until then, the Symphony's musicians were, to me, white and black dots I'd struggled to magnify through binoculars. Yet, when my new classmate and I glanced at each other for the first time, I felt as though I'd known her for a lifetime" (n.p.). This vivid recollection of another person going from being "just a black or white dot" to becoming a person with whom she feels a deep and lasting connection is, perhaps, what allows Smith to speak through Jewish voices with understanding and empathy.

Yet, while Smith's own affinity as a Black woman for Jewish individuals facilitates her creative process, Smith does not impose this mindset onto her characters. Rather, she allows each of them to speak from their own truth through her voice, humanizing each of them as individuals while maintaining the divides that characterized Black–Jewish relationships at this time. As Susan Dominus notes of *Fires in the Mirror* and *Twilight*, "[Smith's] empathetic portraits, collectively, aspired to convince viewers of the legitimacy of seemingly contradictory views" (n.p.). Smith herself has stated that conducting the interviews for the play in the Lubavitch homes reminded her of going to her Jewish friends' unassimilated grandparents' homes when she was a high school student and that, because of this memory, she felt "completely at home in a place that should be so strange" ("In Conversation with Anna Deavere Smith"). Despite this comfort, the play does not pretend to offer reconciliation between the Black and Jewish neighbours in Crown Heights. As Brantley's review of the 2019 version of *Fires in the Mirror* notes, "the sobering takeaway of this production is that the cultural walls that separate the black and Hasidic communities here are so insurmountable as to preclude such identification" ("Review: Reflections That Sear" n.p).

At its core, *Fires in the Mirror* is a story about how people converge and connect. Or, as the testimony of one Jewish woman in the play, Rosalyn Malamud, tells it, "We don't mingle socially because of the difference of food and religion and what have you here. But the people in this community want exactly what I want out of life" (536–7). Richard Schechner notes in his review of Smith's performance, "Roz Malamud speaks with the kind of voice that sounds 'Jewish'" (63). As Malamud underscores throughout her monologue, her understanding of the riots is that the majority of the rioters were not her neighbours but rather Black youths from other parts of New York City whom the Reverend

156   Absorption Narratives

Al Sharpton had recruited (such that she Others the Black New Yorkers involved in the riots on the basis of class in addition to race). Because, in her view, these rioters were from outside Crown Heights, she adds, "My black neighbors? I mean I spoke to them. They were hiding in their houses just like I was. We were scared. I was scared!" (539). For Malamud, being a neighbour means not partaking in the riots on either side, suggesting a certain apolitical ideal as a way of existing harmoniously. Of course, this ideal is neither ideal for racial justice nor, in all likelihood, historically accurate. Nonetheless, her monologue is of interest because it speaks to a recognition of difference to explain why Black and Jewish neighbours do not mingle socially and it also speaks to an absorption of difference through her assertion that her Black neighbours were also hiding in their homes. While she does say, "I spoke to them," her move from "We were scared" to "I was scared!" coupled with her comparison of "just like I was," takes her own feeling to substantiate her claim that all of her neighbours were scared, absorbing any possibility of difference between herself and her Black neighbours. Malamud's assertion, in a sense, dovetails with Cyprian's claim of mutual ignorance of one another between Jews and Indigenous people in *The Master Butchers Singing Club*. Malamud stops short, however, of articulating a fully chiastic relationship of "Our Black neighbors were scared of Jews as we Jews were scared of our Black neighbors."

Smith's use of ventriloquism to allow each character to voice their own truth exemplifies Bakhtinian diglossia. For Bakhtin, diglossia means that "each character's speech possesses its own belief system" (315). As Dorothy J. Hale has argued, we are well served as critics to think of Bakhtinian double speech in terms of Du Bois's model of double consciousness, insofar as both are "defined by a negative capability: [the subject's] self-consciousness about the social identities contained in language allow him to be more than the social languages that define him – but that greater identity formulated through the activity of distanciation, possesses no positive value of its own" (448). *Fires in the Mirror* juxtaposes different beliefs and different ways of talking so as to humanize each character as an individual while also illuminating the impasses among them, resisting the type of flattening of difference that a character such as Malamud, quoted above, might espouse while still allowing contradictory perspectives. Because of the differing beliefs, mutual identification – much less reconciliation – remains asymptotic throughout the play. Through the empathy she establishes with her interviewees, through the written play, and through the performance, Smith sows moments of hope for some sort of identification, but the play creates a stronger sense of the tensions at play rather than resolve

Creole Dreams 157

them. These differences come down to "tribalism," in Smith's terms, or what Rothberg terms "competitive memory" that stems from Black and Jewish relationships to their collective identity. Similar to the point raised by Khalid Muhammad with which Rothberg begins *Multidirectional Memory*, some of the Black activists included in Smith's play also hasten to point out that many more Black people died during slavery than Jews during the Holocaust. Smith has suggested that what made *Fires in the Mirror* so successful was that no two interviewees had the same take on the event; everyone contradicted each other. The playwright says, "Nobody told the same story. Nobody. The Black people said that it was a riot, or a rebellion. The Jews said it was a pogrom. Nobody had the same story. And so, I was able to write a story where I was going back and forth, back and forth, and everybody was expressing a different reality" ("In Conversation with Anna Deavere Smith").

When Smith speaks through the voices of Jewish characters, she inverts the phenomenon of Jewish ventriloquism of Black voices that Glaser discusses. For Smith, the act of both listening to and speaking for the other is related, in her own words, to being "absorbed" by America. In a 2004 interview, Smith stated that she came up with the idea to speak through others' voices on the basis of the interviews she conducted; it had occurred to her that this type of theatre would be a more palatable way for people to discuss race at a time when conversations about race were often eschewed. She went on to state that she believed that this type of documentary theatre could fill in gaps in the ways that the public thinks about race relations. The playwright underscores that her goal is to convey not necessarily what people say (although that will be important for my analysis) but *how* they say it as a way of understanding something about their identities. In her 2005 Ted Talk, Smith stated, "[I] interview people, thinking that if I walked in their words ... that I could sort of absorb America. I was also inspired by Walt Whitman, who wanted to absorb America and have it absorb him" (0:09–0:29). The playwright hopes to walk in the words of people so as to walk *through* such contested spaces as Crown Heights. Smith's testimonial theatre, in her own words, seeks to "absorb" America through inhabiting other people's words, but it is not her intention (nor her effect, in my interpretation of the play) to absorb others' identities. For Smith, as she signals by comparing herself to Whitman, to interview and speak through others is a way of coming to belong – having America absorb her. Crucially, this "America" that absorbs her includes voices of those not born in the US. As Smith recently noted in an interview, "all of the people that I met [for the play] were bothered ... you know a lot of the people were Caribbean American not just African American" ("Spotlight Series"

158   Absorption Narratives

2:57–3:11). In light of the centrality of Guyanese experiences in this play (and the conflict that inspired it), we might push Smith's own avowal further to say that the playwright is seeking to absorb *the Americas* and to have *them* absorb her in *Fires in the Mirror*.

One of the more comedic elements of the play is an anonymous Lubavitcher woman's monologue, in which she tells the story of one afternoon during the Sabbath on which her baby accidentally turned on the radio to a loud station and, since nobody in the observant household could turn off the radio, she asked a young Black boy in the street to come in and coaxed him to turn off the radio. She notes, "and we laughed that he probably thought: And people say Jewish people are really smart and they don't know how to turn off their radios" (473). The humorous account – based on what the woman assumes to be the young Black boy's misunderstanding of the situation – raises the question of why she did not attempt to explain the situation to the young child. She finds humour in the situation that humanizes the unknown child, but she does not attempt to foster a further sense of mutual understanding. The anonymous woman's statement dovetails with Malamud's monologue in that both attempt to cohabitate harmoniously but also make assumptions about their Black neighbours' subjectivities. These perspectives on others – a sort of Jewish ventriloquism in their own right – contrast with what Smith herself accomplishes as a playwright and actor.

The lingering traumas of the Holocaust and US slavery haunt many of the monologues, sometimes explicitly. Reverend Conrad Muhammad, then Minister to Louis Farrakhan, explicitly disavows comparisons between the Holocaust and slavery on the basis of numbers, both the number of years that slavery lasted in the US and the number of lives taken by slavery. Muhammad states:

in the middle passage –
Our women, raped
before our own eyes
so that today
some look like you,
some look like me,
some look like brother...
(*Indicating his companion*)
This is a crime of tremendous proportion.
In fact,
no crime in the history of humanity
has before or since

equaled that crime.
The Holocaust did not equal it
Oh, absolutely not.
First of all,
that was a horrible crime
and that is something that is a disgrace in the eyes of civilized people.
That, uh, crime also stinks in the nostrils of God.
But it in no way compares with the slavery of our people
because we lost over a hundred and some say two hundred and fifty,
million
in the middle passage coming from Africa
to America.
We were so thoroughly robbed.
We didn't just lose six million.
We didn't just
endure this
for, for
five or six years
or from '38 to '45 or '39 to –
We endured this for over three hundred years –
the total subjugation of the Black man. (498)

The minister's words do not underscore the same distinction that Baldwin draws between the fact that the Holocaust occurred in Europe, whereas the US itself enacted slavery. Rather, they signal that slavery was a paradigm that lasted "over three hundred years" and constituted the "total subjugation of the Black man." Muhammad's discourse is exemplary of Rothberg's model of competitive memory through his comparison of the scale of each phenomenon.

For their part, some of the Jewish neighbours thought that the incident had been a pogrom. Reuven Ostrov, assistant chaplain at Kings County Hospital (where Yankel Rosenbaum, the Jewish Australian man killed in the riots, died), asserts in the play, "we had Sonny Carson come down / and we had, um, / Reverend Al Sharpton come down / start making pogroms" (541). Ostrov's monologue tells the story of his foiled attempt to ensure that an autopsy (written and voiced by Smith as "aurtopsy") was not conducted on Rosenbaum because it goes against Orthodox beliefs. For Ostrov, the neighbourhood "had Carson and Sharpton come down," which he describes as "making pogroms." The memory of Jewish persecution in Eastern Europe is thus brought to bear on Black–Jewish tensions in Brooklyn in the 1990s.

160 Absorption Narratives

Some accounts from both the Black and Jewish characters in the play speak to Black–white conflicts while others speak to specifically Black–Jewish tensions. Much of the language used to describe Jewish characters underscores that they are not just perceived as "non-Black" or "white" but as Jewish. Holocaust tropes were invoked by some at Gavin Cato's funeral. Michael Miller, then Executive Director of the Jewish Relations Council, notes in his monologue, "there were cries of 'Kill the Jews' or 'Kill the Jew,' there were cries of, 'Heil Hitler.' There were cries of 'Hitler didn't finish the job'" (516). Miller pivots to point out that Hitler would not have looked kindly on Black people any more than on Jews. Miller affirms, "'To hear in *Crown Heights* – and Hitler was no lover of Blacks – 'Heil Hitler'?" (517). Miller emphasizes *Crown Heights* (through his inflection and Smith's italicization) in a way that presents Crown Heights as a Black space through the aside "and Hitler was no lover of Blacks." Through Miller's speech and through Smith's transcription, Crown Heights metonymically morphs into "Blacks" and Miller underscores that Hitler also propagated anti-Black racism. At the same time, through this aside, Miller also suggests an assumption of the Crown Heights neighbourhood as a place of refuge for Jews in which Jews coexist harmoniously with Black neighbours, an expectation that is betrayed by the cries of "Heil Hitler." While the Black characters in the play mention the Holocaust, the Jewish characters do not speak of slavery in the Americas. Moreover, one character, community organizer Richard Green, insists that the Black children did not know what they were saying when they said "Heil Hitler." Green states:

> And they're not angry at the Lubavitcher community
> they're just as angry at you and me,
> if it comes to that.
> They have no
> role models,
> no guidance
> so they're just out there growin' up on their own
> their peers are their role models
> their peers is who teach them how to move
> so when they see the Lubavitchers
> they don't know the difference between "Heil Hitler"
> and, uh, and uh, whatever else.
> They don't know the difference.
> When you ask 'em to say who Hitler was they wouldn't even be able
> to tell you.
> Half of them don't even know.

Three quarters of them don't even know.
...
Half of them don't even know three quarters of 'em
Just as much as they don't know who Frederick Douglass was. (535)

Green appeals to an ahistorical understanding of the twentieth-century world history (and "particularly Jewish issues") to give context to what Jewish neighbours perceived to be pogroms against them. The analogy that Green draws between Black youths' ignorance of the Holocaust and their ignorance of Frederick Douglass not only seeks to absolve them of wanton anti-Semitism but also casts doubt on their knowledge of African American history. Moreover, the analogy underscores the importance of education as well as the importance of intergenerational conversations. Green goes on to state that, while the youths he works with do not know who Frederick Douglass is, they know who Malcolm X is: "Because the system has given 'em / Malcom is convenient and / Spike is goin' to give 'em Malcolm even more / It's convenient" (535). In some of the characterizations that Black characters in the play offer of Jews, they speak of them as Jews, whereas in other cases they speak of them as white people. In many of the monologues, Jews exhibit rather superficial understandings of Black people and vice versa, an element of the play that is important because it speaks to the possibility that not malice but rather ignorance fuels even the most overtly anti-Semitic and anti-Black assertions made by characters.

While the play is rife with individual monologues that exemplify competitive memory, Smith's juxtaposition of accounts that contradict one another underscores the fallacies of competitive memory. The playwright (and actor, in her own performance of the work) avoids gesturing towards mutual understanding among her characters, instead relying on the dissonance among their accounts to create an ethical, empathetic witnessing among her audience.

On the other hand, absorption is an phenomenon apparent throughout the performances of the play. We recall that Smith absorbs the Americas and has them absorb her. In her performance of the play, in turn, for Schechner, "Smith *absorbs* the gestures, the tone of voice, the look, the intensity, the moment-by-moment details of a conversation. But in so doing, she does not destroy the others or parody them. Nor does she lose herself" (64, my emphasis). Because of the dialogue that facilitates the monologues throughout *Fires in the Mirror*, Smith absorbs some of the characters and identities that make up the people and places of Crown Heights, but she manages to do so in such a way that maintains and recognizes the differences among her subjects.

162   Absorption Narratives

Schechner's characterization of Smith's play recalls my earlier discussion of Du Bois's double consciousness in his approach to the Warsaw ghetto. This double consciousness may also be thought of in Brechtian terms. Smith's performance and Michael Benjamin Washington's revival of the role in 2019 have a *Verfremdung* effect that interpellates, compelling the audience to become witnesses to the tragedy of Cato's and Rosenbaum's deaths and to the tragedies visited upon Black and Jewish communities for centuries. As a *New York Times* review of the revival notes, "There's a generous transparency about Washington's portraiture, a compound of sympathy and contemplation that suggests a warm variation on classic Brechtian remove" ("Review: Reflections That Sear" n.p.). This Brechtian effect, as Brantley suggests, allows for interpersonal identifications between the audience and the characters. Both Smith in her origination of the role and Michael Benjamin Washington's performance in 2019 deliver empathetic performances that are at times humorous and always raise complex questions about identity, coexistence, and belonging.[2]

What changes most between Smith's original performance of the role (and the PBS recordings of it) and Washington's rendition is gender. As Smith has noted, "When you think about it, the story revolves around two men" ("Spotlight Series" 12:49–12:52). At times – most notably through the performance of the anonymous Lubavitcher woman who coaxes a Black child from the neighbourhood to turn off her radio – Washington's gender-bending takes on a comical effect. Similarly, despite Smith's stature and her intensity as an actor, her portrayal of Reverend Sharpton is warm and funny. One thinks of the many caricatured impersonations of Sharpton on programs such as *Saturday Night Live*, but Smith brings a disarming note to her portrayal. In contrast, Washington's delivery of the same lines more closely mirrors Sharpton's intensity in real life. Twenty-seven years after the riots, and with Sharpton less central in the public eye, this intensity takes on a social role of reminding audience members of Sharpton's crucial role at the time of ensuring racial justice. The slight ludic notes of Smith's performance of Sharpton would perhaps be out of place in 2019. Because of the temporal distance from the events of 1991, the 2019 production had the advantage of fewer audience members arriving with opinions a priori about the events but also the disadvantage of having to make the events relevant. Because of both the text itself and Washington's performance, the revival of the play achieves this almost immediately.

What certainly did not change between the 1992 production and the 2019 production was the relevance of the play for racial tensions that were in the foreground of news and public life at the time of the

Creole Dreams   163

performances. *Fires in the Mirror* premiered in 1992 at the time of the Los Angeles riots over the police impunity following Rodney King's beating. As Smith has noted in interviews, this timing made *Fires in the Mirror* more immediately of interest to audiences. What made it of interest, however, was not just the very literal connection of riots based on racial tensions and discrimination but also the historical truths of Black belonging in the US and Black coexistence with other groups. In 2019, movements such as Black Lives Matter and the Movement for Black Lives had grown to combat police brutality against BIPOC. The 2019 production was part of Smith's residency at New York City's Signature Theater, which was also slated to include a production of *Twilight* in spring 2020. *Twilight* focuses on Rodney King's beating and the reactions to the incident and to the police officers' impunity in ways that would have resonated uncannily with the events throughout the US in spring 2020 following the shooting of Breonna Taylor and the killing of George Floyd by police officers.

"To Be Black and to Fly": *The Year My Parents Went on Vacation*

Similar to Anna Deavere Smith's memories of her childhood friendship with a white Jewish girl in Baltimore, *The Year My Parents Went on Vacation* captures, from the perspective of Jewish-identified filmmaker Cao Hamburger, a young Jewish boy's fascination with an Afro-Brazilian neighbour. As we have seen through chapter 4's discussion of Lispector's short story, Blackness occupies a central place in understandings of race in Brazilian society, including among the nation's Jewish community. Moreover, Jewishness occupies a fraught place in ethnic and racial categories in the nation owing to the evolving ideas of racial democracy in Brazil. Film production from Brazil has registered the relationship between Jews and Afro-Brazilians in both documentary and fiction forms. Brazilian documentary filmmaker Cintia Chamecki depicts encounters with Blackness as part of the beginnings of Jewish life in Brazil – spawned by the pursuit of refuge from Eastern European pogroms – in her 2014 film *Danken got*. An interviewee included in the documentary tells of how she exclaimed, upon seeing an Afro-Brazilian person for the first time, shortly after immigrating to Brazil, "He's Black! He's dirty!" The young girl's father responded by taking her hand and the Afro-Brazilian man's hand and touching them to one another, telling his daughter, "See? He is not dirty. He is clean. He is just like you and me." Similar to Roz Malamud's statement that her neighbours were "just as scared" as she was, "just like you and me" begins the documentary film's chronicle of Jewish life in Brazil

164   Absorption Narratives

through incorporating Otherness and exoticism. Decades later, in Cao Hamburger's 2006 film *The Year My Parents Went on Vacation*, set during the 1970 World Cup, Mauro, a young Jewish boy mesmerized by an Afro-Brazilian man's soccer skills, reflects that he wants to "be black and to fly." Hamburger conveys a Jewish affinity with Afro-Brazilian identities that at times verges on appropriation while also creating a model of Black–Jewish encounters that offers new cultural understandings of race in Brazilian society.

In the film, Mauro's parents drop him off at his paternal grandfather's apartment building in Bom Retiro, at the time known as the Jewish neighbourhood of São Paulo. Once he enters the building, however, he discovers that his grandfather is not there because he has passed away. Reluctantly, an elderly neighbour, Shlomo, takes Mauro in and the young boy lives among the inhabitants of this apartment building for weeks as he awaits his parents' return. The film takes place during Brazil's dictatorship, which began in 1964 and lasted until 1985. The repression of dissidence was particularly brutal during Emílio Garrastuzi Médici's leadership, which began in 1969 and was commonly known as the "lead years." Mauro's parents leave him during this time so that he will be protected while they participate in the resistance against the dictatorship. The child of a Jewish man and non-Jewish woman, Mauro has been raised secular and is completely unaware of Jewish culture or beliefs before entering the apartment building in Bom Retiro. At the same time that he learns about Jewish life, he also learns about Greek and Italian communities and comes into contact with Afro-Brazilian character Edgar, who sparks an immediate fascination in the young boy. Mauro gains an awareness of both Jewish difference and Afro-Brazilian difference at the same time in his life – that is, during a confusing and difficult time when his parents are absent fighting against the authoritarian powers in the country. In what follows, I discuss specific moments of the film that suggest that Mauro's awareness of these discrete forms of difference, in addition to coming about at the same time, co-constitute one another.

Soccer becomes an important way of engaging with salient themes of race relations between Jews and Afro-Brazilians. In a moment that emphasizes the tight-knit community in Bom Retiro, Mauro attends a soccer match between the neighbourhood's Jewish inhabitants and the Italians. As Mauro informs viewers through his voiceover from the bleachers, the Jews had a secret weapon: Edgar, the Afro-Brazilian boyfriend of the Greek woman whose family runs a local coffee shop. Edgar already rather mesmerizes Mauro and the other young boys in the neighbourhood because they are envious that he is dating the attractive

Creole Dreams   165

young woman. After seeing the soccer match, Mauro's fascination grows and his voiceover tells viewers, "I wanted to be black and to fly." As critic Carolina Rocha points out in her discussion of this utterance, Mauro's reaction to Edgar's soccer skills "betrays his previous color-blindness" (93). For his part, critic Shawn Stein interprets this moment as indicative of the colorblind thinking that characterized Brazilians of Hamburger's generation (259). I agree with both interpretations and argue that this moment simultaneously evinces an awareness and a na-ivety on Mauro's part vis-à-vis racial difference. A great deal of Mauro's coming of age in the film has to do precisely with encountering ethnic and racial differences as he is immersed in a Jewish community for the first time in his life. In turn, he is becoming more race conscious. The tension between Mauro's racial colorblindness versus "wanting to be Black and fly," in the context of race in Brazil, evokes sociologist Gilberto Freyre's notion of *democracia racial* – racial democracy – an idea that has been increasingly contested but that nonetheless has had enor-mous staying power in notions of Brazilian national identity.

Like much of the film, the scene of the soccer game follows Mauro's gaze. He is seated in the stands and, from his perspective, viewers see different neighbours who make up the team as his narration tells us their names. His narration is interrupted by excited cheers as a mo-torcycle drives up and Edgar hops off. We see Edgar beam and give a double thumbs up through a shot framed by his girlfriend's curly hair and the person sitting next to her in the stands in front of Mauro, emphasizing the perspective of the young boy. The game begins and the camera shows Edgar in the position of goalie blocking the Italians' shots, at which time Mauro informs viewers that the Jews had a "secret weapon" (notably, he uses the third person plural verb form to talk about the Jews rather than the first, grammatically reminding viewers that he is an outsider among the Jews). Throughout the scene, the Ital-ians and Jews scuffle around the court as the shots move from closeups to wider shots, capturing the frenzy and excitement that Mauro finds in the game. The energy slows, however, when the Italians take a pen-alty kick and gather together; the camera turns to Edgar in a shot that is disproportionately long relative to the rest of the shots of the soccer game as he kneels to prepare to block the kick. Edgar crosses himself and, wanting to imitate him, Mauro also crosses himself in the stands, at which point Shlomo, in the upper right corner of the frame sitting be-hind Mauro, slaps him on the back of the head, reminding Mauro and viewers alike that Mauro is, at least for this time that he is spending in Bom Retiro, Jewish. Immediately after, the camera shows Edgar block the kick as Mauro's voiceover states, "Suddenly, I knew what I wanted

166   Absorption Narratives

to be. I wanted to be Black and to fly." The film immediately cuts to Mauro jumping on his bed and practising his goalie skills, as if acting out this desire. Mauro's particular fascination with Edgar thus leads to an appropriation – through mimicking Edgar's movements as goalie – of the Afro-Brazilian man's identity.

The montage of other scenes depicting Edgar and Mauro together emphasize the tumult of the historical moment in which the film is set and the specific care Edgar shows for Mauro. In a later scene in the film, following violence in the streets, Edgar spots Mauro among a crowd of people and takes Mauro home on his motorcycle. Akin to the aesthetics of the earlier scene of the soccer match, shots change frequently to emphasize the chaotic energy of the moment. We see Edgar spot Mauro and move towards him to take him out of harm's way, but Mauro does not see him. From Mauro's perspective, harkening back to his characterization that Edgar is Black and flies, the man swoops in as if out of nowhere to rescue him. In both of these scenes, the frequent cuts back and forth between Mauro and Edgar emphasize the frenzy of soccer and of the military repression at the same time that they suggest an identification between Mauro and Edgar. Through these visual sequences, the film again emphasizes the imbrication between Mauro's awareness of his own difference (both his difference *as* a Jew and his difference from the rest of the Jews in the Bom Retiro apartment building) and his awareness of Edgar's difference as an Afro-Brazilian.

Because of how race has historically been constructed and understood in Brazil, Mauro's fascination with Edgar does not cleave to the same Black–white binary that, in the US, has been shown to compel Jews to avow whiteness in ways that – whether intentionally or not – advance white supremacist and anti-Black attitudes. Yet, Hamburger's retrospective treatment – from the perspective of 2006 – of his young Jewish protagonist's relationship to a Black character in 1970 underscores and at the same time subtly questions the model of racial democracy, the idea that racial mixture in Brazil means that the country is not racist or is less racist than other nations. In the 1970s, the term began to be criticized for the whitewashing inherent in it. Nonetheless, as Thomas Skidmore argued in 1993, the understanding of Brazil as a fundamentally multiracial nation – an idea that has often been used to exculpate the country as a whole from racism – is, in effect, not very different from widespread understandings of the US as a biracial society, as we recall from the previous chapter's discussion of George Reid Andrews and Thomas Skidmore's analyses of race in Brazil.

Similar to racial democracy's recognition yet ultimate eschewal of racial difference and specificity, Mauro goes through a process in which

Creole Dreams 167

he moves from racial colorblindness to acknowledging racial difference, yet through his avowal of "wanting to be Black," his newfound awareness also problematically eschews difference. At the same time that he is becoming or living as a Jew, he describes Edgar as "the Jews' secret weapon" and notes that he himself wants "to be Black and fly." In light of Mauro's obsession with soccer and the film's setting during the 1970 World Cup, his fascination with Edgar evokes the notion of *futebol mulato* ("mulatto football)" that characterized Pelé's stardom in that World Cup and that took root in the model of racial democracy; the concept was enormously important for cultural understandings of Brazilian national identity at that time and undergirded popular understandings of soccer in the so-called *pais do futebol*. As Kittleson (2014) notes in his analysis of how racial democracy converged with soccer, the notion of mulatto football also became increasingly fraught due to the obvious contradictions of racial hegemony's co-optation of ethnic identities. Through the 1960s and up through the 1970 World Cup, when this film was set, this narrative of mulatto football remained largely en vogue.

From Mauro's perspective, Edgar goes from being a figurative Afro-Brazilian soccer legend to being a real person with whom Mauro connects when Edgar rescues Mauro from the tumultuous crowd, a moment that suggests a special affinity between these two characters. Shawn Stein proposes that Hamburger's film "could have been about Japanese Brazilians, Syrian Brazilians, or Lebanese Brazilians (the big groups of immigrants not considered white) but Hamburger chooses to focus on his own roots to reflect on the role of Jews within the topic of Brazilianness" (259). Stein offers an equation between immigrant groups – yet, crucially, not to racially Indigenous or African sectors of society – as a way of exploring whether Hamburger's film ultimately propagates or demystifies the notion of racial democracy. As Stein concludes, the film "draws on multiculturalism to suggest to the spectator the dream of a more inclusive and tolerant future" (262). I submit that the film's treatment of Mauro's astonishment over this Afro-Brazilian character, coupled with the special care that Edgar displays for Mauro, implies that Mauro's story could *not* have been about any ethnic group not considered to be white. Rather, through Mauro's proclamation that the Jews "had a secret weapon" and his desire to emulate Edgar's "ability to fly," the film depicts a specific identification between Jews and Afro-Brazilians. Edgar – like Shlomo – serves as a surrogate parent to Mauro in his parents' absence. Thus, Mauro's shifting understanding of his identity and his place in the world are guided by his encounters with Jews, a militant activist, and an Afro-Brazilian man. The film underscores the centrality of racial, ethnic, and political identifications

168   Absorption Narratives

for Mauro in the absence of his parents. These themes become even more significant in the film in light of the importance of nationality for Mauro and the other inhabitants of Bom Retiro during the World Cup that takes place simultaneously. Through Mauro's fascination with Edgar and the special care that Edgar shows for Mauro, the film suggests a specific identification between Jews and Afro-Brazilians. That is, Bom Retiro is depicted as both the quintessentially Jewish neighbourhood of São Paulo *and* as a space that welcomes immigrants from many different countries as well as Afro-Brazilians. Yet, at the same time, within this melting pot, Hamburger's film tells the story of a particular identification between the young boy who is beginning to learn about his own Jewish roots and the Afro-Brazilian man who begins as a sort of mythological figure for the child (who believes Edgar can fly) and, later, comes to take care of the young boy just as the Jewish inhabitants of his deceased grandfather's apartment building have also taken care of him while his parents are away.

Edgar is a relatively minor character in the film, yet his appearances in key moments – the local soccer match and following the moment of military violence – punctuate Mauro's year of learning about Jewishness. We thus see that his awareness of Afro-Brazilian characters and of Jewishness are simultaneous. In light of how drastically different Mauro and the Jewish inhabitants of his grandfather's apartment building are from Edgar, Mauro likely comes to "betray" (in Rocha's words) his colorblindness *because* of his exposure to difference. Jewish whiteness finds a figurative representation through Mauro's familial identity: Jewishness is and is not part of his identity, insofar as his mother is not Jewish and his parents have not initiated him into any Jewish religious or cultural practices, and yet he is initially assumed to be Jewish because his grandfather is Jewish (that is, until Shlomo comically realizes that Mauro is not circumcised when he discovers the young boy urinating into a houseplant in his home). Yet, despite the fact that Jewish difference is represented as a very different type of difference than Blackness, I maintain that it is certainly by no means coincidental that this young man should spark such a strong identification with an Afro-Brazilian man at the same time that he is learning about Jewish difference. The simultaneity of Mauro's discovery of these particular forms of difference underscores the need to move past such notions as racial democracy. On the one hand, Mauro perpetuates the idea of racial democracy through his desire to appropriate Edgar's identity. Yet, on the other, his awareness of Edgar is bound up in his realization of Jewish difference, an identity to which he in some ways can and in other ways cannot lay claim. The film's depiction of these categories of difference is limited, however, because although Edgar becomes less figurative for Mauro, the audience never hears Edgar speak except to utter a few words that are muffled, and the film does not vest him with much agency as a character. Hamburger reproduces a filmic counterpart of the Jewish literary blackface of which Glaser takes note in US contexts.

Unlike Smith's creation and performance – only a year later – of the contentious riots in Crown Heights, Hamburger's film returns some thirty-five years later to the filmmaker's own neighbourhood to depict a moment that, if tumultuous with regards to politics, was seemingly harmonious vis-à-vis race relations. This retrospective gaze on Bom Retiro's past serves as a way of recapturing a moment when both the political dreams of Mauro's parents and harmonious racial relations might have existed. Today, Bom Retiro is no longer known as a "Jewish neighbourhood." In a sense, Hamburger's revision of the neighbourhood in 1970 signals the diachronic changes by which the neighbourhood became less a refuge for European and lighter-skinned immigrants and more a place for Indigenous immigrants from other countries as well as internal migrants from Brazil. The film also captures a utopic moment suspended in time just before Mauro becomes an exile. In this way, Hamburger's film is strikingly similar to Halfon's novella, in which the narrator becomes aware of race and class differences in his native Guatemala just as he is on the verge of leaving the country. (The obvious distinction, of course, is that the parents of Halfon's narrator are decidedly *not* involved in politics; despite what Mauro's parents say, neither are they). Hamburger's coming-of-age film tells a story marked by political upheaval and by the beginning of racial consciousness – two factors that define and complicate the child subject's self-understanding as Brazilian. At the same time, *The Year My Parents Went on Vacation* is a markedly nostalgic film. Hamburger's film depicts a nostalgia for a moment that was politically tumultuous yet, in the way of interracial dynamics, characterized by a hopeful naivety.

Between Creole Dreams and Wakanda: *Telegraph Avenue*

Similarly, *Telegraph Avenue* is similarly nostalgic – if not revisionist – in its depiction of race relations from the perspective of the early 2000s. While Chabon's work is a novel rather than film, *Telegraph Avenue* is notably cinematic, owing in no small part to the text's many allusions to films as diverse as *Pulp Fiction* and 1970s Blaxploitation films. Published in 2012 and set in the late summer of 2004, Michael Chabon's *Telegraph Avenue* takes its name from the boulevard that both connects

170   Absorption Narratives

and divides Berkeley and Oakland. The novel centres on two couples: a Jewish couple (Nate Jaffe and Aviva Roth-Jaffe) and a Black couple (Archy Stallings and Gwen Shanks). Nate and Archy co-own Brokeland Records, a portmanteau of Berkeley and Oakland. The record store's name is a semantic marker of the neighbouring relationship between the two cities and a nod to the breakdown in the racial utopia of Berkeley/Oakland due to the gentrification that threatens to oust such businesses. For their part, Aviva and Gwen run a midwifery practice delivering babies in home births. Gwen and Aviva have a conflict with a doctor at the local hospital following complications during a birth, which prompts the doctor to scold Gwen, calling Gwen and Aviva's work "voodoo." Gwen responds in anger and the two women fear for the well-being of their licences and practice. Meanwhile, "Brokeland" is on the verge of closing. The two couples' career crises encapsulate the eclipse of the false illusions of a postracial society. Both Archy's "Brokeland Creole dream" and the doctor's racist accusation that Gwen and Aviva practise "voodoo" evoke the Afro-Caribbean models of mixture and spirituality that bear on how Black characters in Berkeley/Oakland in the early 2000s live and are perceived by others.

Telegraph Avenue furthers the focus on comic superheroes and social issues that Chabon began in *The Amazing Adventures of Kavalier and Clay*. In that novel, Chabon poignantly recreates the comic book genre in prose and centres Jewishness in the history of the genre. Chabon's narrative account of the titular characters' creation of an escape artist as a heartbreaking homage to Josef Kavalier's little brother who remained in Prague after the Nazi occupation while Josef was able to come to live with his cousins in Brooklyn centres on the question, "What is the why?" (95). That is, as the characters discuss the superhero they are ideating, it is important that the superhero have a motive and purpose. For The Escapist, the character they create, the "why" is the fight against the Holocaust. For Sarah Chihaya, *Telegraph Avenue* "demands that readers reconsider the nuances of the superhero's depiction in contemporary popular culture and its diverse generic, characterological, and political functions" (n.p.). Put another way, the "why" of *Telegraph Avenue* is race relations within an apparent racial utopia.

Chabon's novel captures its characters in a moment of abeyance between the "Brokeland Creole dream" and "Wakanda," the mythical homeland of the comic book hero Black Panther. In fact, Archy and Nate front a band named "The Wakanda Philharmonic," a nod to the racial harmony of which their friendship is part and parcel. Here, I take into account the role of a Du Boisian double consciousness in Chabon's racial ventriloquism of the novel's Black characters as a way of thinking

Creole Dreams 171

about racial utopias. Afro-futurism – which "Wakanda" almost necessarily evokes – has increasingly been discussed in terms of Du Bois's double consciousness. In 2003, critic and writer Kodwo Eshun submitted, "Alienation ... is a psychosocial inevitability that all Afrodiasporic art uses to its own advantage by creating contexts that encourage a process of disalienation. Afrofuturism's specificity lies in assembling conceptual approaches and countermemorial mediated practices in order to access triple consciousness, quadruple consciousness, previously inaccessible alienations" (298). For Juliet Hooker, "it is ... particularly appropriate to read Du Bois's writings on mixture in light of Afrofuturism, as racial utopias that dare to imagine a world not dominated or defined by whiteness" (119). In *Telegraph Avenue*, the Black character's musings on racial utopia evoke similar notions of racial mixture. While, within the context of a novel penned by a white author, the extent to which its characters' understandings of race could be "not dominated or defined by whiteness" is debatable, the model that Hooker articulates through her reading of racial mixture in Du Bois does find affinity with Archy's Creole dreams, as I discuss further.

In creating the Brokeland world, Chabon draws from his experience as a young child in the planned community of Columbia, Maryland. By his own account, as a child, he was able to see Black and white neighbours coexist harmoniously in this place and came of age thinking that such a racial utopia was the norm for the US – a view that was debunked when he left Columbia for Pittsburgh for college and later moved to L.A. The author positions himself as heir to Black culture and Black history in a way that borders on appropriation. Chabon noted:

> Frederick Douglass, Harriet Tubman, Dr. Charles Drew: in the City of the Future, in 1970, a young Jewish boy could look at the lives of these people and feel connected to them, indebted to them – in a very real way, descended from them. Because if there was one salient fact about the black history that I learned, from the lips of black teachers, as a boy growing up in Columbia, Md., it was this: Black history was my history too. Black music was my music, and black art was my art, and the struggles and the sufferings of black heroes were undertaken not just for the sake of their fellow African-Americans but for my sake, and for the good of us all. ("O.J. Simpson, Racial Utopia")

Chabon earnestly listens to Black voices and considers their viewpoints (a salient feature throughout *Telegraph Avenue*, and one of its greatest assets as a novel). Nonetheless, as we observe through this quotation, Chabon proclaims that he as a "young Jewish boy" was "in a very real

172 Absorption Narratives

way, descended from them" *because* his Black teachers told him that to understand his relationship to Black history and culture this way was "for the good of us all."

In the novel, Chabon recreates the model of a young Jewish boy learning Black history by vesting his Jewish protagonist, Nat Jaffe, with a backstory of having been raised by a Black stepmother who taught him to cook soul food and by creating a close friendship between Nat and Archy Stallings. The novel depicts a scene in which the young Jewish boy Julius Jaffe, son of Nat and Aviva, listens to a history lesson from Luther Stallings, the estranged father of Archy and an erstwhile Blaxploitation actor with ties to the Black Panthers. Luther recounts what the narrator terms *The Secret History of the Black Man in California According to Luther Stallings* for over twenty minutes, beginning with: "Everything got started for us, minute the white man wanted to get some sleep on a train" (*Telegraph Avenue* 314). His girlfriend, Valletta Moore, interrupts him to tell him that nobody is listening to what he's saying, to which Julie responds, "*I'm* listening" (317). Julie absorbs the knowledge of his Black elder in a way that recreates the model of listening and learning that Chabon describes in his own childhood. Like Smith's "deep listening" in *Fires in the Mirror*, this element of the novel also recalls Lugones's "faithful witnessing." Luther tells the story of Pullman porters who traversed the country to Oakland.[3] Similarly, as we recall from chapter 1, a review of the audiobook of *Telegraph Avenue* notes Chabon's "ear for urban vernacular" as a way of explaining his skill for crafting Black voices. Similar to Smith's play, the author creates a literary world in which listening is integral to imagining how others speak.

In Luther's "secret history," the history of Oakland is a synecdoche for the history of California and also a synecdoche of Black life in twentieth-century US: in his description, the Pullman porters were "spreading the lore and the styles across the country, to every place where black people lived, and most of all singing the song of California, to be specific the city of Oakland" (Chabon, *Telegraph Avenue* 315). Nonetheless, as readers learn from Luther's story here and over the course of the novel, this dream of Oakland is, in fact, a dream, and one that is untenable. Luther's story in which "the song of California, to be specific the city of Oakland" becomes a synecdoche of Black life in the US parallels the history of the Black Panthers in which he was involved in the 1970s. As W.J. Rorabaugh has shown, "Newton and Seale's party grew from a movement in Berkeley and Oakland into a national organization with chapters in several large cities" (79). The Berkeley/Oakland border, distilled both in the portmanteau "Brokeland" and in Chabon's use of Telegraph Avenue as the title, connotes the limit of Oakland's geography and the limit of Oakland as the epicentre of the Black American dream. Chabon tellingly defers the backstory from Berkeley in the 1960s to Oakland in the 1970s, despite his own residence in Berkeley. Likewise, in Archy's "Brokeland Creole dream," Brokeland "means you stop drawing those lines."

The salient difference between Luther's "Secret History" and Archy's model is that Luther's is predicated on separatism and Oakland as a refuge for Black folks, whereas Archy's Brokeland is about harmonious coexistence, a difference that signals changes in racial politics that divide the two generations. Archy describes that, "on the old Silk Road ... between Europe and China ... you've got this long, hard journey. ... And every so often, every few hundred miles or so, maybe, you got these oases, right, these caravansaries, where they all get together and chill, hang out, listen to good music, swap wild tales of exaggeration. ... that was kind of our dream. The Brokeland Creole dream" (Chabon, *Telegraph Avenue* 374). His use of the term "Creole dream" connotes the hospitality of the Black–Jewish pair of friends serving as a space that allows convergence and hybridity in a "Creole style." Créolité is characterized by racial mixture and syncretism. In this case, the convergence of Blackness and Jewish whiteness allows for a dreamlike space that Archy describes as Creole. Central to Creole identities is the autochthon. It is only in the space of Brokeland Records' storefront on Telegraph Avenue that this particular convergence of ethnicities and spiritualities can be fostered, and it is only at the present moment in time, as readers become increasingly aware throughout the novel. Like he describes, as he waxes poetic over the caravan stops on the Silk Road, the Brokeland Creole dream is an event as much as a place, confined to the particular moment of convergence. Yet, as we see through the obstetrician's disparaging reference to Gwen and Aviva's practice as "voodoo," this convergence is troubled by those who discriminate against Black characters as well as, I argue, by the overly utopian visions of well-intentioned white characters in the novel, similar to the functioning of *democracia racial* that I discussed in the context of Hamburger's film. In this novel, according to critic Joseph Dewey, Chabon "is interested in how the imagination can cross rather than defend boundaries, transcend rather than define and protect divides, how it can at once create and celebrate community, define commonality and embrace fluidity" (115). In an obvious case of Jewish ventriloquism, Archy serves as a mouthpiece for Chabon's vision of undoing and crossing lines between people.

Chabon's approach to boundaries and Archy's description of Creole as "you stop drawing those lines," anticipate Dean Franco's 2019 study of race and literature in Los Angeles, *The Border and the Line*, in which

174   Absorption Narratives

he discusses metaphor and metonymy in the context of neighbouring relationships between Jews and Chicanxs. For Franco, Blackness is often presented as metonymic and synchronic rather than metaphorical or diachronic. Chabon's idea – voiced through Archy – of a "Brokeland dream" also resonates with Franco's analysis of Los Angeles. What differs between Franco's model and *Telegraph Avenue*, however, is that, unlike in his previous novels, Chabon is *not* "working in the name of Jewishness" to address structural racism. Of course, he sets out to address racism through his chronicle of the oppression and marginalization faced by the novels' Black characters, but Jewishness mostly fades out of focus. For example, the narrator describes Julius: "Julie wanted to die of his own whiteness, to be drowned in the tide of his embarrassment on behalf of all uncool white people everywhere when they tried to be cool" (*Telegraph Avenue* 98). Jewish characters in the novel are not very distinguished from white folks writ large in the novel. This characterization is starkly different from how Chabon depicts Jewish characters in other novels, particularly *The Yiddish Policeman's Union*.

The breakdown of Black–Jewish friendships – Brokeland Records closes, and Gwen decides to leave her midwifery practice with Aviva to go to medical school to become an obstetrician – is also depicted in terms of this Brokeland mixture. The narrator describes Nat's "belief that real and ordinary friendship between black people and white people was possible, at least here, on the streets of the minor kingdom of Brokeland, California. Here along the water margin, along the Borderlands. ... There was no tragic misunderstanding, rooted in centuries of slavery and injustice. No one was lobbing vile epithets, reverting to atavistic tribalisms" (*Telegraph Avenue* 411). Yet, as we see, this moment is fleeting, because Brokeland will close and Gwen will attend medical school. Importantly, this belief belongs to Nat, the idealistic white character who, as we observe here, is perhaps overly idealistic to the point of not appreciating the centuries of slavery and injustice, which he problematically dismisses as "atavistic tribalisms." As the narrator goes on to point out here, "The differences in class and education among the four of them canceled out without regard for stereotype or cultural expectation: Aviva and Archy both had been raised by blue-collar aunts who worked hard to send them to lower-tier colleges. The white guy was the high school dropout, the black woman upper-middle-class and expensively educated" (411). Nonetheless, even within this chiastic defiance of stereotypes or cultural expectations, the intimate, almost familial bonds between Aviva and Gwen, and Nat and Archy, are not tenable. Once the record store closes and the Brokeland Creole dream proves untenable, the novel ends with Titus and Clark (Archy and

Gwen's newborn baby) in the back seat of Archy's car as Titus asks where they are going, to which Archy responds "to Wakanda." As we see through the novel's ending and through Chabon's own account of the impetus for the novel, such a harmonious coexistence is not possible in Berkeley, Oakland, or even in the mythical Brokeland. Archy is left to take Titus and Clark to Wakanda to live out his Brokeland dreams.

The novel's treatment of Luther's backstory as a Blaxploitation actor bridges the novel's interest in cinematic references with the importance of 1970s Black culture in Oakland. For Kendi, Blaxploitation films are interrelated with the idea of Black neighbourhoods as the most "authentic Black experience": "The Black Power movement ... sent creative Black people on a mission to erect Black standards, a new Black aesthetic. Blaxploitation films arrived right on time, with Black casts, urban settings, and Black heroes and heroines: pimps, gangsters, prostitutes, and rapists" (164). The Blaxploitation backstory also conjures a perhaps quirkier connection: the 2003 film *Hebrew Hammer*, a parody of *Shaft* in which the protagonist is the Jewish character Mordecai Jefferson Carver, a "certified circumcised dick" who has to save Hanukkah from the evil Santa Claus. For Goldstein, *Hebrew Hammer* is indicative of a trend in which "during the 1990s and the first years of the twenty-first century, there are suggestions that an increasing number of Jews are becoming frustrated with the constraints of acceptance in white America and are expressing a sense of alienation and disengagement from whiteness" (235). This phenomenon that Goldstein notes dovetails with Glaser's model of "borrowed voices," in which Jewish authors' speaking through racial Others is a function of lamenting the loss of their previous status as the Other. Chabon's engagement with the Blaxploitation genre similarly expresses white Jewish anxieties about race in the US.

Chabon's novel attempts a delicate, and ultimately impossible, balance. It is, at many points, overly optimistic about race in following Archy's model of the Brokeland Creole dream. And yet the novel's ending tells us that, if it is not possible for Nat and Archy to be best friends and business partners in 2004 Oakland/Berkeley, racial harmony between Black and white people anywhere might be impossible. Akin to the author's own account of his realization following the O.J. Simpson verdict that he was out of touch with Black experiences in the US, the novel is about the breakdown of solidarity across racial lines. However, it is also about breaking down these lines. For Chabon, this solidarity is fraught with the ventriloquism of speaking for others. At the same time, this ventriloquism is only possible, *Telegraph Avenue* shows through its narrator and through its characters, by first listening to Black characters. The novel's success in fostering interracial and intercultural solidarity

176 Absorption Narratives

is in many ways asymptotic. White (Jewish) characters can empathize but cannot fully understand their Black friends' plight – hence, Aviva's policy is "What do I know about being Black?" (*Telegraph Avenue* 309). The novel, despite its many instances of Jews speaking for Black characters, shies away from exploring more robust forms of allyship. Nonetheless, if one reads for the ways in which Chabon, his characters, and his narrator listen to Black history, the novel does recalibrate critical understandings of how Jewish literature fosters anti-racism. What this novel does *not* address explicitly is what, if anything, Jewish anti-racism and actively promoting anti-racism *as a Jew* might look like, an elision that is striking within the broader panorama of the works that Chabon published prior to this one. As in the author's account of his own childhood, his Jewish characters focus not on the fact that they are Jewish but on the fact that they are not Black. In this way, Chabon seems to create a model in which Jewish anti-racism eschews one's own ethnic identity and focuses the reckoning on racial oppression against Black US citizens. *Telegraph Avenue*'s 465 pages are replete with specific references to its Jewish characters' cultural and religious specificities, yet when focusing on racism and oppression, the novel does not emphasize its Jewish characters' own experiences with oppression. Unlike the Jewish whiteness of which Karen Brodkin writes that benefits from and perpetuates white supremacy, *Telegraph Avenue*'s Jewish characters avow whiteness in ways that position them as allies to their Black friends and colleagues, minimizing any oppression of their own and thus avoiding any of the "competitive memory" that Rothberg notes.

Conclusions

Through their distinct forms – documentary theatre, fiction film, and the novel – these three works take account of shifting relationships in specific urban spaces between Black and Jewish neighbours. While Smith's play was written and first performed immediately after the moment that it depicts – a uniquely tumultuous flashpoint in Black–Jewish relations – the fact that the play continues to be performed speaks to its quality as a work of literature and its continued relevance for conversations on race and belonging. For their part, *The Year My Parents Went on Vacation* and *Telegraph Avenue* both return – from the perspectives of Generation-X Jewish males in the early twenty-first century – to a particular time (the late 1960s and early 1970s) to contemplate how Black–Jewish relationships then and in the early 2000s relate to political dreams. Their fictional retrospective depictions of Black characters in the 1970s evoke the history of Black–Jewish solidarity in the US civil rights movement and in the anti-dictatorial groups in Brazil alike. Thus, they capture a heyday of ideals and belief in equality, the "working in the name of Jewishness" for anti-racism, as Franco describes, that seemed possible from the perspective of children in the 1970s in ways that do not seem as feasible in the present. *Fires in the Mirror*, in contrast, captures a moment in Brooklyn's history in which Black–Jewish relations are so contentious as to seem dystopic. And yet, as Smith has made clear in her own discussions of the play, her approach to the subject and to her individual characters is rooted in her own familiarity and intimacy with Jewish families from her experience as a Black child in Baltimore. Jewishness comes into contact with Black–white paradigms of race and the idea of racial democracy in Brazil in ways that at times maintain and at times disrupt ideas of white supremacy. The complexities of the shifting logics that undergird racialized thinking throughout the Americas come into greater relief when we examine Jewishness vis-à-vis racial paradigms between these two nations.

These works' respective treatments of Black and Jewish characters challenge long-standing notions of racial mixture that absorb differences, even as such an act of speaking for the Other appropriates the Other. These three cultural agents draw from their own childhood experiences of Black–Jewish encounters so as to reimagine their respective nations' past and present and the place of differing communities therein. Because anti-Black racism remains an enormous issue throughout the Americas, we are reminded of the urgency to think through the possibilities for anti-racism that Jewish–Black coalition offers. In response to the death of George Floyd in Minneapolis, Minnesota, at the hands of police officers in May 2020, Moustafa Bayoumi, a scholar of Arab American literature, published an opinion piece in the *New York Times* referencing the James Baldwin piece with which I opened this monograph. Bayoumi asked "Why Did Cup Foods Call the Police on George Floyd?" and chronicled the policies that have allowed police and city officials to coerce non-Black immigrants into working in their favour and against Black people, "compelling shopkeepers into doing the police's work for them." Bayoumi, like Baldwin before him, reminds us that functions of economic and legal hegemony compel non-Black immigrants into enacting white supremacy as ways of belonging and advancing in society. As these three works from throughout the Americas show, Black–Jewish encounters are always bound up in these hegemonic structures. Yet all three authors – Hamburger through his focus on Mauro as a child, Smith and Chabon through their respective *New York Times* accounts – return to their childhood understandings of how Jewishness fits into Black–white race relations as a way of understanding possibilities for anti-racism.

6 Queering Ethnic Rites of Passage

In the summer of 2018, the Los Angeles group Defend Boyle Heights, an anti-gentrification coalition, boycotted a kosher restaurant after the owner retweeted anti-Latinx and xenophobic statements from then-President Trump. Responses to the case highlighted the neighbourhood's welcoming of Jewish immigrants in the 1930s and the expectation that the Jewish community extend the same hospitality towards other immigrant and minority groups. Similarly, in her 2016 documentary *East LA Interchange*, director Betsy Kalin includes accounts from community members who assert that the Jewish community in Boyle Heights avowed strong support for Latinx civil rights in the 1960s as an expression of affinity and solidarity. Recently, the Boyle Heights Jewish community was depicted in the popular Amazon series *Transparent* (2014–19) through flashbacks that tell the story of the main family's refuge in the neighbourhood after fleeing Germany between the world wars. In another story set nearby in the Los Angeles Echo Park neighbourhood (which came to be known as L.A's "Little Havana" in the 1960s), *One Day at a Time* depicts queer Cuban coming of age similarly to *Transparent*'s treatment of queer coming of age in a Jewish setting.[1] Both series include gendered rites of passages, the Latinx quinceañera and the Jewish bat mitzvah, in a way that shows sexuality and ethnicity sitting uncomfortably with one another for queer adolescents whose grandparents immigrated to the US.[2] The two storylines both situate family as a site of compulsory heterosexuality, feature adolescent characters who negotiate their sexual identities as they grapple with a rite of passage, and use humour as a tactic to question, resist, and at times reify patriarchal norms. Following chapter 5's focus on urban spaces, this chapter centres on the respective television programs' treatments of Los Angeles. In this regard, it is a departure from the rest of the book's comparative readings of works from throughout the Americas. Furthering my discussion of Latinidad in the US in my reading of *Days of Awe*, I argue that a comparative analysis of these two shows reveals the disparate ways in which Latinidad and Jewishness are absorbed into the mainstream. The fluidity of gender in these shows furthers our understanding of the liquidity of race and memory and the ways in which these become absorbed into the mainstream.

Over the course of its five seasons, *Transparent* did not fully seize on the opportunity to make a truly intersectional intervention commensurate with Boyle Heights's rich history. The Pfeffermans' story includes flashbacks to Boyle Heights as a place of refuge for Jewish immigrants in the 1940s (and as the site of protagonist Maura's burgeoning transgender identification) but makes no references to the neighbourhood's importance in the intervening years as a hub of Latinx and Black community organizing and activism, let alone to the commingling of these groups with Jewish communities.[3] The family moved to the Palisades (likely in the 1970s or in the 1980s, since they are shown raising their children there in the early 1990s). There, as Maura remarks to her fellow trans friend Davina in 2014, "they don't let our kind in. ... They only recently started letting in the Jews." Their family story is a common one, in which Jews vacated neighbourhoods like Boyle Heights for whiter neighbourhoods – part of the family's "carefully constructed white world" (12).[4] This whiteness is "carefully constructed" not only in Soloway's representation of the Pfeffermans' world but also in the history of race relations in the twentieth-century US that compelled Jews into avowing whiteness in order to be accepted in neighbourhoods like the Palisades after leaving Boyle Heights.[5] In contrast, *One Day at a Time* – a much more aesthetically conventional, multi-camera situation comedy – celebrates the Cuban presence in Echo Park, a neighbourhood that is gentrifying. The series does take the opportunity to include Jewish characters who reflect on their difference and privilege vis-à-vis Latinx families. Likewise, the show's reflections on colourism and its intersections with queer identities tell a story that is more in line with the legacy of Boyle Heights's welcoming of refugees that *Transparent* seeks to celebrate.

The diachronic stories of urban spaces within Los Angeles are marked indelibly by the complexities of Jewish and Latinx convergence and divergence. Franco notes, "Boyle Heights ... is a dynamically negotiated space, with shifting lines of belonging and exclusion" (28). While *Transparent* circumscribes its depiction of Boyle Heights to the time and space in which the Pfefferman family found refuge there in the 1940s, the intersections of immigrant and queer identities in Los Angeles neighbourhoods are more dynamic than the show suggests. We

180   Absorption Narratives

note the contrasts between what Villarejo describes as a "carefully constructed white world" of the Pfeffermans' present as opposed to their family's past in the "dynamically negotiated space" of Boyle Heights. The "carefully constructed white world" is one in which Jewishness absorbs whiteness and vice versa (here, Jewishness and whiteness are in a chiastic relationship with one another). Bearing this contrast in mind, my comparative discussion of how *Transparent* and *One Day at a Time* treat coming-out narratives seeks to move past delineations between disparate ethnic and racial categories. Specifically, both shows emphasize the particular challenges for coming out presented by dominant majority culture and by the minority cultures to which these characters' families belong.

Rites of passage are particularly salient for immigrant communities in the US insofar as, in addition to marking a watershed moment in an individual's coming of age, they play an important part in maintaining cultural identities related to immigrant communities' countries of origin. Jewish bar/bat mitzvahs and Latinx quinceañeras are two examples of such rites of passage that have been integral to celebrating and preserving ethnic identities among their respective cultures in the US. Moreover, both are patently gendered. *Transparent* uses flashbacks to character Ari's decision to forgo their *bat mitzvah* in such a way that is inexorable and arises from their vexed relationship to their family's immigrant history and their burgeoning queer (and later non-binary) identification as a twenty-something in the series' present.[6] As an adult, Ari reclaims the anti-assimilation of her ancestors through their sexual freedom in the cabarets of Weimar Germany before immigrating to Boyle Heights.[7] Likewise, *One Day at a Time* presents character Elena's process of coming to terms with whether or not to celebrate her quinceañera, which she perceives as a misogynist, patriarchal tradition, as she grapples with coming out. Since Deborah Kaplan had her bat mitzvah in New York in 1922, the bat mitzvah has played an important role in fostering Jewish young women's identification with Judaism as a religion as well as with Jewish culture and ethnicity in the US. To this day, as Mark Oppenheimer has noted, the celebration retains a particular feminist meaning for many Jewish families. For US Latinx families, the quinceañera has long held significance in fostering a connection to one's culture of origin, although this significance has shifted over the decades along with patterns of Latinx assimilation.[8] In this way, in addition to their obvious (though not uncomplicated) importance for gender, both rites of passage have historically been significant for families' maintenance of cultural and ethnic heritage within US racial paradigms that otherwise eschew cultural difference and specificity.

Queering Ethnic Rites of Passage   181

As these shows remind us, representations of racial and ethnic difference in television function within hegemonic understandings of normative culture in ways that dovetail with normative understandings of sexuality. Herman Gray posits, "Television representations of blackness operate squarely within the boundaries of middle-class patriarchal discourses about 'whiteness' as well as the historic racialization of the social order" (9). That is, representations of racial difference are situated within structures of privilege and power that are based on white middle-class heterosexual normativity. Notably, Gray focuses on network television in 1995, and enormous breakthroughs in representation have taken place since then in network television and on streaming platforms. Yet white, middle-class, heteronormative, patriarchal codes continue to orient television's representations of categories of difference and are relevant to the representations I discuss of queer folx and immigrant families, particularly those who do not pass as white. Steven Funk and Jaydi Funk also take note of how whiteness and heterosexuality are similarly codified in television depictions of coming-out stories.[9] Coming-out narratives can reify gender normativity, akin to Gray's model of representations of Blackness that serve to codify existing paradigms of racial hierarchies. Similarly, Kristin Moran has noted that the fact that media is produced for Latinx audiences "does not mean it is necessarily free from replicating many of the narrative tropes found in other programming" (84). Much of the progressive sensibility that these programs may be able to foster is belied by their own affirmation of white, patriarchal, heteronormative cultural paradigms, which we may understand in relation to cultural hegemony.[10] In these shows, despite having parents who do not conform to conventional heteronormativity, the adolescent characters in both series still grapple with their own sexual identifications and with coming out to their families.

The two characters on whose coming-out narratives I focus here – *Transparent*'s Ari and *One Day at a Time*'s Elena – recall Adrienne Rich's model of compulsory heterosexuality and lesbian existence. The assumption of identification with norms of conventional femininity is coded as part and parcel of these characters' families and their ethnic identifications. Ari's and Elena's coming-out stories shed light on the compulsory heterosexuality engrained in their individual families as well as within Jewish and Cuban American culture, respectively. For Adrienne Rich, "the assumption that 'most women are innately heterosexual' stands as a theoretical and political stumbling block for feminism" (26). These shows centre on female-identified (and later non-binary identified, in the case of *Transparent*'s Ari) characters whose life stories go against compulsory heterosexuality and who are being

182   Absorption Narratives

raised by a cross-dressing father (*Transparent*) or a strong single mother (*One Day at a Time*), yet whose lives are still bound by heteronormativity. These shows – helmed by a non-binary showrunner and a woman showrunner, respectively – work both within and against the limits of television as a medium to push the boundaries of sexuality and ethnicity. Likewise, the shows themselves are bound by some of the constraints of heteronormativity within television. In *The Queer Politics of Television*, Samuel Chambers draws from Rich's ideas to linger on the importance of norms themselves as a way of reifying heterosexual culture (65). Heteronormativity is insidious and bound up in hegemonic understandings of culture that pervade the coming-out process, as I underscore throughout my discussions of these two programs.[11] My comparative discussion here of *Transparent* and *One Day at a Time* provides a modest attempt to think through the queer politics of television by acknowledging the necessary limits of each individual show.

A comparative discussion of these two shows raises necessary questions about whiteness and queer sexualities. Both Ari and Elena are light skinned; yet, Jewish immigrants to the US, such as Ari's grandparents and Cuban Americans, have vexed (although very different) relationships to whiteness in ways that further problematize their sexuality and their relationships to their own cultures. For José Esteban Muñoz in *Disidentifications: Queers of Color and the Performance of Politics*, "queer desires, perhaps desires that negate self, desire for a white beauty ideal, are reconstituted … we thus disidentify with the white ideal" (15).[12] Such disidentification with the white ideal necessarily includes a reckoning with white supremacist racial paradigms.[13] Muñoz's model of disidentification that insists that identity is a fiction bears indelibly on my discussions of how these adolescent characters negotiate their own coming-out processes.

With regard to their aesthetics, the two shows' treatments of coming-out processes drastically differ. *One Day at a Time* is faithful in its form to the original 1970s show from which it is adapted: the thirty-minute episodes include a laugh track and multiple cameras. In contrast, *Transparent* is much more aesthetically radical for a television show: the show has always been difficult to categorize formally; it incorporates aspects of camp and melodrama in an unmistakably cinematic television show. The last season (which also sees Ari now identify as non-binary and no longer includes Jeffrey Tambor, a known sexual harasser, in the main role of Maura), takes the form of musical theatre. In many ways, the formal aspects of the two series could not be more different. Yet, the aesthetic forms mirror the respective content of each of the shows, which is paradoxically similar. In their own ways,

Transparent and *One Day at a Time* constitute feminist, gender-queer approaches to television, but with their own limitations. Not only does *Transparent* differ formally from a conventional family sitcom, but, as Joshua Louis Moss argues, sitcom conventions are tacitly invoked in *Transparent* to highlight the changes occurring within the family. Moss notes, "Maura struggles with her new identity, often falling back on her established patriarchal status when confronted or in trouble. These comedic sequences suggest the familiar sitcom parent comically out of touch with both her children's needs and the contemporary pop culture landscape she clings to" (76–7).[14] In this regard, *Transparent* engages with some of the codes of the family sitcom format that *One Day at a Time* is remaking.[15] *One Day at a Time* furthers the feminist innovations made by the 1970s version by bringing immigration, racial difference, and queer identifications to bear on the show's understanding of gender. With Norman Lear lending his expertise on some episodes, the show also continues the legacy that he established in such shows as *All in the Family* by addressing uncomfortable questions of race and racism in humorous, innovative ways. Within each of their aesthetic forms, both shows are, to an extent, limited to the gender norms of television and of society. At the same time, however, each manages to innovate and break new ground in television representation. In my discussion of the shows, I focus specifically on their emphases on previous generations' immigration stories and how these bear on queer adolescents' coming-out processes.

"Torture in a Dress": *Transparent*

Since its debut in 2014, *Transparent* has generated myriad discussions on the points of contact between Jewishness and gender and sexuality. The series repeatedly depicts the two as inexorable from one another. As the 2003 edited volume *Queer Theory and the Jewish Question* argues, categories of gender normativity and Jewish difference have shared histories. The editors posit in their introduction "Strange Bedfellows": "If gender provided a ready interpretive grid through which nineteenth-century science could detect and interpret the racial difference of the Jew, the masculine/feminine axis was also being fit to another emerging taxonomy of difference: the modern discourse of sexuality with its 'specification' and 'solidification' of individuals … into distinct sexual personages" (3). *Transparent* makes clear throughout its run that Jewishness necessarily takes into account the negotiation of gender and sexuality. One of the strengths of the show is that it treats the points of contact between sexuality and Jewishness in ways that are deferential to

184   Absorption Narratives

the fact that the two are, at times, analogous and, at others, co-constitutive. The episodes of the show that I discuss here focus on the gendered elements of becoming a Jewish woman in such a way as to grapple with the patently gendered (and limiting) aspects of Jewish identifications. This element of the series recalls Janet Jakobsen's essay in the aforementioned volume, "Queers Are Like Jews, Aren't They?" Similarly, Soloway's series not only depicts characters who largely exceed the limits of the identities with which they are associated by others, but also call into question these categories themselves. While *Transparent*'s main characters do not "come out" as Jewish within the show, they do take on new relationships to Judaism and Jewishness as they grapple with their sexual identities. In keeping with Sedgwick's characterization, both Jewishness and sexuality are vexed but nonetheless essential to Ari's (and Maura's) coming-out story – specifically in the outward showing, performative aspects of identification.

However, while the series breaks meaningful ground in transgender representation (the casting of a cisgender actor in the main role, an oversight the show corrected in its fifth and final season after Tambor was ousted from the show), it falls short of attaining the very intersectionality that it acknowledges and at which it pokes fun. The show's emphasis on Maura's womanhood – in a still patriarchal role of provider and authority figure within her family unit – often overshadows the subjectivities of other woman-identified characters: in particular, her two daughters and her ex-wife. Joey Soloway commented in a speech at the Toronto International Film Festival that they wanted to be associated with the female gaze: "You know what's crazy is that it's been FORTY YEARS since Mulvey named the Male Gaze and no one has claimed being the namer of the Female Gaze yet! I really want that. I want it to be like MULVEY: MALE GAZE, SOLOWAY: FEMALE GAZE!" ("The Female Gaze"). To be sure, *Transparent* breaks meaningful new ground in terms of destabilizing the male gaze. Yet, as Amy Villarejo asks, "If Soloway carefully and deliberately constructs a way of looking at Maura that is expressive of Soloway's own feminist queer-politics (for now, call it trans-affirmative and genderqueer), why does that gaze not extend to the three other women in the Pfefferman clan?" (11). While this shortcoming that Villarejo acknowledges improves over the course of the series, episodes showing Ari's cancelled bat mitzvah depict Maura in the role of a patriarchal authority figure who, despite her closeness with her youngest child, did not provide the guidance that Ari sought in their formative years.

Transparent Season 1, Episodes 6–10 – two of which include flashbacks to 1994, the year of Ari's would-be bat mitzvah (six, "The Wilderness,"

Queering Ethnic Rites of Passage   185

and eight, "Best New Girl") – all reference the unresolved conflicts sparked by the cancelled bat mitzvah. At this point in the series' progression, main character Mort has begun transitioning to Maura and we see her children launched into an exploration of their respective gender and sexual identifications. Throughout the series, sexuality is presented as part and parcel of the family's Jewish identity and its backstory of emigration from Germany after the sexual freedom of Weimar Germany came to a screeching halt upon the Nazi takeover. Within these five episodes in particular (6–10), then-Mort's struggles with his gender identity and his desire to cross-dress in 1994 are coupled with Ari's discomfort with the gendered bat mitzvah. In the scenes set in the present day, Ari decides that they want to enrol in gender studies courses and subsequently begins to date a transgender man (whom they introduce to their siblings and boast, "that man has a vagina"). The show's diachronic story of Ari's bat mitzvah and their present are interlaid so as to couple the cancelled bat mitzvah with their burgeoning sexual and gender fluidity. In this five-episode arc, we see Maura repeatedly attempt to bond with her child on the basis of their shared gender fluidity. Yet gender fluidity, although a point of identification, is also a source of tension between the two in a dynamic in which Maura often reverts to an authoritative, patriarchal figure despite her transition.

These attempts to bond with her child are shown to be rooted in both characters' decades-long questioning of their Judaism and their gender identifications. The scenes set in the present depict Ari asking Maura for financial support to enrol in gender studies courses, saying that they are inspired by her. Maura asks if it is because she is a renowned scholar (a retired professor of political science), which Ari dismisses to say that they are inspired by Maura's transition. This moment speaks to a generational divide in which, while Maura is transgender, she does not connect this personal experience to her academic persona. The exchange recalls Moss's interpretation of the show's tacit invocation of family sitcom humour based on the out-of-touch patriarch.[16] In the first flashback to 1994, we see Ari on the verge of tears as they hold a frilly dress that they are devastated at the thought of wearing. Presenting as a tomboyish adolescent, Ari is wearing sport shorts with their hair pulled back in a ponytail and bemoans, "This is torture. It's torture in a dress." Maura responds that she thinks that it is a beautiful dress; from the perspective of what we know about Maura in the present, we understand that Maura (Mort in this scene) is envious of the dress that her child is supposed to wear for the ceremony. After proclaiming that they do not want to wear the dress and participate in the bat mitzvah, Ari asks Maura, "Do you actually believe in God?" to which Maura responds,

186 Absorption Narratives

"That has nothing to do with your bat mitzvah!" Maura goes on to assert – in a somewhat effeminate posture with her fingertips daintily brushing her clavicle – that she struggles with the pain and suffering. Ari responds by listlessly sinking down the wall as they lament, "So if there is no god, I mean honestly, like, everything we do, no one sees it." The parent's and child's shared conflicts with categories of gender and sexuality thus cede to their shared doubts about spirituality. Ari complains about the dress and insists that they have not memorized the Torah verses, yet they recite them perfectly for the caterer who turns up at the house unaware that the event is no longer happening. As we will see in the later scenes set in the present, Ari begrudges Maura for having fostered doubts rather than having inculcated a stronger sense of belief and having served as a spiritual role model.

Mort and Ari's emphasis on the dress that Ari would (not) wear for the bat mitzvah anticipates the tenth episode's visual emphasis on Maura's dress and Star of David that she wears for the first shiva she attends as a woman. Over the course of these five episodes, we see Maura become gendered as a Jewish woman for the first time. In the episode prior to the one that depicts Ari's cancelled bat mitzvah, Maura prays over a seder as the mother of the family. She fumbles to light the candles and then through the blessing, which she realizes is the Hanukkah prayer and not the Shabbat prayer. In a later episode, she attends ex-wife Shelly's husband Ed's funeral, a coming-out event of sorts for her as she appears (fashionably late and in a limousine) in women's clothing for the first time in front of many of Shelly's relatives and friends. Ari comments here that Maura is wearing a "sparkly Star of David" necklace and adds somewhat derisively, "Since when are you into Judaism?" Like their earlier exchange in 1994, Maura and Ari's gender identifications are again couched in terms of their fraught relationships to Judaism and, like the dress in the 1994 scene, prompted by frilly adornment. The question stems from their rancour over her parents' allowing them to cancel their bat mitzvah, over which they confront both parents during their stepfather's shiva. That Ari should bring up the subject during a shiva again equates Jewish practices – here, the mourning ritual – with gender identification through focusing on both Ari's own gender fluidity and Maura's cross-dressing during Ari's adolescent years.

As we come to see over the course of these episodes, Ari's cancelled bat mitzvah is bound up in issues of both her own sexual orientation and Maura's gender identification. We learn that Maura wanted to cancel the bat mitzvah in part so that she could go to a cross-dressing camp with her friend. Shelly, however, is incensed over the prospect of cancelling the bat mitzvah and reproaches Maura, "I want you to be a man! And save the goddamn day." We see Maura's face grow long as Shelly storms out of the room. Shelly's anger and frustration in this scene are echoed decades later when Ari finally asks at their stepfather's shiva why they allowed them to cancel the bat mitzvah.[17] Shelly, already annoyed that her ex-spouse is using her husband's funeral as an opportunity to come out as trans (in an outfit completed by the sparkly star of David), erupts in anger and yells at Ari, "So that your father could go to cross-dressing camp!"

The flashback scenes of young Ari at home alone – at times with their siblings – evoke their parents' neglect as Maura and Shelly were both focused on Maura's sexual identifications in ways that distracted them from their parenting. On the day of the would-be bat mitzvah, Ari is alone at home and ends up on the beach with a stranger. The final scene of the episode juxtaposes shots of Ari in a cave on the beach and shots of Maura in dress at camp while an upbeat tango-inspired track plays. Gaby Hoffman – rather than Emily Robinson, the young actress portraying the twelve-year-old Ari in the rest of the flashback scenes – steps in to act as Ari as the tango reaches its crescendo. Ari (Robinson) crawls towards adult Ari (Hoffman) as the stranger kisses the adult Ari to pull him away from Ari. The young Ari steps in to save the adult Ari, visually emphasizing the need for Ari as a child to fend for themself. This performance tacitly couples Ari's sexuality and bat mitzvah with her family history, since the other role that Gaby Hoffman will play in the series is that of Ari's own grandmother (Maura's mother) in Boyle Heights after immigrating from Germany.

The backstory of Ali's cancelled bat mitzvah, interspersed with Maura's first seder as a woman and her attending her ex-wife's funeral wearing a Star of David necklace, creates a storyline in which both Ari and Maura look to gendered religious rites to understand better their sexuality. For Moss, "The canceled bat mitzvah by a transgender woman is also ironic. The female version of the bar mitzvah was a recent development towards gender equality in Reform and Conservative Jewish culture. Mort's cancellation of the event suggests a paradox, a severing of assimilated Jewish cultural life at the moment each of the Pfeffermans begin to explore their individual sexual identities" (87). Yet, for both, either these rites are overly rigid in their gender roles or the individuals' understandings of them are somehow impressionistic and removed from the original meanings of the rites themselves. In fact, much of the show's depiction of Judaism – despite being focused on religious rites – might more properly be thought of as Jewishness, rather than Judaism. Similarly, as Roberta Rosenberg notes, "*Transparent* offers a

188   Absorption Narratives

window into a world where secular Jews (and even their rabbi) struggle, sometimes succeeding and sometimes failing to create a spiritual
world of Jewish ritual living that will provide them with the ability
to do '*lech lecha*,' a going forth as courageous adults into a challenging
world" (78). In these episodes, Ari laments their own aimlessness in life
and begrudges their parents for not having inculcated more aspects of
Jewish life in them as a child.

The climax of the conflict surrounding Ari's bat mitzvah culminates
in her confronting Maura and asking why Maura gives them money
(something she does not do for her other adult children), to which
Maura responds, "because you cannot *do* anything." Maura steps into
the role of an authoritative patriarch in this moment to admonish her
child and also becomes the centre of attention at Shelly's second husband's shiva. Ari leaves angry, although they come back later and reconcile with their parents.

As the show will later make clear during its the second season
through the flashbacks to Weimar Germany, the Pfeffermans' Jewish
identifications, even when patently religious, have more to do with
cultural identifications as children and grandchildren of immigrants
and as part of a diasporic community than with spirituality. While later
episodes of the show depict the family's time in Boyle Heights after
fleeing Germany, the show does not depict that neighbourhood's Latinx populations, which were already present at that time and grew in
importance over the decades. Nor does the show engage with present-day issues of immigration and refuge. Like the show's storylines
in the present, the backstories in both 1994 and the 1930s and 1940s
emphasize genderqueer identifications, yet despite the importance of
immigration for this family's backstory, the topic is not taken up in the
show's present.

"I'm Coming Out": *One Day at a Time*

One Day at a Time is very conscious of the importance of Latinx representation in television. Touted as the frontrunner of Latinx television
programs in recent years, the show explicitly tackles stereotypes and
perceptions of Latinx communities in nearly every episode. As a queer
Latinx adolescent, Elena finds herself in tension with the gender codes
both of mainstream, hegemonic culture and of her own Cuban American family. For purposes of my discussion of Elena's quinceañera, I
focus on the show's first season, the finale of which centres on the event
itself. This season premiered on Netflix in January 2017 and immediately met with popular and critical acclaim, leading the streaming

platform to renew the show for two seasons before deciding not to do a fourth season. *One Day at a Time* was then taken up by Pop Network, which aired the fourth season before CBS decided to do so beginning in October 2020. *One Day at a Time* has garnered headlines such as "Norman Lear's New *One Day at a Time* Has a Latin Flavour" (Keveney 2017). Yet, these exoticizing glosses are misleading because the Netflix series goes far beyond just being a "Latinx version" of the acclaimed, groundbreaking 1970s series. Calderón Kellet's series offers meaningful insights into intersectional understandings of gender, ethnicity, and sexuality. In fact, Keveney quotes Calderón Kellet as stating, "1975 sexism is different than 2016 sexism." The reboot tackles loaded issues of mental health, immigration, single mother Penelope's PTSD from her service in Afghanistan, and queer identifications, continuing the legacy of the original series' innovative consideration of single motherhood. In addition to *One Day at a Time*'s focus on Cuban American experiences, Calderón Kellett's version maintains the original show's family structure of a single mother with son and daughter, but adds the single mother's mother, Lydia, portrayed by the iconic Rita Moreno. This character adds the energy and dynamism of the EGOT-winning actress.

Because of Lydia's presence, the children on the show – Elena and her younger brother, Alex – are in effect being raised by two women. The generation gap between Lydia and Penelope and their differing perspectives often causes them to butt heads over what is best for Penelope's children in ways that sometimes recall conflicts between heterosexual parents. Lydia's role in the family evokes a characteristic of many Latinx families in which grandparents often live with the nuclear family, so the show's inclusion of this character is also an important element of Cuban American and Latinx family structures. Rather than having an authoritative father figure propel much of the conflict and humour, the family is patently matriarchal. This family structure thus debunks monomaternalism, understood as the idea – rooted in heterosexist belief systems – that every child should have only one mother. As Shelley Park notes, this idea works "by giving us a personal stake in claiming to be a child's 'real' mother and thus the only mother who counts" (14). The structure of the family thus works against heterosexist, patriarchal assumptions. Elena's father only appears in two episodes and is not accepting of her sexual orientation.

At the same time, however, Lydia espouses conventional and patriarchal viewpoints on gender roles, such that this two-mother parenting structure is also heteronormative in some ways. Yet, when Elena comes out to her, Lydia is effusively supportive and works through any issues she has with her granddaughter's homosexuality on religious

190   Absorption Narratives

bases by quoting Pope Francis's famous "who am I to judge" line. Her conservatism, however paradoxically, allows her to accept Elena's homosexuality more readily than Penelope. Lydia's character also couples Latinidad with Catholicism. Similar to *Transparent*'s treatment of Judaism in relation to Jewish ethnicity and memories of immigration, *One Day at a Time* emphasizes Catholicism's role in Latinx identities. Yet, the show does not underscore the religious elements of the quinceañera. Characters state that "Cubans go to church" in contrast to Protestants, suggesting that Catholicism is such a part of Cuban American life as to conflate the two by setting up a binary between "Protestant" and "Cuban." Like in *Transparent* (in which Ari's sister, Sarah, feels during her wedding reception that she has made a huge mistake in marrying her college lover and proclaims, "I hate her fucking family, these fucking WASPS"), religious identity is important because it is tied to a marginalized identity and to a family history of immigration.

The show couples Latinidad – and issues of Latinx immigration to the US – with sexuality. As del Río and Moran highlight, "Latinas featured in scripted programming are often narrowly defined by a limited binary that pits the hypersexual young Latina against the asexual grandmotherly figure or the untouchable immigrant. ... *One Day at a Time* challenges these characterizations through its three female lead characters by working within and against this narrative device" (14). Del Río and Moran make note of other television characters – including *The Office*'s Oscar Martinez and *Grey's Anatomy*'s Callie Torres – whose intersecting queer and Latinx identification serve to reify heteronormativity. In contrast, *One Day at a Time*, while at times bound up in the compulsory heterosexuality of television, nonetheless defies the patriarchal, heterosexual norms of television by allowing Elena to embrace elements of Cuban American culture that she identifies as misogynistic.

In the show's first episode, Elena asserts to her mother and grandmother, "I don't want to be paraded around in front of the men of the village like a piece of property to be traded for two cows and a goat," in a characteristically indignant rejection of what she perceives to be a patriarchal practice. *One Day at a Time* takes a common sitcom trope – a "rebellious" teenager and the generation gaps with parents and grandparents – to make Elena a fleshed-out, sympathetic character who grapples with her identity in a supportive family, albeit not without struggles. Crispin Long notes that "[Elena's] battle with her family, especially her grandmother, over whether to have a *quinceañera* ... leads to subtle conversations about gender roles and heritage, and to Elena's eventual realization that she is a lesbian. Ideas that would normally be relegated to an "issues episode" ... are part of the emotional fabric of the show, and handled with a light but sensitive touch" (n.p.). In this way, *One Day at a Time* deviates from the norms of the sitcom to foreground serious family and political issues and to maintain its focus on these conflicts over the course of multiple episodes (and even seasons) rather than resolve them neatly. Similarly, Jacinta Yanders notes, "Very real concerns of the Latinx diaspora are foregrounded in a way that's far removed from the 'Very Special Episode' of years past. Viewers don't get the sense that the Alvarez family will necessarily overcome every roadblock. Instead, these problems are ongoing struggles" (145). *One Day at a Time* works within the sitcom format to push the genre's boundaries so that "issues" episodes – in my focus here, coming out and immigration – are not relegated to a half-hour storyline and neatly resolved at the end. Rather, these issues take centre stage throughout the show's first season and affect the everyday dealings of the family.

By the end of the first episode, however, Elena agrees to the quinceañera because her mother tells her the event is important to her because she wants people to see her as a strong single mother who is pulling everything together. This matriarchal family thus resignifies the quinceañera to make it a celebration of a single mother's triumph over hardships. At the season's end, Elena attends her quinceañera in a white pantsuit that her grandmother tailors for her out of the quinceañera dress that she had previously made for her and the party becomes a coming-out party for Elena as queer (she walks out onto the dance floor to the song "I'm Coming Out"). While her father had promised to dance with her at the party even though he has been grappling with her sexual orientation, he leaves the party after seeing Elena's pantsuit, and Penelope dances with her daughter in another gender-bending element of the celebration.

Earlier in the season, Lydia suspects that Elena is queer because of her close relationship to a friend from school, Carmen, in the first season's fifth episode, "Strays." While Lydia's suspicions that Elena is queer do turn out to be true, the family soon comes to learn that Carmen has been sleeping at their house because her own family has been detained and is going to be deported. When Penelope insists that Carmen has spent enough time in their home and needs to go home, the girls seem panicked and dramatically say goodbye to one another, leading audiences to suspect that they are teenage lovers who cannot bear to be separated. Once Carmen is caught trying to sneak back into their apartment, Elena becomes irate with her mother. In this way, through a relationship that is very different from Lydia's own, the show underscores an intergenerational identification between Cuban immigrants of Lydia's generation and their grandchildren's generation, among which Latinx immigrants

192   Absorption Narratives

tend to be from Central America and Mexico and often face discrimination or even deportation, such as Carmen's family. The episode begins with Penelope entering the family's apartment to find Elena and Carmen asleep under the same blanket on the living room couch. Lydia comments to Penelope that she suspects that there is something "queer" between the two girls as Carmen begins spending more and more time at their home, virtually always depicted walking around the apartment wrapped together in the same large blanket. Certainly, two teenage girls depicted right next to each other is conventional in family sitcoms, but the image of these two wrapped in a blanket together and embraced establishes a visual coding of Elena in intimate relationships with other females, in contrast to her later foray into heterosexuality. After first describing herself to her younger brother as bisexual, she briefly flirts with and kisses a boy with whom she establishes a friendship and who agrees to be her quinceañera escort. Aside from the time that she kisses him, the two are shown spending time together but are much more distanced.

Present for Carmen's return to the Álvarez home and the discovery of her parents' deportation is Penelope's boss, Leslie Berkowitz, whom Penelope has invited to their house because it is his birthday and no one else has offered to celebrate with him. Her hospitality here is another reason for the episode's title, "Strays." Berkowitz identifies as Jewish; in another episode, after he reveals that he often dreamed of writing parodies of beloved songs, Lydia sings a song to him to the tune of "Hava Nagila." Throughout the series, he is lovingly touted as a straight white man who benefits from certain privileges (as the two characters discuss explicitly, he was able to attend medical school whereas Penelope was not) but who is extraordinarily empathetic and aware of his own privilege. Here, *Transparent*'s lack of engagement with Latinx characters comes into greater relief: while *One Day at a Time* incorporates a Jewish character into its depiction of Cuban American rites of passage, *Transparent* does not include Latinx characters in its consideration of Jewish sexualities.

Queering Ethnic Rites of Passage

Despite this difference, both *One Day at a Time* and *Transparent* depict gendered rites of passage with a strong emphasis on intergenerational relationships and family histories of immigration. This similarity is important to my reading of *Transparent*'s depiction of Boyle Heights because the show also depicts the history of this neighbourhood so as to highlight intergenerational relationships. Gaby Hoffman, the actor who portrays Ari in the show's present, also plays the role of Maura's mother in 1940s Boyle Heights after she and her family escaped Germany and found refuge in Los Angeles. Thus, the show tacitly couples intergenerational relationships with the storied spaces once inhabited by Jews in Los Angeles. While *One Day at a Time*'s Lydia chides Elena's balking at a quinceañera, *Transparent*'s Shelly rebukes her then-husband Mort's insistence that it is not her bat mitzvah with "Oh yes, it is my bat mitzvah." Mothers and grandmothers are bonded together in both works through these rites of passage. Previous generations' stories of immigrating to the US loom large in these stories.

The narrative pivot in *One Day at a Time*'s "Strays" episode between a possible lesbian relationship and the experience of deportation patently couples immigration with queer identification, as do *Transparent*'s flashbacks to earlier generations in the Pfefferman family that emigrated from Germany. In this regard, queer immigrant experiences are shown to be similar in Cuban American and Jewish American cases. For Anna Dempsey, "Soloway and [their] team weave together a Weimar Jewish transgender historical narrative with a Cold War US history of immigration and twentieth-century archival film and television to create a fictional account of the twenty-first century late-in-life 'coming out' of Mort Pfefferman as Maura" (803–4). This "weaving" of which Dempsey speaks is intimately connected to past generations' experiences of immigrating to the US and forming part of minority groups.

As a way of addressing the enormous trauma placed on their families by fleeing Germany or, in Lydia's case, coming to the US alone as a minor through the Pedro Pan Operation, both shows use humour to make their characters' stories palatable and engaging. Both shows derive much of their humour from other characters teasing Ari's and Elena's "wokeness." For example, when Ari tells their brother and sister that their date is trans, her sister scoffs and says, "Fucking Ali, Jesus Christ," balking at Ari's embrace of gender fluidity as typical of their personality, and their brother responds, "So, four out of five Pfeffermans now prefer pussy." As Jack Halberstam states of this line, "It is a great line and like much of the humor in the show, perfectly delivered. Eschewing the sit-com laugh-line humor for a more self-deprecating style that mixes defeat and disappointment in healthy doses with wry self-awareness, *Transparent* actually hits a few new notes for comedy." Similarly, *One Day at a Time* pokes fun at Elena through her banter with Lydia. When she says that she does not want to be paraded around the village for two cows and a goat, Lydia responds that Elena certainly thinks that she is worth a lot. The humour here is particularly telling: both shows, while they break significant ground in representation, also

194 Absorption Narratives

grapple with the challenges and complexities of intersectionality insofar as their characters often find their sexual identifications and ethnicities at odds with one another. Through their use of humour at the expense of such topics as intersectionality and gender-inclusive language, these series suggest a latent conservatism in their explorations of sexuality and ethnicity. In this way, both series continue the problem that Newcomb and Hirsch noted over forty years ago in their analysis of "the obvious ways in which [television] maintains dominant viewpoints" (571).

Yet, these points of humour can also be interpreted as serving to disarm viewers who may be ignorant towards or biased against LGBTQ characters. Soloway has stated that they sought to put into praxis an aesthetic of the "funcomfortable," that is, to entertain at the same time that they make viewers uncomfortable by prompting them to question their assumptions. Soloway's avowed endeavour to amuse while making viewers somewhat uncomfortable recalls Bakhtin's model of the seriocomic. For Bakhtin, "reduced laughter in carnival literature by no means excludes the possibilities of sombre colours within a work ... it is not their final word" (166). The dry humour of these seeks not to give final authority to the figures who utter them – older siblings, parents, and grandparents – but to push the boundaries of how their LGBTQ characters might be perceived in hegemonic codes. As in Bakhtin's model of dialogism, laughter functions to contest monolithic or authoritative figures (including authors and directors themselves). In *Transparent* and *One Day at a Time*, humour works to question heteronormative, racist, and anti-Semitic paradigms of representation within the conventional modes of televised serial comedy. In these instants in which jokes are at the expense of doubly marginalized subjects, the humour of the situation is codified within norms of acceptance. Lydia pokes fun at Elena's feminist and genderqueer expressions of self, but fiercely protects and accepts who she is when Elena comes out to her, while Ari's sister, who scoffs at their pronouncement that her date has a vagina, is at that moment also in a relationship with a woman. Thus, as in Bakhtin's discussion of reduced laughter, the shows' ludic treatment of serious subjects is not their final word. Rather, such uses of humour may serve to disarm viewers, both because the comic relief conforms to common expectations of sitcoms and because it makes light of subjects that are difficult to broach for some viewers.

Both shows' stories about queer rites of passage culminate in a breakdown in father-daughter relationships. When Ari attempts to confront Maura about the cancelled bat mitzvah, their encounter devolves into a screaming match in the middle of Shelly's husband's shiva. After seeing

Elena's suit for her quinceañera, her father leaves the party, abandoning her for the father-daughter dance. Penelope, Lydia, and Alex join her on the dance floor, visually emphasizing Lydia's role as a replacement for a father in the nuclear family. While Elena's relationship with her father is left in shambles, Ari returns to reconcile with both of her parents after storming out of the shiva. While Ali's family unit, in the present, has reconciled, the story of Elena's quinceañera ends with her absent father. Yet, both families are, at the end of the shows' respective first seasons, helmed by two women.

Despite these dramatic moments, these shows use humour both to conform with and to push the boundaries of situation comedy. Perhaps surprisingly, it is the more aesthetically normative of the two shows – *One Day at a Time* – that ends its first season with an unresolved family conflict: Victor leaves Elena's quinceañera and does not return, whereas Ari comes back to their childhood home (where they had spent the weekend of their would-be bat mitzvah alone) after their stepfather's shiva to find both their two parents and their siblings all joined around the table. While the next seasons will bring further familial disruption to the Pfeffermans, it is perhaps paradoxical that the show that seeks to destabilize the male gaze nonetheless returns to the nuclear family – now helmed by a trans woman but still relying on her as the authoritative figure. Indeed, it would not be until Jeffrey Tambor (who himself proclaimed in accepting his Emmy for his role as Maura that he hoped to be the last cisgender actor) was ousted from the show that it completely eschewed the norms of sitcom television to produce its final "season" as an extended musical theatre episode.

If the aesthetics of these two shows hold substantial potential to break new ground in inclusion and representation, I conclude that such potential is to be found in their opening credits. Both include montages of photos and film reels and are unmistakably flamboyant in their own ways: *Transparent* incorporates footage of gendered rites of passage, family celebrations, and beauty pageants paired with a slightly melancholic instrumental. To set the tone of the flash-back episode, "Best New Girl" uses the first verse of Bob Dylan's "Oh Sister" and evokes a strong sense of longing through the lines, "Oh Sister, when I come to lie in your arms / you should not treat me like a stranger." *One Day at a Time* includes images of Cuba and of Cubans in Echo Park and updates its original theme song from the 1970s version to add a salsa beat and Gloria Estefan lends her iconic voice to the lyrics. As Manuel Avilés-Santiago has noted, the opening credits evoke nostalgia: "The visuals of the credits include a montage of images of the cast and the production team. The use of real photos of the cast and production

196   Absorption Narratives

team (e.g., weddings, graduations, social events, etc.) induces a false nostalgia of shared moments, intended to make the audience see the characters as part of a shared past" (68–69). The importance of nostalgia for both of these shows further emphasizes the importance of intergenerational exchanges that are essential for fostering gender and ethnic identifications among these characters as they come of age or remember their coming of age. The nostalgic, exuberant tones that the shows' credits establish also create a framework for disidentification. These sequences show families, ethnicities, and gender identifications that, as the episodes themselves emphasize, orient the young characters' identities but also problematize them.

Throughout these story arcs, Elena and Ari must grapple with the ways in which their families' minority cultures and mainstream hegemony define gender norms. Moreover, the seemingly feminist structures of their families – having a transgender parent or having a single mother – provide a framework in which to come to terms with their own individual identities but are also normative and hierarchical in their own ways. Even when these families' pasts are bound up in resistance and defiance of hegemonic norms, they still present generation gaps and obstacles for their young protagonists. But what is potentially radical and liberating about these stories is that they not only suggest a more optimistic future but rewrite history in a way that centres genderqueer and immigrant experiences. Yet, perhaps *Transparent* would have been even more radically inclusive had its depiction of the Pfefferman family's story not moved so hastily from Boyle Heights to the Palisades – skipping over Echo Park – but instead lingered in a space such as the Álvarez household. After all, as Franco and Kalin have reminded us, this is the legacy of Boyle Heights. And, as Archy Stallings reminds us in *Telegraph Avenue*, the Creole dream is that "you stop drawing those lines."

Epilogue: Can Fiction Unite the Ununitable?

Across the Américas, centuries of racialized memories passed down over generations bear on encounters between people and are manifest within individuals, creating syncretic spaces in which identities are constantly negotiated and renegotiated. Across the Atlantic and across the globe, chiastic relationships are created and contested among race, memory, and identity. These narratives show that individual and group identities necessarily coalesce in relation to racial Others – in many cases because the racial Other is part of the self. If Archy Stallings's Creole dream is to "stop drawing those lines," a question that remains unanswered in these pages is how we stop drawing those lines without absorbing difference. Can individuals and groups be united without eschewing the differences between them?

Chicana author Luz Alma Villanueva asks, in the context of considering Israeli–Palestinian tensions from the space of contemporary California, whether art is capable of uniting the ununitable. Her 1994 collection of short stories, *Weeping Woman: La Llorona and Other Stories*, centres predominantly on Chicanx characters in the US–Mexico borderlands. One story in the collection, "Sabra," tells of Israeli character Judith's time as an artist in residence in California, where she has a turbulent, passionate interlude with a German sculptor named Frank. During their sexual encounter, Judith is haunted by her own memory of killing a Palestinian child as part of her service in the Israeli army. Her family's experience with the Holocaust surfaces as a repressed inherited trauma in response to her intimate encounter with the German man. She has a complicated memory of fighting in the name of Israel *because of* her family's history with the Holocaust. Thus, the violence visited upon Arab Palestinians is brought into question. Within the context of a collection of short stories focused on the US–Mexico borderlands and set in California, Villanueva brings memory of German

198 Absorption Narratives

and Jewish atrocities into the living present and into conversation with the contentious debates on land rights and belonging in the context of the US–Mexico border. Villanueva creates a narrative in which Chicana self-expression and belonging in the borderlands takes into account Jewish experiences of expulsion and diaspora. "Sabra" takes into account both the need for Jewish refuge in a post-Holocaust world and the harm caused by Jewish occupation of Palestine. Villanueva not only creates an analogy between Israel–Palestine and the US–Mexico border but extends the map of the movement of memory into California as the place of convergence between the German character and the Israeli character. In this way, the author brings the Americas – specifically, California – to the fore of conversations about memory and land disputes.

Set in an idyllic space that houses writers and artists, Villanueva's story lends itself to interpretation as a reflection – perhaps even a self-aware one – of fiction's capacity to bridge differences between groups. That is, just as the artists' retreat constitutes a space in California that allows for the creation of art, the story itself seeks to create a space for reflection about specific forms of difference and the traumas and oppressions they carry along with them. When Judith and Frank meet and she suggests that they might not get along because she is from Israel, he responds, "We're artists, aren't we? Aren't artists supposed to transcend history, unite the ununitable?" (85). In posing this question to Judith, Frank seeks not to exculpate himself from any complicity with which Judith might be imputing him for being a non-Jewish German but rather to suggest that art can serve as a way for individuals who find themselves on opposite sides of a moment of history as complex as the Holocaust to find aspects of their human experiences that unite them. Once they have sex, Judith is immediately triggered and pictures the face of the Palestinian child whom she killed. She begins crying and, as Frank seeks to console her, she asks her if she can keep his diamond earring; they trade earrings and comfort one another in the space of the California artists' residence.

Within the broader context of a collection focused on Chicanx characters, "Sabra" evokes the parallels between white settler colonialism in the US that took away land from Mexico in what is now California, on the one hand, and the ongoing Israeli–Palestinian conflict on the other. Judith's reminds herself, "I am a Sabra" as she encounters Frank and as she finds herself thousands of miles away from home, haunted by both previous generations' traumatic memories of the Holocaust and by her own repressed memory of having killed others to defend Israel. Villanueva's story crafts a multilayered exploration of the ongoing significance of the Holocaust and the Israeli–Palestinian conflict not only

Epilogue: Can Fiction Unite the Ununitable? 199

for Jews but also for other oppressed groups around the world. "Sabra" provocatively questions the ways that Holocaust memory is transmitted and – oftentimes – thought of as the *sine qua non* of memory in the twentieth century through having Judith's trauma stem not from the brutality of the Holocaust but from her own acts of atrocity. In this way, the text forges a solidarity along racialized lines of Chicanx–Palestinian affinities yet also humanizes Judith and acknowledges the complexities of fighting for Israel. Villanueva thus approximates Frank's aspiration as an artist to "unite the ununitable." Now twenty years since its publication, "Sabra" remains relevant as political conversations worldwide seek to make sense of how the Israeli–Palestinian conflict relates to broader conversations of racial justice and solidarity. Villanueva's story offers particular insights into how the conflict resonates with global questions of the Holocaust and of paradigms of racial oppression. As we have seen throughout the texts discussed here, "uniting the ununitable" is a necessary endeavour that is not always feasible. The negotiations between what is united, what is absorbed, and what remains are constantly in flux and in dispute.

Two recent films took up the issue of Black–Jewish relations in New York and Los Angeles. The critically acclaimed 2019 film *Uncut Gems* – directed by Josh and Benny Safdie – centres on protagonist Howard Ratner, a middle-aged Jewish man who works in New York City's diamond district and is addicted to gambling. Ratner buys a large, rare opal from Ethiopia (the titular "uncut gem") and is convinced that auctioning the gem will save him from the financial troubles in which he finds himself due to his gambling. When Boston Celtics player Kevin Garnett enters Ratner's business and Ratner shows Garnett the opal, Garnett senses that the gem could bring him good luck, and Ratner lets him borrow it. The film begins with images of Jewish miners in Ethiopia and transitions to Ratner's daily, basketball-obsessed life in which he interacts with Kevin Garnett (played by himself) and his assistant, portrayed by Lakeith Stanfield. The film makes clear that any profit that Ratner might gain from his byzantine scheming is at the cost of Black people who are involved. To this point, in an editors' conversation in *Jewish Currents* about the film, Arielle Angel noted that "what's uncomfortable ... is the film positioning this old, pernicious Jewish character as a figure of contemporary American capitalism" ("An Unserious Man" n.p.). What the critic terms "uncomfortable" is Ratner's assimilation into contemporary capitalism. In the conversation in *Jewish Currents* about the film, once the "uncomfortable" element is mentioned, the discussion immediately turns to race. Angel states that, other than Ratner, the rest of the Jewish characters in the film "read to me as part of

200   Absorption Narratives

this newer quasi-racialized demographic – post-Soviet émigrés, Iranian Jews, the Kardashians – that's intersecting with blackness and whiteness in ways we're still trying to figure out how to talk about" ("An Unserious Man" n.p). Throughout the Americas, we are still trying to figure out how to talk about these "quasi-racialized" demographics that intersect with Blackness and whiteness. As *Uncut Gems* and the *Jewish Currents* discussion of the film make clear, these fraught intersections are inexorable from conversations about class and privilege.

In 2022, Netflix released the comedy *You People*, co-written by Jewish comedian Jonah Hill and Black comedian Kenya Barris, in which a young Jewish man and young Black woman fall in love with each other. The film was criticized for, among other things, missing the opportunity to explore the identity embodied by the film's own leading actress, Lauren London, who is Black and Jewish. (Barris has also been criticized for this same elision in his long-running television series *Black-ish* starring Black Jewish actress Tracee Ellis Ross). The film revisits early 1990s points of contention in Jewish–Black relations (a discussion of Farrakhan) as a way of creating insurmountable differences between the Black and Jewish leads. Hill and Barris's romantic comedy cannot break the formula of the genre and therefore relies on the trope of "opposites attract" and has the mother of the Jewish man and the father of the Black woman befriend each other to bring their children back together. The romantic comedy "unites the ununitable" but necessarily eschews and absorbs the differences between groups. The film suggests, still in 2022, an inability to imagine a more dynamic (and authentic) model of the relationship between Jewishness and racial alterity.

As the responses to *Uncut Gems* and *You People* show, mainstream culture lacks a capacious understanding of intersecting identities of Jewishness and race to account for the complexities of lived experiences and identities. If, as Arielle Angel noted, so many people are "still trying to figure out how to talk about" Jews of colour, it stands to reason that Hill and Barris would eschew that topic. Another film, albeit a very different type, that shows (and critiques) a static understanding of Jewish relationships with racial alterity is the 2007 Peruvian documentary *The Fire Within*, directed by filmmaker Lorry Salcedo Mitrani. The documentary examines Jews in Iquitos, Peru, a small city in the Amazonian region to which Sephardic businessmen arrived in the nineteenth century during the rubber boom. There, many had children with local Indigenous women, and their descendants today, the documentary emphasizes, have often had their Jewish identities denied to them by figures of religious authority in urban centres such as Lima. The documentary hinges on the "conversion" process through which

Epilogue: Can Fiction Unite the Ununitable? 201

these Indigenous Jews, who already self-identify as Jewish, "become" Jewish in a more formal sense. While the film did not reach a large audience and was modestly distributed, it is an important instance of representation of Jews of colour and the challenges that many Jews of colour throughout the Americas continue to face to be recognized and accepted as Jews.

Indeed, during the time that I have spent writing these pages, cultural and literary conversations have become increasingly nuanced in their account of dynamics between Jewishness and categories of racial alterity in the Americas. In July 2022, Ojibe-Jewish author David Treuer penned an opinion piece for the *New York Times*, "Adrift Between My Parents' Two Americas," in which he concludes:

> This country is a terrible one, and this country is not. This country has done its best to take and conquer and kill my Native life, and at the same time it has saved my father's life and created mine. There is a great ugliness on the land and also a great beauty. This country would and will do its worst at the same time it embodies the most nurturing habits our civilization has to offer. There is no reconciling these contradictions; they cannot be reduced or done away with. I must, *we* must, find a way to contain both. (n.p.)

Fifty-five years after Baldwin remarked on the differential meaning of the US for Black and Jewish citizens, Treuer notes that the nation remains two different places for Jewish Holocaust refugees and for Native Americans. Treuer's insistence that we "find a way to contain both" compels us to resist narratives that absorb the historical truths and lived realities of Jewish and Native American individuals.

At the same time, over the past several decades, we have also seen a plethora of narratives that have emerged to contemplate and contest the ways in which Jewishness, Indigeneity, and Blackness mutually inform one another throughout the Americas. Literature that addresses racial ventriloquism to consider these questions persists and thrives. In March 2024, Percival Everett's novel *James* was released and reimagined the character of Jim from Mark Twain's *Adventures of Huckleberry Finn*. The uproariously funny novel furthered, in a sense, the brilliant provocation of race sensibilities for which Everett became known with *Erasure* ("erasure" being a phenomenon that we might consider akin to "absorption") through racial ventriloquism. Everett inverts Twain's ventriloquism of Jim's character by representing Jim and other Black enslaved characters as speaking more like white people when no white characters are around and changing their speech to African American

202 Absorption Narratives

Vernacular English whenever white folks are around. James even gives lessons to other Black characters in how to speak in ways that make white people feel intellectually superior to them. At one point in the novel, James and Huck find themselves present for a pantomime in which two white characters – one of whom has proclaimed that James is his slave since Huck is too young to own slaves and has just referred to him as a cannibalistic "savage" from Borneo – begin reciting lines from Shakespeare. The other causes a ruckus by proclaiming, "I am a Jew. Hath not a Jew eyes" (121), quoting Shylock's lines from *The Merchant of Venice*, because those are the only lines he has memorized from Shakespeare. Cultural productions from throughout the Americas continue to provoke and prompt reflection on the basis of centuries-old tropes (the "cannibalistic" "savage" and the Shylock figure) through speaking through the racial Other.

Often, it seems that the closer film and literature come to uniting disparate categories of racial identities, the more complicated it becomes to discuss how these discrete categories and the points of overlap between them are defined. If Francisco Goldman's Flor asks, "What is it we absorb," I ask, what is it that we as readers and audience members absorb from fiction that contemplates these complicated points of contact? What is it we absorb from stories that eschew these points of contact? If there are any answers to these questions of how Jewishness bears on how race is constructed throughout the Americas, I have sought to show that these answers are to be found not within national or regional boundaries, but by reading between the lines and between geographical boundaries. For it is beyond these borders that we begin to discern the ways in which fiction might be able to unite the ununitable. These narratives remind us of the necessity to continue grappling with and reimagining the ways in which encounters between individuals and categories have informed and will continue to inform intergroup dynamics as well as self-understanding within the paradigm of centuries of coloniality.

Notes

Chapter 1

1 Earlier, in 1921, James Weldon Johnson's narrator in *Autobiography of an Ex-Colored Man* had noted that, "in the discussion of the race question the diplomacy of the Jew was something to be admired; he had the faculty of agreeing with everybody without losing his allegiance to any side. He knew that to sanction Negro oppression would be to sanction Jewish oppression and would expose him to a shot along that line from the old soldier, who stood firmly on the ground of equal rights and opportunity for all men" (89). For Johnson's narrator, it is wise for the Jewish character to oppose Jewish oppression because it is understood to part and parcel of Black oppression. Catherine Rottenberg notes in her reading of the novel that, "what the narrator does not reveal is that the smoking compartment is, undoubtedly, for whites only ... the Jew is present in this scene and thus seems to be accepted as white ... His 'Jewishness,' which he does not attempt to conceal, seems to stand in the way. the narrator, in stark contrast, must only not only conceal is 'Blackness,' but is also silenced; he watches and listens as 'the Negro' is discussed. Moreover, he would not even be physically present if it were not for his ability to 'pass'" (309–10).

2 Because *The Plot Against America* does not explicitly engage with Jewish–Native encounters, I do not discuss the novel at length in this monograph. Nonetheless, the fact that the novel is concerned with Jewish "absorption" into mainstream US culture reveals the importance of this concept as a mechanism of forced assimilation in the broader context of anti-Semitism and Nazism. Cord Jefferson's 2023 film *American Fiction*, adapted from Percival Everett's 2001 novel *Erasure*, references *The Plot Against America* in a tongue-and-cheek reference to academic discussions about race in literature. Protagonist Monk Ellison, a Black creative writing professor, defends himself to his colleagues against accusations from white students that his

204   Notes to pages 4–18

discussions of race offended them, during which one colleague points out that Monk had previously asked a German student whether his family were Nazis when teaching *The Plot Against America*.

3 I am indebted to Lewis Gordon for the term "Jewish investment in whiteness." Gordon uses the term to talk about the Anti-Defamation League's downplaying of the anti-whiteness as anti-Semitism: "They're against Jewish investment in whiteness. So, an anti-white language is being translated into an anti-Jewish language. And this leads to another problem, because it leads to, despite those Jews saying that they're not investing in a racial identity, their Jewish identity is about religion, nevertheless, their membership in American society depended on a racial identity" ("Re-thinking Black-Jewish Relations").

4 Elsewhere, playwright OyamO creates a Jewish character in his 1995 play *I Am a Man* who arrives in Memphis during the days leading up to Martin Luther King Jr.'s assassination there in an effort to help the garbage collectors' union's negotiations with the mayor. This character rejects the mayor's attempt to placate the Black union leader by quoting William Faulkner's 1953 *Ebony* piece "If I Were a Negro," in which Faulkner expounds what he would do if he were a Black man in the South at that time. Faulkner inhabits the voice of a Black man and OyamO's character cites Faulkner by repeating this ventriloquism. OyamO's play – while not part of the corpus that I study here – thus creates a *mise-en-abime* of ventriloquism between Black and white (one of them Jewish) characters. The fact that OyamO and Smith both use Jewish voices in their plays highlights the necessity of imagining other voices to understand narratives of belonging and racial identities in the literary imagination of the Americas.

5 Throughout *The Signifying Monkey*, Gates makes several references to cultural anthropologist Melville Herskovits, the child of Jewish immigrants to Ohio and a Ph.D. student of Franz Boas, whose work on African influences on African American life has long been understood to be fundamental to African American Studies.

6 In his 2016 book *Confluence Narratives*, Antonio Luciano de Andrade Tosta studies a corpus similar to the one I study here (that is, inter-American and more contemporary, whereas Sommer focuses on nineteenth and early-twentieth-century Latin American texts), including a chapter on Jewish fiction from Argentina and Brazil. *Confluence Narratives* argues that these texts, rather than "foundational" fictions, are "formational" fictions because of their insistence on the maintenance of difference.

7 The cultural model of "civilization" versus "barbarism" that Friedenberg notes here comes from nineteenth-century Argentine author and politician Domingo Faustino Sarmiento, whose work *Facundo* is subtitled

Notes to pages 18–24 205

"Civilization and barbarism" and is tied to a political and cultural project of welcoming European immigrants to Argentina as a way of whitening the nation. Sarmiento is one of the figures whom Juliet Hooker studies in her monograph *Theorizing Race in the Americas* (2019).

8 Tuck and Yang characterize Cooper's novels as narratives of "adoption," which they equate to absorption: "the easy absorption, adoption, transposing of decolonization is yet another form of settler appropriation" (3).

9 We may also think of adjacency in the context of human geography. Human geographer Doreen Massey advocates for "geographies of responsibility" in which, in her discussion of London, "Londoners have begun to assume an identity, discursively, within the self-conception of the city, which is precisely around mixity rather than a coherence derived from common roots" (6). Similarly, Ash Amin has advocated for what he terms a politics of propinquity, an approach that advocates for "a politics of place that ... makes for a vision and a set of political priorities established out of an open but fair power-play between agonistic actors and their competing and often conflicting claims" (39). These geographical conceptualizations of identity and place push our critical understandings of the connection between place and identity by foregrounding difference so as to focus on the ethical relationships between different groups and the place they inhabit. This critical understanding of human geography is fundamental to the concepts of racial mixture that have long characterized understandings of race throughout Latin America to the point that they organize national identity. In turn, I seek to bring this paradigm of difference to bear on my discussions of English-language and North American texts as well.

10 In his 1985 discussion of Du Bois and "the illusion of race," Anthony Appiah noted, "Race, we all assume, is, like all other concepts, constructed by metaphor and metonymy; it stands in, metonymically, for the Other; it bears the weight, metaphorically, of other forms of difference. ... Talk of 'race' is particularly distressing for those of us who take culture seriously. For, where race works ... it works as an attempt at a metonym for culture" (35–6).

11 Graff Zivin is mindful of differences between North American and Latin American Jewish experiences: "Within the context of Latin America, not only do Jews possess distinct histories relative to their European and North American counterparts, but they also come to occupy new spaces within the cultural landscape on a symbolic level" (2).

12 As Diego von Vacano argues, it is often speculated that the figure of Fray Bartolomé de las Casas – the instigator of the so-called Black Legend through his creation of terms and concepts for racial categorizations in colonial Latin America – had Jewish origins, a biographical detail that,

206 Notes to pages 24–7

for von Vacano, points to the cross-pollination between race and religion stemming back to the emergence of racial categories. For von Vacano, the ambiguities of las Casas's lineage – and the inevitability of conversations about racial origins and morality as a way to ascertain any individual's lineage in the context of the Inquisition, created "a context where nascent racial characteristics such as blood lineage were thought to have moral implications" (31). Put another way, from their inception, categories of racial difference in Latin America have been bound up in preoccupations about morality and religiosity. The very figure attributed with the emergence of race and Empire – and the points of mutual imbrication between the two – is himself bound up in these interstices.

13 The complexities of racial hybridity and the implications of racial mixture vis-à-vis Jewishness have been studied more in Caribbean contexts than elsewhere in the Americas. For this reason, aside from my consideration of Obejas's novel, I do not explore Caribbean works as the focus of my analysis here. The editors of the volume *Caribbean Jewish Crossings: Literary History and Creative Practice* (Charlottesville, VA: University of Virginia Press, 2020) frame their endeavour by first offering literary examples that invoke the Holocaust as a way of addressing Black experiences in the Caribbean. Both *Calypso Jews* and *Caribbean Jewish Crossings* take account of Black–Jewish encounters in the Caribbean as a way of decentring the US in conversations on Black–Jewish relations in the Americas. Similarly, I seek here to recalibrate this critical understanding further through a critical comparison of North, Central, and South American works of fiction.

14 In *Revolutionary Visions*, I provided the following précis of Jameson's model of allegory: "Fredric Jameson's now rather infamous model of Third World allegory is put forth in 'Third-World Literature in the Era of Multinational Capitalism.' Jameson explains there the postmodern affinity for allegory in its capacity to celebrate discontinuities: 'The allegorical spirit is profoundly discontinuous, a matter of breaks and heterogeneities, of the multiple polysemia of the dream rather than the homogeneous representation of the symbol'" (73). I avoid this critical approach because of the problems that many responses to Jameson have evoked in doing so (most notably Aijaz Ahmad). Jean Franco responded to Jameson stating that "not only is 'the nation' a complex and much contested term, but in contemporary Latin American criticism it is no longer the inevitable framework for either political or cultural products" (130). Additionally, as Robert Tally recapitulates in a reference entry in *Global South Studies*, "Jameson's intent, if not necessarily his outcome, was to grapple with the emergence of a Global South that could maintain itself as qualitatively different from the metropolitan powers of the age of imperialism in the context of an increasingly dominant system of globalization. The controversy

Notes to pages 27–32   207

over Jameson's intervention into Third-World literature thus becomes a key moment in the critical apprehension of the processes and effects of globalization with respect to literature, politics, and cultural studies more broadly" (4).

15 As I discuss further elsewhere in this monograph, Rothberg's model of competitive memory discusses so-called "competition" between two experiences of oppression – namely, the Atlantic slave trade and the Holocaust. In the summer of 2019, Congresswoman Alexandria Ocasio-Cortez faced a great deal of controversy when she referred to detention centres on the US border as "concentration camps." (This was, it is worth noting, a few months after she announced that she had discovered she herself had Sephardic ancestors). The United States Holocaust Memory Museum issued a statement in which they cited a Holocaust survivor living in the US who took issue with the analogy. A group of academics – most of whom specialize in Jewish studies (myself included) – responded with an open letter noting the importance of analogy for the study of history. For his part, Vine Deloria critiqued anthropologist "Mr. Farb," who claimed that genocide had "civilized" Native Americans by drawing a comparison to the genocide against Jews. Deloria notes, "Farb's basic assumption is that somehow Indians have risen to civilized heights by being the victims of four centuries of systemic genocide. Under these assumptions to European Jews should be the most civilized people on Earth from their graduate course in gas ovens given by Eichmann" (67).

16 Figueroa's provocative discussion of destierro's bourgeois and colonial underpinnings calls into question how we might grapple critically with experiences of Jewish exile in the cultural imaginary of the Americas, particularly when contrasted – as it often is in the works that I analyse here – with Black and Indigenous communities' experiences of being uprooted. French Jewish critic Maurice Blanchot has noted that exile is often the mode through which Jewish subjects come into contact with the world around them and understand themselves as citizens of the places where they seek refuge. Blanchot submits, "The words exodus and exile indicate a positive relation with exteriority, whose exigency invites us not to be content with what is proper to us (that is, with our power to assimilate everything, to identify everything, to bring everything back to our I)" (127).

17 Since Spitzer's memoir is not a work of fiction, I do not offer a sustained close reading of his text; my discussion centres on works of fiction.

18 In keeping with Anzaldúa's deliberate use of both English and Spanish in her original text, I have not translated into English the words she wrote in Spanish.

19 In a inter-American approach similar to the one that Taylor takes and that I take here, political theorist Juliet Hooker takes into consideration José

208 Notes to pages 32–43

Vasconcelos alongside Frederick Douglass, W.E.B. Du Bois, and Domingo Faustino Sarmiento on the grounds that they are all "hemispheric thinkers" because, "they (to differing degrees) looked to the other America as a source of inspiration or contrast, and engaged with political or philosophical problems central to the Americas, such as the legacy of slavery, mestizaje (racial mixture), multiracial democracy, and so on" (2). Hooker's intervention also insists that, rather than comparison, juxtaposition is a generative method to hemispheric thinking on race. In a similarly comparative approach, each of my chapters pairs texts from Latin America with texts from North America to generate a side-by-side understanding of how Jewishness bears on racialization throughout the Americas. As Anzaldúa and Taylor also do with models that absorb difference, I seek to disaggregate what has been absorbed by models of mixture.

Chapter 2

1 Native American identities in *Northern Exposure* serve more as a relief against which to consider Jewish alterity than as an identity category in their own right, despite the variety of Native American characters included in the show. As Sara R. Horowitz's reading of another episode underscores, "one's identity as a Jew travels wherever one goes, melding into the American landscape while still preserving its distinctiveness" (60). Fleischman's Jewishness is melded into this landscape and, paradoxically, preserves its distinctiveness, particularly when Jewishness comes into contact with Indigeneity.

2 I would be remiss not to note here that Elaine Miles often questioned and rejected the dialogue that had been written for her character. Miles also gained considerable notoriety among the Native American community in the 1990s for her portrayal of Whirlwind. Her influential role in the show and in early 1990s popular culture in the US thus has a particular relationship to the model of Jewish ventriloquism. Marilyn serves largely as a foil character for Joel Fleischman's anxieties about belonging in the US, but the actress and the character alike also push back against a role in which she serves predominantly as a mouthpiece for the white Jewish protagonist. In their discussion of *Northern Exposure*, Diana George and Susan Sanders note that even the show's seemingly progressive elements in some of its representations of Native American characters "are still set within the context of network television, and as such are part of a discourse which in the end tends to serve dominant ideologies" (444).

3 Perera's novel centres on an upper-class child's experiences in 1950s Guatemala. Like Perera's novel, Luis Argueta's 1994 film *El silencio de Neto /*

Neto's Silence also tells the story of an upper-class, non-Indigenous child protagonist as he experiences coming of age against the backdrop of political turmoil in Guatemala, specifically the 1954 coup that ousted President Jacobo Árbenz. In light of the works' shared focus on upper-class, non-Indigenous protagonists, we may understand a certain equivalence between this social status and a lack of political consciousness, a wilful silence of sorts – one that will also pervade my analysis of Halfon's *Tomorrow We Never Did Talk About It* later in this chapter. As Georgia Seminet posits in her interpretation of Argueta's film, "Neto is implausible as a representative for the disenfranchised sectors of society that were/are seeking, indeed fighting for, a greater voice in Guatemalan politics" (54). If, in Seminet's reading of Argueta's film, Neto is "implausible as a representative," this implausibility as an authentic representative for the struggle of disenfranchised sectors of Guatemalan society is complicated when we consider films centred on light-skinned Jewish children in Guatemala. *Neto's Silence* shares with *Rites* a similar dynamic between Indigenous domestic workers and wealthy, light-skinned children. Neto's family maid tells Neto that in Guatemala everyone is Indigenous, to which Neto responds that he is not Indigenous. Argueta's film posits a stark separation between Neto and the rest of the nation along ethnic lines. In light of the contrast between Neto and the maid in this exchange, his social class also sets him apart. Like Perera's narrator, Neto is upper class and reckons with his coming-of-age process that is likewise punctuated by Guatemala's political conflict. Yet Neto is not Jewish; classism and colorism do set Neto apart from the domestic workers in Neto's family. Such accounts evoke the points of contact between ethnicity and social class that characterize the Ladino sector of Guatemalan society.

4 The novel also anticipates Mexican Costa Rican filmmaker Guita Schyfter's 1993 film *Novia que te vea* (*Like a Bride*), in which two young women – one Sephardic and one Ashkenazi – befriend one another in 1960s Mexico as college students and recount their shared experiences of being excluded from playing with other children on the playground because, the other children shouted at them, they "killed Christ." In Schyfter's film, the same characters in their college years feel similarly Othered as they observe an Easter procession on campus in which the Jews, rather than the Romans, are depicted as having killed Christ. The character who laments being depicted in this way as a Jew goes on to become an archaeologist who studies Indigenous cultures in Mexico as a way of feeling a stronger sense of connection to the country in which she was born. Relationships between Jews and Indigenous characters have figured as a subtle plot point in other Mexican films. The tragicomic film *Cinco días sin Nora / Nora's Will* (2008) includes as one of its funniest moments a scene in which Fabiana,

210 Notes to pages 47–61

the family's Indigenous housekeeper, places a rosary on the defunct body of Jewish Nora in hopes that her soul will be saved. Likewise, the similarly themed *Morirse está en hebreo / My Mexican Shiva* (2007) depicts the matriarch's heated encounter with the domestic staff whom she scolds for using the same knife for dairy and meat, informing them that to mix the two is a sin as she furiously scrapes the tainted food into the trash. The Indigenous housekeeper replies that wasting food is also a sin. In these films, the religious and cultural differences between Jews and Indigenous people are brought to light.

5 As I have studied elsewhere, both Burman's and Jodorowsky's films emphasize circumcision as a marker of difference. *El abrazo partido* shows its main character, Ariel, quip to the rabbi that his birth certificate – which he needs to be able to prove Polish ancestry to emigrate from Argentina – is nicked on the corner, "like the bris" that the same rabbi performed on him as an infant. As I argued in my reading of Jodorowsky's (2014) film, Jewish circumcision is patently racialized in contrast to mestizo Chileans in that film. The film's main character, Alejandro, masturbates on the beach next to his classmates, and all of the boys who have darker skin than his have bananas between their legs, whereas Alejandro's phallus is in the form of a mushroom, provoking the other boys' ridicule. The film's visual language couples difference between Jewish whiteness and Indigeneity in line with the difference of being circumcised or not.

6 Alcalá's novel is not the first work of fiction to depict a Mexican Jew who expresses identification with the Tarahumara: Schyfter's film *Like a Bride* includes a scene in which its protagonist Rifke asserts that "great Mexican family" is inclusive of cultural minorities; she enumerates "the otomís, the coras, the Tarahumaras, the huicholes, the náhautls, the Jews." The character lists these groups to state that they all belong in Mexico as a way of responding to an anti-Semitic character who condescendingly Others her as a Jewish woman in 1960s Mexico City. The same character goes on to study archaeology and Indigenous populations in Mexico after learning that many of the nation's Indigenous communities, like her own family from Germany, immigrated to Mexico City from other places. As I have argued elsewhere, Rifke's description here of the "great Mexican family" in a way that accounts for the particularities of the groups she names also tacitly contests the notion of Vasconcelos's cosmic race by advocating for the maintenance of difference rather than its absorption (Pridgeon 2021).

7 The "Lost Tribes of Israel" refers to the ten Hebrew tribes who took possession of the Promised Land, Canaan, after Moses's death and were later assimilated into other groups. Native Americans are sometimes included among groups believed to be part of the ten lost tribes.

Notes to pages 63–8   211

8 The Lindbergh reference also recalls Schyfter's film *Novia que te vea*, which opens with images of its Turkish protagonist's parents arriving in Mexico City to a train station flanked with posters of Charles Lindbergh, a visual reminder that the Americas both welcomed and Othered Jews.

9 Eppelsheimer notes that Fidelis's (and later Eva's and Delphine's) daily life of making sausages recalls the popular maxim of not letting people see how sausages or laws are made.

10 Deborah Lea Madsen's "On Subjectivity and Survivance" also studies *The Crown of Columbus* alongside *The Heirs of Columbus*, arguing that Erdrich and Dorris's novel is a narrative of survival, whereas Vizenor's text is a "narrative of survivance," in line with the author's own model of survivance "in the context of and desirability of this notion of selfhood in a Native American Indian context" (1).

11 While Halfon never names Guatemala directly, we can be all but certain that *Tomorrow We Never Did Talk About It* is set in Guatemala because of the references to the 1976 earthquake at the novel's beginning and the increased paramilitary activity in 1981 as the government forces sieged guerrilla strongholds. Both are events in keeping with Guatemalan history.

12 In her recent reading of *Tomorrow We Never Did Talk About It*, Magdalena Perkowska notes that these questions "revelan que este niño ya ha asimilado la distinción racista y clasista entre ladinos e indios, entre los que son sus pares y los otros. Sin saberlo, no obstante, toca con sus preguntas una herida histórica y social que el padre no puede o no quiere explicar" ("reveal that this boy has already assimilated the racist and classist distinction between *Ladinos* and *indios*, between those who are his peers and Others. Without knowing, nonetheless, his questions touch on a social and historic wound that his father either cannot or does not want to explain to him," my trans, 608). Perkowska's interpretation of the novel focuses on childhood memory and not on elements of race and ethnicity. This conclusion takes for granted that the narrator and his family, as Jews, readily form part of the category of Ladino, a notion that I seek to consider here.

13 Ilan Stavans notes in his afterword to the English short story version of "Tomorrow We Never Did Talk About It" that "the fact that they are going to the United States makes clear where their loyalties are" (loc. 275). That is, the family is against the guerrillas' struggle. However, the narrator does not comprehend – much less articulate – how his family fits into the political conflict.

14 While Marianne Hirsch's notions of postmemory related to the Holocaust have been widely embraced in critical considerations of political disappearance in the Southern Cone, the intricacies of memory within Jewish populations during moments of political conflict have not been sufficiently theorized.

212   Notes to pages 69–70

15 Salvadorean author Horacio Castellanos Moya's *Insensatez* (2004) is set in a country that is most likely Guatemala (but whose name, like in Halfon's novel, is never actually uttered), where the narrator works on a report that is most likely the REMHI (*Informe sobre la Recuperación de la Memoria Histórica*, "Recovery of Historical Memory") report. The bishop overseeing the human rights report is murdered, as happened in Guatemala to Bishop Juan Gerardi, the subject of Francisco Goldman's non-fiction *The Art of Political Murder* (2007). Rey Rosa's *El material humano/Human Matter* (2009) also recounts its narrator's experiences working in the archives for the human rights commission; the author addresses issues of authoritarianism more figuratively in his science-fiction novel *Cárcel de árboles* (1997). These authors deal with issues of historical memory – specifically, the silences and omissions that exist in the transmission of memory – but, unlike Halfon's work, do so from an adult perspective rather than from that of a child. Moreover, while Castellanos Moya and Rey Rosa were both almost immediately embraced and celebrated academically, Halfon has yet to receive significant attention within literary criticism, despite his above-mentioned editorial accolades. At age fifty, Halfon is over a decade younger than Castellanos Moya or Rey Rosa; while not a substantial age difference, we may consider Halfon to be the harbinger of a new, younger generation of authors.
16 While we want to avoid conflating the narrator and the author, the two often seem interchangeable due to Halfon's use of autofiction. Autofiction is also prevalent throughout Halfon's works in the expansions and additions that he creates when translating works from one language to another. This is the case for *Tomorrow We Never Did Talk About It*, whose English version "Tomorrow We Never Did Talk About It" is a short story that consists only of the last section of the novel.
17 In the way of films: *Voces inocentes* (Mexico, 2004), *Machuca* (dir. Andrés Wood, Chile, 2004), *Infancia clandestina* (dir. Benjamín Avila, Argentina, 2011), *Los rubios* (dir. Albertina Carri, Argentina, 2002), and *O ano em que meus pais sairam da feria* (dir. Cao Hamburger, Brazil, 2006). Novels include Laura Alcoba's *La casa de los conejos* (Argentina, 2006), Alejandro Zambra's *Formas de volver a casa* (Chile, 2011), and Andrés Neuman's *Una vez Argentina* (Argentina, 2004). Both Hamburger's film and Neuman's novel, in their explorations of childhood, focus specifically on Jewish topics vis-à-vis Brazil and Argentina's political struggles of the 1970s. *Machuca*, for its part, was co-written by the director Andrés Wood and the Jewish Chilean author Roberto Brodsky. Brodsky also wrote the 2007 novel *Bosque quemado*, which, like Halfon's novel, recounts its childhood narrator's exile from his home country after the military takes over.

Notes to pages 70–6   213

18 See, for example, Luis Martín Cabrera's analysis of recent Argentine fiction in which the younger generation presents a "betrayed inheritance" of their parents' political legacy.

19 If we consider the broader panorama of twenty-first century Latin American cultural production that draws from the childhood perspective to explore issues of political conflict, Halfon's novel also closely resembles *Machuca* (2004) in its depiction of an upper-class boy's experiences during the days leading up to Chile's military coup in 1973. Unlike *Machuca*, however, Halfon's narrator sees violence and death only obliquely, whereas *Machuca* centres on a close friendship between two young boys, one the upper-class student of a parochial school and the other the inhabitant of one of Santiago's shantytowns whose home is decimated and who disappears. The novel's lack of development of a similar storyline is likely due to the snippet-like structure of the novel, which, as I mentioned previously, is marked throughout by silences and omissions.

20 Halfon treats anti-Semitism and Nazism more directly in his novel *El boxeador polaco / The Polish Boxer* (Bellevue, 2008).

21 Perkowska also places *Tomorrow We Never Did Talk About It* in dialogue with recent Southern Cone novels dealing with childhood memory. Argentine novelist Patricio Pron's recent novel *El espíritu de mis padres sigue subiendo en la lluvia*, for example, also focuses on silences and the breakdowns in the transmission of memory. Whereas Halfon's narrator's father breaks his promise to discuss the conflict with him tomorrow, Pron's narrator's father lies unconscious in a coma for most of the novel's diegesis, likewise impeding a pending conversation about what took place during a moment of political upheaval. Geoffrey Maguire concludes his analysis of Pron's novel: "the protagonist ... exercises his right to creatively account for the fissures in his own past by means of a process which is posited as entirely justifiable when the familial stories one inherits are fragmentary, incomplete, and objectively unknowable" (225). In this vein, Halfon uses silences and the foreclosure of the possibility of resolution via one's parents' discursive interventions. In this sense, we are reminded of Arias's assertion that recent Central American fiction often evinces a lack of collective memory, in this case – like in Pron's novel – through explicit mentions of the breakdown in transmission of family history.

22 Levinson does not pay much attention to either Brodsky or his narrator's Jewish identity in her analysis of the novel.

23 While this child may be *mestizo*, the fact that the narrator refers to him this way strongly suggests that he does not belong to the category of Ladino to which the narrator's childhood friends – who live in fancy houses and attend the same school as he – undoubtedly belong. When mentioning these

214 Notes to pages 76–127

friends, categories of race and ethnicity are absent, whereby we surmise that this child is darker and likely would not pass as Ladino.

Chapter 3

1 Argentine author Ricardo Feierstein's 1994 novel *Mestizo*, mentioned in the introduction, is also a detective novel and uses the term "Mestizo" to refer to Jewish Argentine hybridity.

2 In a similar vein, Cuban American literary critic Gustavo Pérez Firmat considers his own and others' "life on the hyphen" in line with Ortiz's transculturation, putting forth his own thinking of "biculturation" in which "the two cultures achieve a balance that makes it difficult to distinguish between the dominant and subordinate culture" (5). Pérez Firmat himself acknowledges that the perhaps overly optimistic implications of his model might be perceived as assimilationist. In this regard, the hyphen, I submit, is another form of absorbing parts into a whole, akin to a such model as cosmic race (a comparison that Pérez Firmat himself later makes).

3 Curiously, Goldman spells "Anne Hunt" with an "e" in *The Long Night of White Chickens* and "Ann Hunt" without in *Monkey Boy*.

Chapter 4

1 The novel was adapted to a film just two years after its publication. While I am not primarily interested in focusing on the adaptation, I mention it briefly for the racial implications of the casting choices. As a young man, Coleman is portrayed by biracial actor Wentworth Miller. Curiously, rather than a Black or Jewish actor, Anthony Hopkins portrayed Coleman Silk in his older years in the film version. In this way, the film perpetuated a long-standing problem of whitewashing in film adaptations, in which literary characters of colour are portrayed by white actors in film adaptations. This whitewashing of a character who is Black or, if one thinks of Coleman Silk's later passing as Jewish, the "gentilewashing" (if I may) of this character might be thought of as a visual counterpart of ventriloquism, in which white faces take on the experience and subjectivity of non-white characters. One character who remains racially unchanged from the novel to the film adaptation is Coleman Silk's mother, portrayed by none other than the actress-playwright Anna Deavere Smith, whose ideas about ventriloquism between Black and Jewish identities I mentioned in the introduction and will address further in chapter 4. The actress delivers a powerful performance that, like in *Fires in the Mirror*, evokes the impassioned complexities of Black–Jewish negotiations. The film casts Mili Avital, an Israeli actress, in the role of young Iris.

Notes to pages 127–78   215

2 As Jennifer Glaser argues, "Critical accounts of *The Human Stain* often lose sight of the fact that Roth's novel is not only a novel about race but also one about literary history and the Jewish academic within the multiracial academy" (loc. 2441).
3 Dragulescu also takes account of Du Boisian double consciousness in Coleman Silk's character development.
4 Roth's open letter to Wikipedia makes note of the fact that the word "passing" does not ever appear in *The Human Stain*.
5 Glaser notes that "Silk can say things that Roth can't: the most vociferous critiques of the multicultural university come from Silk's mouth. While the narrator Zuckerman clearly blames the college administration for his friend's downfall, he, like Roth himself, ironically deflects responsibility for his criticism" (loc. 2510).
6 Jonathan Freedman interprets Leni as "the reverse of Coleman Silk: a Jew who passes for a Levantine or South American as a way of denying her identity as a white woman" (210).

Chapter 5

1 For Rothberg, "in essaying to create a map contoured by relationships of heterogeneity, Du Bois removes Holocaust memory (and African American life) from the respective risks of stultification and banalization attendant upon hyperbolic discourses of uniqueness or similarity" (121).
2 My discussion of Washington's performance is based on my viewing of the play at the Signature Theatre on December 8, 2019.
3 Interestingly, the father of Coleman Silk in *The Human Stain* was also a Pullman porter. As his sister tells Nathan Zuckerman, their father's occupation as a porter had a great deal to do with his interest in language and literature that he fostered in his children,

Chapter 6

1 Whereas *Transparent* has already ended its run – replete with a fifth season in the form of a musical in which Ari comes out as non-binary – *One Day at a Time* is still producing new episodes. (At the time of this writing the show is in between its fourth and fifth seasons). The show has changed platforms from Netflix to Pop Network to CBS. The episodes on which I focus were aired on Netflix with each season released as a whole, akin to *Transparent*'s streaming on Amazon. According to del Río and Moran, this format allows the show to dedicate more careful detail to individual characters breaking ground in representation of Latinx characters. They submit, "*One Day at a Time* offers a potential change of course for the general

216 Notes to pages 178–9

market representation of Latinidad, one that is specific in its cultural logic, working against the flattening of difference, and both critically acclaimed and renewed by Netflix" (6–7). While still maintaining many of the norms of sitcom television and of hegemonic US culture, these shows certainly push past many of the boundaries of television formats.

2 Latinx communities in Boyle Heights have been depicted in the recent series *Gentefied* as well as in *Vida*. *Vida* emphasizes the points of contact between sexuality and Latinidad. Similar to my consideration of the bat mitzvah and quinceañera in queer contexts, the show's third season includes an episode in which character Marcos has a "double quinceañera" for his thirtieth birthday – dubbed a "queerceañera" by the show's characters. The film *Quinceañera* is set in Echo Park and studies the Latinx rite of passage in that neighbourhood. Sociologist Bernard Beck has offered a comparative reading of the exuberant bar/bat mitzvah culture in *Keeping Up with the Steins* in contrast with the more solemn depictions of the quinceañera in *Quinceañera*.

3 One exception is in the premiere episode of season 3. While working in a call centre, Maura receives a call of distress from a Black caller, and goes in search of them in South Los Angeles, where she attempts to speak in Spanish to the Latinx store workers in a mall to help find the caller. Yet, as Horvat notes, this moment "portrays the character as almost hyperbolically incapable of navigating any terrain except the one in which the show normally takes place" (469).

4 Deborah Dash Moore noted that, in the postwar years, "American Jews consciously narrowed their collective boundaries, redefining what it meant to be Jewish" (19). Insofar as this narrowing included racial boundaries, the postwar US to which the Pfeffermans immigrated consisted of Jewish communities that were increasingly avowing whiteness as a way of shedding Otherness in order to come to be accepted as part of middle-class society. For her part, in *How Jews Became White Folks*, anthropologist Karen Brodkin examines her own Jewish family – specifically, her immigrant grandmother's embrace of racist language and attitudes to refer to Black people – and concludes, drawing from Toni Morrison, that her grandmother's racism shows that "one could become an American by asserting one's own white superiority over African Americans" (19).

5 For the first four seasons, this character's name is "Ali," and they are female-identified, yet at the end of the fourth season their mother informs their siblings that they are "not trans, but not comfortable being a woman," and in the fifth season their name is "Ari." I use the name Ari and the gender-neutral pronouns they/them/theirs to refer to this character.

Notes to pages 180–3   217

6 In season 3, episode 2, Ari is teaching a course on gender and sexuality in which they focus on their own family's past in the sexual freedom of Weimar Germany and proclaims that "Berlin between the two World Wars was a much freer place than America is today." They ask their students, "How many of you have had the ominous feeling that your very essence is taboo to those around you?" and add, "so the Jewish people have this escape legacy." They thus reclaim the condition of marginalization that compelled Jewish diaspora.

7 Verdín and Camacho submit, "Since the need to differentiate from Whites or Blacks has not been as great in the 21st century, the meaning ascribed to the quinceañera tradition evolved to reflect the Hispanic family's changing minority position and subsequent expectations" (190).

8 Funk and Funk submit, "Ultimately, the 'coming out' narrative rendered in American television since the 1990s has been used to tell cisgender people that trans* people are essentially the same as they. This sameness rhetoric renders gender performance and gender differences invisible. This 'gender blind' ideology, however, can be just as damaging as the 'color blind' ideology that allows aversive racism to flourish" (897).

9 Understood as "the 'spontaneous' consent given by the great masses of the population to the general direction imposed on social life by the dominant fundamental group; this consent is 'historically' caused by the prestige (and consequent confidence) which the dominant group enjoys because of its position and function in the world of production" (Gramsci 12).

10 Similarly, in "The Epistemology of the Console," Lynne Joyrich asks, "Is there a way to 'think TV' without thinking just like it, a way to understand how we literally 'think through' its epistemological forms without only reproducing the forms of this mass-reproduced medium?" (17).

11 Similarly, José Quiroga noted in his 2000 book *Tropics of Desire*, "Not content to remain within a world defined by categories, many Latino American works are not so interested in the violence of identity but in its negotiations" (159).

12 In the first episode of the second season of *One Day at a Time*, Elena realizes that she has never been the object of discrimination, unlike her brother who is disparaged for being Latinx. (On a field trip, another child yells at him, "Go back to your country.") She asks, "Wait, am I passing?" when Penelope and Lydia point out that she and her brother are, in Penelope's words, "different shades."

13 Funk and Funk discuss Maura's coming out in *Transparent* in terms of Judith Butler's notion of dispossession.

14 This exchange anticipates a moment in the second season of the show in which Ari's professor/love interest, Leslie (portrayed by actor Cherry

218   Notes to pages 183–7

Jones), admonishes Maura for her sexist dismissal of women's and gender studies as a field of academic enquiry before her transition.

15 This element of subtle yet often present patriarchal authority with which Maura as a character continues to be vested in order for the show to work as television comedy finds a parallel in the fact that a cisgender actor portrayed Maura for the first four seasons. Damien Riggs notes, referring to Tambor's portrayal of Maura, that "it is important to keep in mind that the positive reception of the series perhaps tells us more about the terms on which transgender people are offered space within the media, rather than necessarily reflecting a wholesale shift in public attitudes" ("Does Transgender Reality Really Shine Through in *Transparent*?") For his part, Jack Halberstam notes that "the show seems to orient too much to a straight audience."

16 Rosenberg interprets this moment of the episode: "And here we have the conflation of the sexual and spiritual, as Mort is forced to do two things he's incapable of doing: be a believing Jew who affirms the importance of this spiritual rite of passage and become the 'heroic man' who can overcome the will of a capricious adolescent daughter and 'save the day'" (82)

17 The siblings' reactions here anticipate the comments they will later make to one another at the end of season 4 when they suspect Ari is transitioning to become non-binary. While floating in the Dead Sea on a family trip to Israel, Maura tells the rest of the family that Ari "is not trans. She's just not comfortable being a woman," to which their sister responds proclaiming, "She's a they!" Their brother responds to speculate that Ari is not there with the rest of the family because they are taking some time alone to explore their gender, "which would be very they," and their sister adds, "It's so them!"

Works Cited

Alcalá, Kathleen. *Spirits of the Ordinary: A Tale of Casas Grandes*. Harvest Books, 1998.

Aldama, Arturo J. *Disrupting Savagism: Chicana/o, Mexican Immigrant, and Native American Struggles for Self-Representation*. Duke University Press, 2001.

Alonso, María. "Marvellous Syncretism in Kathleen Alcalá's Trilogy about the Sonoran Desert." *ES: Revista de Filología Inglesa*, vol. 32. 2011, pp. 7–25.

Amin, Ash. "Regions Unbound: Towards a New Politics of Place." *Geografiska Annaler. Series B, Human Geography*, vol. 86, no. 1, 2004, pp. 33–44.

Andrews, George Reid. "Brazilian Racial Democracy, 1900–90: An American Counterpoint." *Journal of Contemporary History*, vol. 31, no. 3, 1996, pp. 483–507.

Antebi, Susan. "Renegotiating Corporeality and Alterity: Carnal Inscription as Jewishness in David Toscana's 'Santa María Del Circo' and Mario Vargas Llosa's 'El Hablador.'" *Hispania*, vol. 88, no. 2, 2005, pp. 267–77.

Anzaldúa, Gloria. *Borderlands: The New Mestiza = La Frontera*. Aunt Lute Books, 2012.

Appiah, Anthony. "The Uncompleted Argument: Du Bois and the Illusion of Race." *Critical Inquiry*, vol. 12, no. 1, 1985, pp. 21–37.

Argueta, Luis, dir. *Neto's Silence / The Silence of Neto*. Maya Media, 1994.

Arias, Arturo. "Post-identidades post-nacionales: Transformaciones en la constitución de las subjetividades globalizadas." *Revista de Crítica Literaria Latinoamericana*, vol. 35, no. 69, 2009, pp. 135–52.

– *Taking Their Word: Literature and the Signs of Central America*. University of Minnesota Press, 2007.

Avilés-Santiago, Manuel G. "'This Is It!' [Is It?]: The Marketing of Nostalgia on Netflix's *One Day at a Time*." *Journal of Latin American Communication Research*, vol. 7, no. 1–2, 2019, pp. 60–78.

Bakhtin, Mikhail M.. *Dialogic Imagination: Four Essays*. Trans. Michael Holquist. University of Texas Press, 1981.

220   Works Cited

Baldwin, James. *Negroes Are Anti-Semitic Because They're Anti-White*. 1967,
Retrieved from https://archive.nytimes.com/www.nytimes.com/books
/98/03/29/specials/baldwin-antisem.html.

Bauman, Zygmunt. *Modernity and the Holocaust*. Polity, 2017.

Bayoumi, Moustafa. "Why Did Cup Foods Call the Cops on George Floyd?"
New York Times, June 17, 2020, "Opinion," accessed May 28, 2024, https://
www.nytimes.com/2020/06/17/opinion/george-floyd-arab-muslims
-racism.html.

Beck, Bernard. 2007. "Outcasts of Echo Park, Heroes of Brentwood:
Quinceanera, Keeping Up with the Steins and Coming of Age in Ethnic L.A."
Multicultural Perspectives, vol. 9, no. 2, 2007, pp. 26–8.

Behar, Ruth, dir. *Adio kerida = Goodbye dear love*. Women Make Movies, 2002.

Benítez Rojo, Antonio. *The Repeating Island: The Caribbean and the
Postmodern Perspective*, translated by James E. Maraniss, Duke University
Press, 1996.

Bényei, Tamás. "What the Raven Said: Genealogy and Subjectivity in
Mordecai Richler's *Solomon Gursky Was Here*." *Commonwealth: Essays and
Studies* (Société d'Étude des Pays du Commonwealth), vol. 25, no. 2, Spring
2003, pp. 95–111, 117.

Bianet Castellanos, M. "Introduction: Settler Colonialism in Latin America."
American Quarterly, vol. 69, no. 4, 2017, pp. 777–81.

Birkle, Carmen. "Of Sherlocks, Shylocks, and the Shoah: Ethnicity in Jewish
American Detective Fiction." *Sleuthing Ethnicity: The Detective in Multiethnic
Crime Fiction*, edited by Dorothea Fischer-Hornung and Monika Mueller,
Fairleigh Dickinson University Press, 2003, pp. 53–80.

Blair, Elizabeth. "Whodunwhat? The Crime's the Mystery in Gerald Vizenor's
The Heirs of Columbus." *Loosening the Seams: Interpretations of Gerald Vizenor*,
edited by A. Robert Lee, Bowling Green State University Popular Press,
2000, pp. 155–65.

Blanchot, Maurice. "Being Jewish." *The Infinite Conversation*, translated by
Susan Hanson, University of Minnesota Press, 1993, pp. 123–9.

Boyarin, Daniel, and Jonathan Boyarin. "Diaspora: Generation and the
Ground of Jewish Identity." *Critical Inquiry*, vol. 19, no. 4, University of
Chicago, 1993, pp. 693–725.

Boyarin, Jonathan. "Europe's Indian, America's Jew: Modiano and Vizenor."
Boundary 2, vol. 19, no. 3, Duke University Press, 1992, 197–222.

Boyarin, Daniel, Daniel Itzkovitz, and Ann Pellegrini. "Strange Bedfellows:
An Introduction." *Queer Theory and the Jewish Question*, Columbia University
Press, 2003, pp. 1–18.

Brand, Joshua, dir. *Northern Exposure: The complete series*. 2020. DVD.

Brantley, Ben. "Review: Reflections That Sear in a Reborn 'Fires in the
Mirror.'" *The New York Times*, November 11, 2019, accessed November 19,

2020, https://www.nytimes.com/2019/11/11/theater/fires-in-the-mirror-signature.html.

Brodkin, Karen. *How Jews Became White Folks and What That Says about Race in America*. Rutgers University Press, 1999.

Buiza, Nanci. "Rodrigo Rey Rosa's *El Material Humano* and the Labyrinth of Postwar Guatemala: On Ethics, Truth, and Justice." *A Contracorriente: A Journal on Social History and Literature in Latin America*, vol. 14, no. 1, 2016, pp. 58–79.

– "Trauma and the Poetics of Affect in Horacio Castellanos Moya's *Insensatez*." *Revista de Estudios Hispánicos Revista de Estudios Hispánicos*, vol. 47, no. 1, 2013, pp. 151–72.

Burman, Daniel S., dir. *Lost Embrace | El abrazo partido*. Axiom Films, 2004.

Calderón Kellett, Gloria, et al. *One Day at a Time*, Netflix, 2017–20.

Cano, Luis C. "Cárcel de árboles, de Rodrigo Rey Rosa, y la meta-ciencia-ficción." *Revista Iberoamericana*, vol. 78, no. 238, 2012, pp. 389–403.

Carini, S. "La reelaboración del trauma a través del archivo en *El material humano* de Rodrigo Rey Rosa y 'La isla' de Uli Stelzner." *Tonos Digital* 27 (2014).

Carr, Matthew. "Book Reviews: The Long Night of White Chickens by Francisco Goldman (London, Faber and Faber, 1993)." *Race & Class*, vol 35, no. 3, SAGE Publications Ltd., January 1994, pp. 95–6, https://doi.org/10.1177/030639689403500313.

Casteel, Sarah Phillips. *Calypso Jews: Jewishness in the Caribbean Literary Imagination*. Columbia University Press, 2016.

– "Jews among the Indians: The Fantasy of Indigenization in Mordecai Richler's and Michael Chabon's Northern Narratives." *Contemporary Literature*, vol. 50, no. 4, 2009, pp. 775–810.

– "Sephardism and Marranism in Native American Fiction of the Quincentenary." *Multiethnic Literatures in the US*, vol. 37, no. 2, 2012, pp. 59–81.

Chabon, Michael. "O.J. Simpson, Racial Utopia and the Moment That Inspired My Novel (Published 2012)." *The New York Times*, September 27, 2012, https://www.nytimes.com/2012/09/30/magazine/michael-chabon-telegraph-avenue.html.

– *Telegraph Avenue*. Harper Collins, 2012.

– *The Yiddish Policemen's Union*. Harper Collins, 2007.

Chambers, Samuel A. *The Queer Politics of Television*, London, I.B. Tauris, 2014.

Chase, David, dir. *The Sopranos. Season 4*. 2014.

Chenillo, Mariana, dir. *Cinco días sin Nora / 5 days without Nora*. 2013.

Chihaya, Sarah. *Superhumanity: Refiguring the Superhero*. November 1, 2012, accessed August 20, 2021, https://www.alluvium-journal.org/2012/11/01/superhumanity-refiguring-the-superhero/.

222   Works Cited

Climent-Espino, Rafael. "Jogos de Alteridade Em A Menor Mulher Do Mundo de Clarice Lispector." *Romance Notes*, vol. 49, no. 3, The University of North Carolina at Chapel Hill, Department of Romance Studies, 2009, pp. 339–46.

Colvin, Michael. "Cannibalistic Perspectives: Paradoxical Duplication and the Mise En Abyme in Clarice Lispector's 'A Menor Mulher Do Mundo.'" *Luso-Brazilian Review*, vol. 41, no. 2, University of Wisconsin Press, 2004, pp. 84–95.

Cornejo Polar, Antonio. "Mestizaje, Transculturation, Heterogeneity." *The Latin American Cultural Studies Reader*, edited by Ana Del Sarto, Alicia Rios, and Abril Trigo, Duke University Press, 2004, 116–19.

Coronil, Fernando. "Introduction." *Cuban Counterpoint: Tobacco and Sugar*. Fernando Ortiz. Translated by Harriet de Onís. Duke University Press, 1995, pp. iv-lvi.

Craft, Linda J. "La adopción internacional como modelo ficticio en *The Long Night of White Chickens* de Francisco Goldman." *Mesoamérica*, vol. 18, no. 34, Centro de Investigaciones Regionales de Mesoamérica, 1997, pp. 667–80.

daFonseca-Wilheim, Corinna. "Review: Chutzpah? An Afro-Cuban-Yiddish Opera Worth a Schlep." *New York Times* "Music," September 7, 2018, https://www.nytimes.com/2018/09/17/arts/music/review-hatuey -memory-fire-montclair-state-peak-performances.html Accessed 23 May 2024.

de Andrade Tosta, Antonio Luciano. *Confluence Narratives: Ethnicity, History, and Nation-Making in the Americas*. Rowman & Littlefield, 2016.

de Paula Rabelo, Adriano. "O enigma da diferencia: Un incômodo antropológico e social em 'A menor mulher do mundo', de Clarice Lispector." *Revista de Estudos Acadêmicos de Letras*, vol. 12, no. 8, 2019, pp. 80–9.

Delgadillo, Theresa. *Spiritual Mestizaje: Religion, Gender, Race, and Nation in Contemporary Chicana Narrative*. Duke University Press, 2011.

Deloria, Vine Jr. *Custer Died For Your Sins: An Indian Manifesto*. University Press of Oklahoma, 1988.

del Río, Esteban, and Kristin C. Moran. "Remaking Television: *One Day at a Time*'s Digital Delivery and Latina/o Cultural Specificity." *Journal of Communication Inquiry*, vol. 44, no. 1, January 1, 2020, pp. 5–25.

Dempsey, Anna M. "Jill Soloway's *Transparent*: Transgender Memory and a Tale of Two Cities." *Gender & History*, vol. 30, no. 3, 2018, pp. 803–19.

Dewey, Joseph. *Understanding Michael Chabon*. The University of South Carolina Press, 2014.

Dominus, Susan. "The Health Care Monologues." *The New York Times*, September 30, 2009, accessed May 28, 2024, https://www.nytimes.com /2009/10/04/magazine/04smith-t.html.

Works Cited   223

Dragulescu, Luminita M. "Race Trauma at the End of the Millennium: (Narrative) Passing in Philip Roth's *The Human Stain*." *Philip Roth Studies*, vol. 10, no. 1, 2014, pp. 91–109.

Drews, Julián. "'"La Inseguridad En El Archivo: Insensatez de Horacio Castellanos Moya y El Material Humano de Rodrigo Rey Rosa." *Istmo: Revista Virtual de Estudios Literarios y Culturales Centroamericanos* vol. 22, 2011.

Du Bois, W.E.B. "The Negro and the Warsaw Ghetto." *Jewish Life*, vol. 6, no. 7, 1952, pp. 14–15, accessed November 3, 2020, https://search.alexanderstreet.com/preview/work/bibliographic_entity%7Cbibliographic_details%7C4392606

– *The Souls of Black Folk*. A.C. McClurg & Co., 1903. Gutenberg eBook accessed January 28, 2021, https://www.gutenberg.org/files/408/408-h/408-h.htm.

Eppelsheimer, Natalie. "'A World Where Butchers Sing Like Angels': German Poetry, Music, and (Counter)History in Louise Erdrich's *The Master Butchers Singing Club*." *Studies in American Indian Literatures*, vol 27, no. 3, University of Nebraska Press, 2015, pp. 52–81.

Erdrich, Louise. *The Master Butchers Singing Club*. Harper Collins, 2003.

Eshun, Kodwo. "Further Considerations on Afrofuturism." *CR: The New Centennial Review*, vol. 3, no. 2, 2003, pp. 287–302.

Everett, Percival. James. Doubleday, 2024.

Faulkner, Sandra L. and Michael L. Hecht. "The negotiation of closetable identities: A narrative analysis of lesbian, gay, bisexual, transgendered queer Jewish identity." *Journal of Social and Personal Relationships*, vol. 28, no. 6, 2011, pp. 829–47.

Feldman, Jeffrey D. "The Jewish Roots of Anthropology." *Anthropological Quarterly*, vol. 77, no. 1, Winter 2004, pp. 107–25.

Figueroa, Yomaira. "After the Hurricane: Afro-Latina Decolonial Feminisms and Destierro." *Hypatia*, vol. 35, no. 1, Cambridge University Press, 2020, pp. 220–9.

Fitz, Karsten. "The Native American Trickster as Global and Transcultural Principle in Gerald Vizenor's 'The Heirs of Columbus.'" *Amerikastudien / American Studies*, vol. 47, no. 2, 2002, pp. 257–67.

Franco, Dean. "Portnoy's Complaint: It's about Race, Not Sex (Even the Sex Is about Race)." *prooftexts*, vol. 29, no. 1, 2009, pp. 86–115.

Franco, Dean J. "Being Black, Being Jewish, and Knowing the Difference: Philip Roth's 'The Human Stain'; Or, It Depends on What the Meaning of 'Clinton' Is." *Studies in American Jewish Literature (1981-)*, vol. 23, Penn State University Press, 2004, pp. 88–103.

Franco, Dean J. *The Border and the Line: Race, Literature, and Los Angeles*. Stanford University Press, 2019.

Fraser, David. *Honorary Protestants: The Jewish School Question in Montreal, 1867–1997*. University of Toronto Press, 2015.

224 Works Cited

Freedman, Jonathan. *Klezmer America: Jewishness, Ethnicity, Modernity.* Columbia University Press, 2008.

Freidenberg, Judith Noemí. *Invention of the Jewish Gaucho: Villa Clara and the Construction of Argentine Identity.* University of Texas Press, 2009.

Funk, Steven, and Jaydi Funk. "Transgender Dispossession in *Transparent*: Coming Out as a Euphemism for Honesty." *Sexuality & Culture*, vol. 20, no. 4, December 1, 2016, pp. 879–905.

Gates, Henry Louis. *The Signifying Monkey: A Theory of African-American Literary Criticism.* Oxford University Press, 2014.

– *Thirteen Ways of Looking at a Black Man.* Penguin Random House, 1995.

George, Diana, and Susan Sanders. "Reconstructing Tonto: Cultural Formations and American Indians in 1990s Television Fiction." *Cultural Studies*, vol. 9, no. 3, Routledge, October 1995, pp. 427–52.

Glaser, Jennifer. *Borrowed Voices: Writing and Racial Ventriloquism in the Jewish American Imagination.* Rutgers University Press, 2016. Kindle file.

Goldman, Francisco. *The Long Night of White Chickens.* Grove Press, 1992.

– *Monkey Boy.* Grove Press, 2021.

Goldman, Dara. "Next Year in the Diaspora: The Uneasy Articulation of Transcultural Positionality in Achy Obejas's *Days of Awe*." *Arizona Journal of Hispanic Cultural Studies*, vol. 8, 2004, pp. 59–74.

Goldstein, Eric L. *The Price of Whiteness: Jews, Race, and American Identity.* Princeton University Press, 2008.

Gräbner, Cornelia. "'But How to Speak of Such Things?': Decolonial Love, the Coloniality of Gender, and Political Struggle in Francisco Goldman's *The Long Night of White Chickens* (1992) and Jennifer Harbury's *Bridge of Courage* (1994) and Searching for Everardo (1997)." *Journal of Iberian and Latin American Studies*, vol. 20, no. 1, Routledge, January 2014, pp. 51–74.

Graff Zivin, Erin. *Anarchaeologies: Reading As Misreading.* Fordham University Press, 2020.

– *The Wandering Signifier: Rhetoric of Jewishness in the Latin American Imaginary.* Duke University Press, 2008.

Gramsci, Antonio. *The Prison Notebooks.* International Publishers, 1971.

Grandin, Greg. *The Blood of Guatemala: A History of Race and Nation.* Duke University Press, 2000.

Gray, Herman. *Watching Race: Television and the Struggle for "blackness."* University of Minneapolis Press, 1995.

Gutiérrez Mouat, Ricardo. "El lenguaje de los derechos humanos en tres obras de ficción: *La Muerte y La Doncella, Insensatez y El Material Humano*." *A Contracorriente: A Journal on Social History and Literature in Latin America*, vol. 11, no. 1, 2013, pp. 39–62.

Halberstam, Jack. "*Transparent* (2014): The Highs, the Lows, The In-betweens," Bullybloggers. January 7, 2015, accessed November 9, 2020, http://

bullybloggers.wordpress.com/2015/01/07/transparent-2014-the-highs-the
-lows-the-inbetweens/.

Hale, Dorothy J. "Bakhtin in African American Literary Theory." *ELH (English Literary History)*, vol. 61, no. 2, 1994, pp. 445–71.

Halfon, Eduardo. "Dicho Hacia El Sur." *Sam no es mi tío: Veinticuatro crónicas migrantes y un sueño americano*, edited by Diego Fonseca and Aileen El-Kadi, Alfaguara, 2012, pp. 133–42.

– *Tomorrow We Never Did Talk About It*. Pre-Textos, 2011.

Hall, Stuart. "Creolité and the Process of Creolization." *Creolizing Europe*, edited by Encarnación Gutiérrez Rodríguez and Shirley Anne Tate, Liverpool University Press, 2015, pp. 12–25.

Hamburger, Cao, dir. *O Ano em que meus pais saíram de férias / The year my parents went on vacation*. SBS2, 2006.

Hardin, Michael. "The Trickster of History: *The Heirs of Columbus* and the Dehistorization of Narrative." *MELUS*, vol. 23, no. 4, 1998, pp. 25–45.

Hecht, Michael L.Ye, et al. "Looking through *Northern Exposure* at Jewish American Identity and the Communication Theory of Identity." *Journal of Communication*, vol. 52, no. 4, December 2002, pp. 852–69.

Hirsch, Marianne. *Generation of Postmemory: Writing and Visual Culture After the Holocaust*. Columbia University Press, 2012.

Hooker, Juliet. *Theorizing Race in the Americas: Douglass, Sarmiento, Du Bois, and Vasconcelos*. Oxford University Press, 2019.

Horowitz, Sara R. "Kaddish – The Final Frontier." *Studies in American Jewish Literature*, vol. 29, Penn State University Press, 2010, pp. 49–67.

Horvat, Anamarija. "Streaming Privilege: Addressing Intersectionality in *Transparent*." *Critical Studies in Television*, vol. 14, no. 4, 2019, pp. 468–72.

"In Conversation with Anna Deavere Smith – Annual David M. Rubenstein Lecture." 2019. accessed August 11, 2021, https://www.amacad.org/news /conversation-anna-deavere-smith.

Irizarry Díaz Guillermo B. "Subjetividades Precarias y Resarcimiento Literario En *The Long Night of the White Chickens* de Francisco Goldman." *Istmo: Revista Virtual de Estudios Literarios y Culturales Centroamericanos*, vol. 27–28, 2014, pp. 1–23, https://www.academia.edu/12000551/_Subjetividades _precarias_y_resarcimiento_literario_en_The_Long_Night_of_White _Chickens_de_Francisco_Goldman. accessed 29 July 2021.

Itkovitz, Daniel. "Passing Like Me: Jewish Chameleonism and the Politics of Race." *Passing: Identity and Interpretation in Sexuality, Race, and Religion*, edited by Maria Sanchez and Linda Schlossberg, NYU Press, 2001, pp. 38–63.

– "Secret Temples." *Jews and Other Differences: The New Jewish Cultural Studies*, edited by Daniel Boyarin and Jonathan Boyarin (University of Minnesota Press, 1997), pp. 176–202.

Jakobsen, Janet R. "Queers Are like Jews, Aren't They? Analogy and Alliance Politics." *Queer Theory and the Jewish Question*, edited by Daniel Boyarin,

Works Cited

Daniel Itzkovitz, and Ann Pellegrini, Columbia University Press New York, 2003, pp. 64–89.

Jáuregui, Carlos A. *Canibalia: canibalismo, calibanismo, antropofagía cultural y consumo en América latina*. Iberoamericana Vervuert, 2008.

Jodorowsky, Alejandro. *La danza de la realidad = La danse de la réalité*. Pathé Distribution, 2014.

Jones, Nicholas R. *Staging Habla de Negros: Radical Performances of the African Diaspora in Early Modern Spain*. Penn State University Press, 2019.

Joyrich, Lynne. "The Epistemology of the Console." *Queer TV: Theories, Histories, Politics*, edited by Glyn Davis and Gary Needham, Routledge, 2009, pp. 16–44.

Kakutani, Michiko. "Books of the Times: Setting Out with a Dream and a Lot of Sausages." *The New York Times*, February 4, 2003, accessed August 20, 2021, https://www.nytimes.com/203/02/04/books/books-of-the-times-setting-out-with-a-dream-and-a-lot-of-sausages.html.

Kalin, Betsy, dir., Vanessa Luna Bishop, producer. *East LA Interchange*, Bluewater Media. 2015.

Kandiyoti, Dalia. *The Converso's Return: Conversion and Sephardi History in Contemporary Literature and Culture*. Stanford University Press, 2020.

– "Sephardism in Latina Literature." *Sephardism: Spanish Jewish History and the Modern Literary Imagination*, edited by Yael Halevi-Wise, Stanford University Press, 2012, pp. 235–55.

Kaplan, Brett Ashley. "Anatole Broyard's Human Stain: Performing Postracial Consciousness." *Philip Roth Studies*, vol. 1, no. 2, Purdue University Press, 2005, pp. 125–44.

Kaye/Kantrowitz, Melanie. *The Colors of Jews: Racial Politics and Radical Diasporism*. Indiana University Press, 2007.

Kendi, Ibram X. *How to Be an Antiracist*. Random House, 2020.

Keveney, Bill. "Norman Lear's New 'One Day at a Time' Has a Latin Flavor." *USA Today*, January 3, 2017, accessed October 3, 2020, https://www.usatoday.com/story/life/tv/2017/01/03/norman-lear-netflix-one-day-at-a-time-cuban/95904230/.

Kittleson, Roger Alan. *The Country of Football: Soccer and the Making of Modern Brazil*. University of California Press, 2014.

Kotcheff, Ted. Dir. *The Apprenticeship of Duddy Kravitz*. Astral Films, 1974.

Koffman, David S. "The Unsettling of Canadian Jewish History: Towards a Tangled History of Jewish–Indigenous Encounters." *No Better Home? Jews, Canada, and the Sense of Belonging*, University of Toronto Press, 2021, pp. 81–113.

– *The Jews' Indian: Colonialism, Pluralism, and Belonging in America*. Rutgers University Press, 2019.

Kokotovic, Milos. "Testimonio Once Removed." *Revista de Estudios Hispánicos*, vol. 43, no. 3, 2009, pp. 545–62.

Kroll-Bryce, C. "A Reasonable Senselessness: Madness, Sovereignty and Neoliberal Reason in Horacio Castellanos Moya's Insensatez." *Journal of Latin American Cultural Studies*, vol. 23, no. 4, 2014, pp. 381–99.

Larsen, Neil. *Reading North by South: On Latin American Literature, Culture, and Politics*. University of Minnesota Press, 1995.

Lesser, Jeffrey. "How the Jews Became Japanese and Other Stories of Nation and Ethnicity." *Jewish History*, vol. 18, no. 1, Springer, 2004, pp. 7–17.

Levinson, Hilary. "Thinking Postmemory through Translation in Roberto Brodsky's 'Bosque Quemado.'" *Revista Canadiense de Estudios Hispánicos*, vol. 39, no. 3, 2015, pp. 589–611.

Lindstrom, Naomi. "Judaic Traces in the Narrative of Clarice Lispector." *Latin American Jewish Cultural Production*, edited by David William Foster, Vanderbilt University Press, 2009, pp. 83–96.

Lispector, Clarice. "The Smallest Woman in the World," translated by Elizabeth Bishop, *The Kenyon Review*, vol. 26, no. 3, 1964, pp. 500–6.

Lomnitz, Claudio. *Nuestra América*. FCE - Fondo de Cultura Económica, 2018.

Long, Crispin. "The Sitcom Triumphs of 'One Day at a Time.'" *The New Yorker*, August 21, 2018, accessed May 24, 2024, https://www.newyorker.com/recommends/watch/the-sitcom-triumphs-of-one-day-at-a-time#:~:text=If%20you%20believe%20that%20the,some%20evidence%20to%20the%20contrary.

Lugones, María. *Pilgrimages/Peregrinajes: Theorizing Coalition Against Multiple Oppressions*. Rowman & Littlefield Publishers, 2003.

Lush, Rebecca M. "Turning Tricks: Sexuality and Trickster Language in Vizenor's *The Heirs of Columbus*." *Studies in American Indian Literatures*, vol. 24, no. 2, University of Nebraska Press, 2012, pp. 1–16.

Madsen, Deborah Lea. "On Subjectivity and Survivance: Re-Reading Trauma through *The Heirs of Columbus* and *The Crown of Columbus*" *Survivance*," edited by G. Vizenor, University of Nebraska Press, 2008, https://archive-ouverte.unige.ch/unige:87783.

Maguire, Geoffrey. "Bringing Memory Home: Historical (Post)Memory and Patricio Pron's El Espíritu de Mis Padres Sigue Subiendo En La Lluvia (2011)." *Journal of Latin American Cultural Studies*, vol. 23, no. 2, 2014, pp. 211–28.

María Elena Martínez. *Genealogical Fictions: Limpieza de Sangre, Religion, and Gender in Colonial Mexico*. Stanford University Press, 2013.

Marshall, Paule. *Triangular Road: A Memoir*. Basic Civitas Books, 2009.

Massey, Doreen B. "Geographies of Responsibility." *Geografiska Annaler. Series B, Human Geography*, vol. 86, 2004, pp. 5–18.

Mignolo, Walter D. "La colonialidad a lo largo y a lo ancho: El hemisferio occidental en el horizonte colonial de la modernidad." *La colonialidad del saber: Eurocentrismo y ciencias sociales: Perspectivas latinoamericanas*, CLASCO, 2000, pp. 34–52.

Works Cited

Moore, Deborah Dash. Introduction. *American Jewish Identity Politics*, edited by Moore, University of Michigan Press, 2008, pp. 1–22.

Moran, Kristin. "'If They're Trying to Say Something About My Culture … I'm Confused': Recognizing and Resisting Authenticity in Latino-Themed Television." *Mass Communication & Society*, vol. 18, no. 1, February 1, 2015, pp. 79–96.

Morrison, Alastair. "*Solomon Gursky Was Here*: A History by Hunger." *Canadian Literature*, vol. 209, Summer 2011, pp. 127–40.

Moss, Joshua Louis. "'The Woman Thing and the Jew Thing': Transsexuality, Transcomedy, and the Legacy of Subversive Jewishness in *Transparent*" *From Shtetl to Stardom: Jews and Hollywood*, edited by Steven J. Ross, Michael Renov, and Vincent Brook, Purdue University Press, 2017, pp. 73–98.

Muñoz, José Esteban. *Disidentifications: Queers of Color and the Performance of Politics*, vol. 2, University of Minnesota Press, 1999.

Newcomb, Horace, and Paul M. Hirsch. "Television as a Cultural Forum." *Quarterly Review of Film Studies*, Summer 1983, pp. 561–73, web.mit .edu/211.432/www. readings/tv%20as%20a%20cultural%20forum.pdf.

Obejas, Achy. *Days of Awe*. Ballantine Books, 2008.

Ortiz, Fernando. *Cuban Counterpoint, Tobacco and Sugar*, translated by Harriet de Onís, Duke University Press, 1995.

Osborne, Stephen D. "Legal and Tribal Identity in Gerald Vizenor's *The Heirs of Columbus*." *Studies in American Indian Literatures*, vol. 9, no. 1, University of Nebraska Press, 1997, pp. 115–27.

Park, Shelley M. *Mothering Queerly, Queering Motherhood: Resisting Monomaternalism in Adoptive, Lesbian, Blended, and Polygagmous Families*. State University of New York Press, 2015.

Parrish, Timothy L. "Ralph Ellison: The Invisible Man in Philip Roth's 'The Human Stain.'" *Contemporary Literature*, vol. 45, no. 3, Board of Regents of the University of Wisconsin System, University of Wisconsin Press, 2004, pp. 421–59, https://doi.org/10.2307/3593533.

Perera, Victor. *The Cross and the Pear Tree: A Sephardic Journey*. University of California Press, 1996.

– *Rites: A Guatemalan Boyhood*. Mercury House, 1994.

Pérez Firmat, Gustavo. *Life on the Hyphen: The Cuban-American Way*. University of Texas Press, 2012.

Perkowska, Magdalena. "Infancia e historia: actos de la memoria en *Dios tenía miedo* de Vanessa Núñez Handal y *Mañana nunca lo hablamos* de Eduardo Halfon." *Revista de Estudios Hispánicos*, vol. 51, no. 3, 2017, pp. 595–620.

Pratt, Mary Louise. *Imperial Eyes: Travel Writing and Transculturation*. 2nd ed., Routledge, 2008.

Pridgeon, Stephanie. *Revolutionary Visions: Jewish Life and Politics in Latin American Film*. University of Toronto Press, 2021.

Pron, Patricio. *El espíritu de mis padres sigue subiendo en la lluvia*. Mondadori, 2011.

Quiroga, José A. *Tropics of Desire: Interventions from Queer Latino America*, vol. 12, NYU Press, 2000.

Rama, Angel. *Writing across Cultures: Narrative Transculturation in Latin America*, edited and translated by David Frye, Duke University Press, 2012.

Reinelt, Janelle. "Performing Race: Anna Deavere Smith's Fires in the Mirror." *Modern Drama*, vol. 39, no. 4, University of Toronto Press, 1996, pp. 609–17.

"Re-Thinking Black-Jewish Relations" Podcast episode transcript. Association for Jewish Studies, accessed August 7, 2021, https://associationforjewishstudies.org/publications-research/adventures-in-jewish-studies-podcast/re-thinking-black-jewish-relations-episode-transcript.

Rich, Adrienne. "Compulsory Heterosexuality and Lesbian Existence." *Journal of Women's History*, vol. 15, no. 3, 2003, pp. 11–48.

Richler, Mordecai. *The Apprenticeship of Duddy Kravitz*. 1959. Emblem Editions, 2001.

– *Solomon Gursky Was Here*. Penguin, 1990.

Riggs, Damien. "Does Transgender Reality Shine through *Transparent*?" *ABC News*, January 14, 2015, accessed 9 November 9, 2020, https://www.abc.net.au/news/2015-01-15/riggs-does-transgender-reality-shine-through-transparent/6017234.

Roach, Joseph R. *Cities of the Dead: Circum-Atlantic Performance*. Columbia University Press, 1996.

Rocha, Carolina. "Children's View of State-Sponsored Violence in Latin America." *Representing History, Class, and Gender in Spain and Latin America*, edited by Carolina Rocha and Georgia Seminet, Palgrave MacMillan, 2012, pp. 83–100.

"Rodrigo Rey Rosa by Francisco Goldman," translated by Ellie Robins, *BOMB Magazine*. October 1, 2013, accessed August 19, 2021, https://bombmagazine.org/articles/rodrigo-rey-rosa/

Rorabaugh, W.J. *Berkeley at War: The 1960s*. Oxford, 1989.

Rosenbaum, Yudith. "Uma estranha descoberta: leitura do conto 'A menor mulher do mundo', de Clarice Lispector." *Literatura e Sociedade*, vol. 20, no. 20, June 20, 2015, pp. 148–56.

Rosenberg, Roberta. "The Importance of Jewish Ritual in the Secular, Postmodern World of *Transparent*." *Jewish Film & New Media*, vol. 5, no. 1, 2017, pp. 75–101.

Roth, Philip. *The Human Stain*. Jonathan Cape, 2000.

– "An Open Letter to Wikipedia." *The New Yorker*, accessed June 3, 2021, https://www.newyorker.com/books/page-turner/an-open-letter-to-wikipedia#:~:text=Dear%20Wikipedia%2C,to%20ask%20to%20have%20removed.

230   Works Cited

Rothberg, Michael. *Multidirectional Memory: Remembering the Holocaust in the Age of Decolonization*. Stanford University Press, 2009.

Rottenberg, Catherine. "Race and Ethnicity in 'The Autobiography of an Ex-Colored Man' and 'The Rise of David Levinsky': The Performative Difference." *Multiethnic Literatures of the US*, vol. 29, no. 3/4, 2004, pp. 307–21.

Rubinstein, Rachel. "Found in Translation: Hatuey, Cuba, and the Jews." *Digital Yiddish Theater Project*, September 21, 2018, accessed August 20, 2021, https://web.uwm.edu/yiddish-stage/found-in-translation-hatuey-cuba-and-the-jews.

Russo, Bernadette V. "Deconstructing the Master's House with His Own Tools: Code-Switching and Double-Voiced Discourse as Agency in Gerald Vizenor's *Heirs of Columbus*." *Studies in American Indian Literatures*, vol. 29, no. 4, University of Nebraska Press, 2017, pp. 58–75.

Sánchez Prado, Ignacio. "La Ficción y El Momento Del Peligro: Insensatez de Horacio Castellanos Moya." *Cuaderno Internacional de Estudios Humanísticos y Literarios (CIEHL)*, vol. 14, 2010, pp. 79–86.

Savin, Ada. "The Burden and the Treasure: Victor Perera's Sephardic Family Chronicle." *Prooftexts*, vol. 18, no. 3, 1998, pp. 225–37.

Schechner, Richard. "Anna Deavere Smith: Acting as Incorporation." *TDR (1988–)*, vol. 37, no. 4, 1993, pp. 63–4.

Schyfter, Guita, dir. *Novia que te vea = Like a bride*. Desert Mountain Media, 1993.

Sedgwick, Eve Kosofsky. *Epistemology of the Closet*. University of California Press, 1990.

Seminet, Georgia. "A Child's Voice, a Country's Silence." *Representing History, Class, and Gender in Spain and Latin America Children and Adolescents in Film*, edited by Carolina Rocha and Georgia Seminet, Palgrave MacMillan, 2012, 63–81.

Silverstein, Stephen. *The Merchant of Havana: The Jew in the Cuban Abolitionist Archive*. Vanderbilt University Press, 2016.

Skidmore, Thomas E. "Bi-Racial U.S.A. vs. Multi-Racial Brazil: Is the Contrast Still Valid?" *Journal of Latin American Studies*, vol 25, no. 2, Cambridge University Press, 1993, pp. 373–86.

Smith, Anna Deavere. "Fires in the Mirror." *Shared Stages: Ten American Dramas of Blacks and Jews*, edited by Joanne B Koch and Sarah Blacher Cohen, State University of New York Press, 2007, pp. 465–544.

– "The First Time a White Person Wrote 'Love' to Me." *The New York Times*, March 13, 2018, accessed August 20, 2021, https://www.nytimes.com/2018/03/13/arts/television/anna-deavere-smith-notes-from-the-field.html.

– "Four American Characters." *TED*, February 8, 2005, accessed August 18, 2021. https://www.ted.com/talks/anna_deavere_smith_four_american_characters?language=en.

Socolovsky, Maya. "Deconstructing a Secret History: Trace, Translation, and Crypto-Judaism in Achy Obejas's 'Days of Awe.'" *Contemporary Literature*, vol. 44, no. 2, 2003, pp. 225–49.

Soloway, Jill. "The Female Gaze." September 11, 2016, accessed May 24, 2024, www.toppleproductions.com/thefemale-gaze.

Soloway, Joey. *Transparent*, 2014–2019.

Sommer, Doris. *Foundational Fictions: The National Romances of Latin America*. University of California Press, 1991.

– "Mosaic and Mestizo: Bilingual Love from Hebreo to El Inca." *Jewish Studies Quarterly*, vol. 2, no. 3, Mohr Siebeck GmbH & Co. KG, 1995, pp. 253–91.

Spivak, Gayatri. "Can the Subaltern Speak?" *Colonial Discourse and Post-Colonial Theory*, edited by Patrick Williams and Laura Chrisman, Columbia University Press, 1993, pp. 66–111.

"Spotlight Series: Anna Deavere Smith and Saheem Ali Talk *Fires in the Mirror* at Signature Theatre." *YouTube*, uploaded by Signature TheaterNY, October 31, 2019, accessed August 18, 2021, https://www.youtube.com /watch?v=zd4XymweEEg.

Springall, Alejandro, dir. *My Mexican Shivah*. Emerging Pictures, 2007.

Stavans, Ilan. Afterword. *Tomorrow We Never Did Talk About It*, translated by Anne McLean. *The Massachusetts Review*, e-book ed., vol. 1, no. 3, 2016. ebook published by Working Titles.

– "Introduction" in *Mestizo: A novel*, translated by Stephen A Sadow, University of New Mexico Press, 2000.

– "Introduction" in *Tropical Synagogues: Short Stories by Jewish-Latin American Writers*, Holmes and Meier, 1994, pp. 1–38.

Stein, Shawn. "'O Ano Em Que Meus Pais Saíram de Férias' de Cao Hamburger: Desmistificação Ou Propagação Do Mito de Democracia Racial?" *Hispania*, vol. 97, no. 2, American Association of Teachers of Spanish and Portuguese, 2014, pp. 256–63.

Tally, Robert Jr. "Fredric Jameson and the Controversy over 'Third-World Literature in the Era of Multinational Capitalism.'" *Global South Studies: A Collective Publication with the Global South*. Web. November 9 2017, accessed 30 August 2018.

Tarica, Estelle. "Where You Don't Belong: On The Construction Of Cultural 'Otherness' In Leo Spitzer's *Hotel Bolivia*." *Journal of Latin American Cultural Studies*, vol. 15, no. 1, March 2006, pp. 17–37.

Taylor, Diana. *The Archive and the Repertoire: Performing Cultural Memory in the Americas*, Duke University Press, 2003.

Treuer, David. "Adrift Between My Parents' Two Americas." *New York Times Magazine*, July 18, 2022, accessed January 18, 2024, https://www.nytimes .com/2022/07/18/magazine/american-patriotism.html#:~:text=David%20 Treuer%20is%20an%20Ojibwe,for%20the%20National%20Book%20Award.

232 Works Cited

Tuck, Eve, and K. Wayne Yang. "Decolonization Is Not a Metaphor." *Decolonization: Indigeneity, Education & Society*, vol. 1, no. 1, September 1, 2012.

"An Unserious Man." *Jewish Currents*, January 23, 2020, accessed September 1, 2021, https://jewishcurrents.org/an-unserious-man/.

Uzendoski, Andrew. "Speculative States: Citizenship Criteria, Human Rights, and Decolonial Legal Norms in Gerald Vizenor's *The Heirs of Columbus*." *Extrapolation* 57, no. 1–2, 2016, pp. 21–50.

Vargas Llosa, Mario. *The Storyteller*, translated by Helen Lane. Farrar, Straus, and Giroux, 1989.

Vasconcelos, José. "La raza cósmica" accessed May 15, 2024, https://enriquedussel.com/txt/Textos_200_Obras/Filosofos_Mexico/Raza_cosmica-Jose_Vasconcelos.pdf.

Venkatesh, Vinodh. "'Yo No Estoy Completo de La Mente': Ethics and Madness in Horacio Castellanos Moya's *Insensatez*." *Symposium*, vol. 67, no. 4, 2013, pp. 219–30.

Veracini, Lorenzo. *Settler Colonialism: A Theoretical Overview*. Palgrave Macmillan, 2010.

Verdín, Azucena, and Jennifer Camacho. 2019. "Changing Family Identity Through the Quinceañera Ritual." *Hispanic Journal of Behavioral Sciences*, vol. 41, no. 2, 2019, pp. 185–96.

Villanueva, Alma Luz. *Weeping Woman: La Llorona and Other Stories*. Bilingual Press/Editorial Bilingüe, 1994.

Villarejo, Amy. "Jewish, Queer-Ish, Trans, and Completely Revolutionary: Jill Soloway's *Transparent* and the New Television." *Film Quarterly*, vol. 69, no. 4, 2016, pp. 10–22.

Vinson, Ben. *Before Mestizaje: The Frontiers of Race and Caste in Colonial Mexico*. Cambridge University Press, 2018.

Vizenor, Gerald. *The Heirs of Columbus*. Wesleyan University Press, 1991.

Von Vacano, Diego. *The Color of Citizenship: Race, Modernity, and Latin America*. Oxford University Press, 2012.

Walton, David. *Michael Chabon's "Telegraph Avenue" Is Rich, Funny*. cleveland.com, September 2012, accessed August 10, 2021, https://www.cleveland.com/books/2012/09/michael_chabons_telegraph_aven.html..

Warren, Kay B. *Indigenous Movements and Their Critics: Pan-Maya Activism in Guatemala*. Princeton University Press, 1998.

Weldon, James Johnson. *Autobiography of an Ex-Colored Man*. Gutenberg EBook, 2004 [1912].

Williams, Claire. "More Than Meets the Eye, or a Tree House of Her Own: A New Look at a Short Story by Clarice Lispector." *Portuguese Studies*, vol. 14, Modern Humanities Research Association, 1998, pp. 170–80.

Winant, Howard. *The World Is a Ghetto: The Making of a New World Racial Order*. BasicBooks, Plymbridge, 2002.

Works Cited   233

"Writers On the Fly: Eduardo Halfon." *YouTube*, uploaded by Iowa City UNESCO City of Literature, December 6, 2010, accessed May 8 2017, www.youtube.com/watch?v=9kaKeV1aoYc.

Yanders, Jacinta. "We Can't Have Two White Boys Trying to Tell a Latina Story: Nostalgia, Identity, and Cultural Specificity." *Netflix Nostalgia: Streaming the Past on Demand*, edited by Kathryn Pallister, Lexington, 2019, pp. 137–52.

Yanes Gómez, Gabriela. "El Entramado de Una Larga Noche: 'Guatemala No Existe.'" *Mesoamérica*, vol. 18, no. 34, December 1997, pp. 637–49.

Zamora, Lois Parkinson. *The Usable Past: The Imagination of History in Recent Fiction of the Americas*. Cambridge University Press, 1997.

Index

accident of racism, 135–6

Adió (Behar), 34

adoption, 80, 103–4, 106–7

adoption narratives, 80, 106–7

"Adrift Between My Parents' Two Americas" (Treuer), 201

Adventures of Huckleberry Finn (Twain), 201–2

African descendants, in Brazil, 124

Afro-Brazilians, race relations between Jews, 164–5

Afro-futurism, 171

Alcalá, Kathleen, 33, 39, 55–6. See also *Spirits of the Ordinary*

Aldama, Arturo, 21–2

allegory, 13, 15, 17, 27, 206n14

allegory of difference, Jewishness and, 15

Alonso, María, 53

Amazing Adventures of Kavalier and Clay, The (Chabon), 170

American Fiction (film), 203n2

American Pastoral (Roth), 127

Americas, Spanish Conquest of the, 22–3

Amin, Ash, 205n9

Anarchaeologies (Graff Zivin), 64

Anderson, Benedict, 80

Andrade Tosta, Antonio Luciano de, 204n6

Andrews, George Reid, 123, 166

Angel, Arielle, 199, 200

anti-Black racism, 130, 160–1

anti-Semitism, 71–2, 104, 130

anxiety of origins, 87

Anzaldúa, Gloria, 31–3, 51

Appiah, Anthony, on race, 205n9

Apprenticeship of Duddy Kravitz, The (Richler), 85–7

appropriation, 171

Árbenz, Jacobo, 208n3

archival fiction, 87

Archive and the Repertoire, The (Taylor), 32

Arendt, Hannah, 152

Argentine gaucho (figure), 17–18

Argueta, Luis, 208n3

Arias, Arturo, 43, 67

armed conflict, 68

Art of Political Murder, The (documentary), 105, 108, 212n15

Ashkenazim, Sephardic Jews contrasted with, 44

Atwood, Margaret, 90

Autobiography of an Ex-Colored Man (Johnson), 203n1

autofiction, by Halfon, 212n15

236   Index

Avilés-Santiago, Manuel, 195
Avital, Mili, 214n1

Baartman, Sara, 120
Bakhtin, Mikhail M., 11–12, 156, 194
Baldwin, James, 3, 159, 201
barbarism, civilization versus, 204n7
Barris, Kenya, 200
bat mitzvahs, 180, 184–8
Bauman, Zygmunt, 29, 145
Bayoumi, Moustafa, 177
Beck, Bernard, 216n2
Behar, Ruth, 78, 135, 136
"Being Jewish" (Blanchot), 68
Benítez Rojo, Antonio, 7, 82
Bényei, Tamás, 88
Bhabha, Homi K., 153
Bianet Castellanos, M., 18, 40
bias, humour disarming, 194
Birkle, Carmen, 111
Black bodies, fetishization of, 121, 125
Black characters, Lispector
   dehumanizing, 125
Black culture, in Oakland, 175
blackface, Jewish literary, 152
Black folks, Jewish Americans
   contrasted with, 3
Black–Jewish relations, 9–10, 174–5,
   199–200
Black Lives Matter, 163
Blackness: Jewish identities absorbing,
   130–1; Jewishness contrasted with,
   126–8, 133, 135–6, 163; whiteness
   converging with, 125
Black Panther (comic book), 170
Black Panthers, 172
Blair, Elizabeth, 96
Blanchot, Maurice, 68, 207n16
Blaxploitation films, 172, 175
Blood of Guatemala, The (Grandin), 69
blood purity (pureza de sangre), 5,
   23, 44, 48, 54, 64; crypto-Judaism

resulting from, 25; expulsion from
   the Iberian Peninsula challenging,
   24; Vinson on, 83, 141
Bolivia, Jewish experiences in, 40
Bom Retiro, in São Paulo (Brazil),
   164, 168–9
Border and the Line, The (Franco), 173
Borderlands (La frontera) (Anzaldúa),
   31, 32
Borrowed Voices (Glaser), 22, 105, 152
Bosque quemado (Brodsky), 75, 212n17
Boyarin, David, 15
Boyarin, Jonathan, 15, 38
Boyle Heights, in Los Angeles
   (California), 178–9, 188, 192, 216n2
Brantley, Ben, 162
Brazil, 124, 163, 166
Bring the Pain (comedy special), 151
Brodkin, Karen, 5, 130, 132, 176, 216n4
Brodsky, Roberto, 75, 212n17
Broyard, Anatole, 131–2
Burman, Daniel, 49, 210n5
Butler, Judith, 101

Calibán (Retamar), 91
Calypso Jews (Casteel), 206n13
Camacho, Jennifer, 217n7
Canada, 84–5, 92
cannibalism, 83–4, 90–2, 125–6
Cárcel de árboles (Rosa), 212n15
Caribbean, Sephardic Jews in, 9
Caribbean Jewish Crossings, 206n13
Carson, Sonny, 159
caste (casta), 8, 12, 23–5, 44, 107, 141
Casteel, Sarah Phillips, 9, 87, 90, 111,
   206n13
Castellanos Moya, Horacio, 67, 77,
   212n15
Castro, Fidel, 144, 146
Catholicism, 55–6, 58, 104, 106, 109
Cato, Angela, 152
Cato, Gavin, 152, 160

Index 237

Central American literature, 67–8, 73

Chabon, Michael, 10–11, 34–5, 81–2, 150, 171–2; *The Amazing Adventures of Kavalier and Clay* by, 170; detective fiction contributed to by, 112; Franco contrasted with, 174. See also *Telegraph Avenue*; *The Yiddish Policemen's Union*

Chambers, Samuel, 182

Chamecki, Cintia, 163

chiasmus, 13–14, 40

Chihaya, Sarah, 170

childhood perspective, 70–1, 212n17, 213n19

Chippewa, 14, 58

Christopher Unborn (*Cristóbal Nonato*) (Fuentes), 94

Cinco días sin Nora. See *Nora's Will*

circumcision, 48–9, 113, 210n5

cities, race relations reflected in, 151–2

Cities of the Dead (Roach), 153

civilization, barbarism versus, 204n7

Climent-Espino, Rafael, 120

Clinton-Lewinsky scandal, 128

Cold War, 193

colonialism, settler. See settler colonialism

colonization, Jewishness and, 97

colorblindness, 165, 167

Color of Jews, The (Kaye/Kantrowitz), 129

colour line, 20–1

Columbia (Maryland), 171

Columbus, Christopher, 93–4, 100

Colvin, Michael, 122

coming-out narratives, 181–3, 191

competitive memory, 161, 207n15; *The Master Butchers Singing Club* undoing, 65; Rothberg on, 29; *Telegraph Avenue* avoiding, 176

compulsory heterosexuality, coming-out narratives recalling, 181–2

Confluence Narratives (de Andrade Tosta), 204n6

contact zones, 6–7, 111

converso (figure), 24, 55

Converso's Return, The (Kandiyoti), 55

Cooper, James Fenimore, 19, 80, 205n8

Cornejo Polar, Antonio, 28, 51

Coronil, Fernando, 27

cosmic race, 8, 31–2, 50–1, 143

cosmopolitanism, Jewishness associated with, 101–2

Craft, Linda J., 105

creolization, 26

Cristóbal Nonato (Fuentes). See *Christopher Unborn*

Cross and the Pear Tree, The (Perera), 42

cross-dressing, 52–3

Crown Heights, in Brooklyn (New York), 9–10, 115, 152, 155–7, 160

Crown of Columbus, The (Dorris and Erdrich), 65, 211n10

crypto-Judaism, 39, 63–4; blood purity resulting in, 25; Judeo-Indigenous contrasted with, 141; national identities and, 51; white privilege and, 142

Cuban Counterpoint (Ortiz), 27

Cuban identity, Jewishness within, 144

cultural memory, *The Heirs of Columbus* challenging, 97

cultural schizophrenia, *The Long Night of White Chickens* evoking, 106

Dafoe, John, 86

darstellen. See rhetoric as trope

daughter-father relationships, 194–5

Days of Awe (Obejas), 25, 34, 119, 139–41, 144–8; *The Human Stain* compared with, 137–8; national identities focused on by, 139; translation in, 136–7, 142–3

decolonization, 19, 21, 80

238 Index

"Decolonization Is Not a Metaphor"
(Tuck and Yang), 80
Defend Boyle Heights (group), 178
Delgadillo, Theresa, 32, 51, 55
Deloria, Vine, Jr., 17, 207n15
Del Río, Esteban, 190, 215n1
democracia racial. See racial
democracy
Dempsey, Anna, 193
deportation, 191–2
destierro. See dis-landing
detective fiction, 83, 96, 110–12, 117
Dewey, Joseph, 173
diaspora, 138–9, 188
diglossia, racial ventriloquism
exemplifying, 156
dis-landing (*destierro*), 28–31, 69,
138–9, 144, 207n16
displacement, 13, 30–1, 40, 55, 78, 101
dispossession, 29–30, 40
Dogs of Paradise, The (Posse), 94
Dominus, Susan, 155
Dorris, Michael, 65
double consciousness, 12, 128, 152,
156, 162, 170–1
Douglass, Frederick, 161
Dragulescu, Luminita, 130, 131
drinking, in Canada, 92
Du Bois, W.E.B., 12, 20–1, 128, 152,
156, 162
Dylan, Bob, 195

East LA Interchange (documentary),
35, 178
Echo Park, in Los Angeles
(California), 178
El abrazo partido (film), 210n5
El boxeador polaco (The Polish Boxer)
(Halfon), 213n20
El camino (The Way) (film), 70
*El espíritu de mis padres sigue subiendo
en la lluvia* (Pron), 213n21

El hablador (The Storyteller) (Vargas),
38–9
El material humano (Human Matter)
(Rosa), 212n15
El silencio de Neto (Neto's Silence)
(film), 70, 208n3
Epistemology of the Closet (Sedgwick), 33
"Epistemology of the Console, The"
(Joyrich), 217n10
Eppelsheimer, Natalie, 59, 62
Erasure (Everett), 201, 203n2
Erdrich, Louise, 14, 33, 39, 96; *The
Crown of Columbus* by Dorris
and, 65, 211n10; foil characters
written by, 60; *The Last Report on
the Miracles at Little No Horse* by,
62. See also *The Master Butchers
Singing Club*
Eshun, Kodwo, 171
Estefan, Gloria, 195
Esu (god), 13
ethnic identity, of Perera, 43–4
ethnicity, 76, 142; academic
understandings of, 148–9; gender
and, 48–9; translation linked
with, 147
"Europe's Indian, America's Jew"
(Boyarin), 38
evangelism, 58
Everett, Percival, 201, 203n2
exile, 70, 138–9, 207n16; Jewish
experiences defined by, 30–1, 144;
state violence contrasted with,
76–7; *Tomorrow We Never Did Talk
About It* showing, 68–9
expulsion from the Iberian
Peninsula, 23–5, 40

Facundo (Sarmiento), 204n7
faithful witnessing, 154, 172
father-daughter relationships, rites
of passage impacting, 194–5

Faulkner, Sandra L., 61, 204n5
Feierstein, Ricardo, 18, 214n1
Feldman, Jeffrey, 115
feminist innovations, *One Day at a Time* furthering, 183
Fernández Retamar, Roberto, 91
fiction: archival, 87; auto, 212n15; detective, 83, 96, 110–12, 117; human rights, 95–6; North American, 95–6; racial Others in, 9–11; syncretism and, 9–10
Fievel Goes West (film), 18
Figueroa, Yomaira, 30, 69, 139, 144, 207n16
Fires in the Mirror (play), 9–10, 35, 153–6, 158–60, 177; absorption in, 161–2; differences flattened in, 157; Los Angeles and, 163; as verbatim theatre, 152
Fire Within, The (documentary), 200
First Nation groups, Jewish groups enmeshed with, 89–90
"First Time a White Person Wrote 'Love' to Me, The" (Smith), 154
Fitz, Karsten, 95
Floyd, George, 163
foil characters, Erdrich writing, 60
Foucault, Michel, 80
Foundational Fictions (Sommers), 17, 80, 88
Frames of War (Butler), 101
Francis (pope), 190
Franco, Dean J., 49, 128, 179, 206n14; *The Border and the Line* by, 173; Chabon contrasted with, 174; Los Angeles focused on by, 150; on metaphors, 20
Fraser, David, 85
Freedman, Jonathan, 16, 24–5, 52, 133–4, 215n6
Freidenberg, Judith Noemí, 17–18
Freyre, Gilberto, 8, 123, 165

Funk, Jaydi, 181, 217n8
Funk, Steven, 181, 217n8
futebol mulato. See mulatto football

García Márquez, Gabriel, 87–8
Garcilaso, El Inca, 94
Garnett, Kevin, 199
Gates, Henry Louis: *The Signifying Monkey* by, 12–13, 95, 204n5; *Thirteen Ways of Looking at a Black Man* by, 132; wandering signifiers considered by, 12–13
gender: ethnicity and, 48–9; race and, 32–3; sexuality and Jewishness and, 183–4
gender identification, Judaism and, 185–6
Genealogical Fictions (Martínez), 23
genealogy, 27–8, 59, 82–3, 87–8, 90–4, 96–7
genocide of Native Americans, the Holocaust linked to, 59–60, 79
Gentefied (series), 216n2
geographies of responsibility, 205n9
George, Diana, 208n2
Gerardi, Juan, 212n15
Gerchunoff, Alberto, 17
Gilroy, Paul, 153
Glaser, Jennifer, 111, 127, 128, 214n2, 215n5; *Borrowed Voices* by, 22, 105, 152; *The Human Stain* read by, 136; on passing, 130–1
Glissant, Edouard, 26
Global South Studies (Tally), 206n14
Goldman, Francisco, 4, 11, 34, 81–2, 202, 212n15; Guatemala characterized by, 104–5; Latinx Jews written by, 103; *Monkey Boy* by, 99, 103, 107, 109, 214n3; on political violence, 108; syncretism addressed by, 109. See also *Long Night of White Chickens, The*

240   Index

Goldstein, Eric, 6, 175
Gómez, Gabriela Yanes, 101
González Echevarría, Roberto, 87
Gordon, Lewis, 204n3
Gräbner, Cornelia, 100, 141
Graetz, Roger, 118
Graff Zivin, Erin, 64, 205n11
Grandin, Greg, 69
Gray, Herman, 181
Green, Richard, 160
Guatemala, 42–3, 49, 73, 211n11;
    ethnic categories in, 69; Goldman
    characterizing, 104–5; Halfon on,
    74; Jews in, 66–7; US differentiated
    from, 101–2
Guatemala City, New York City
    contrasted with, 107–8
Guggenheim Fellowship, 67
Gursky, Bernard, 85, 118
Gutiérrez Mouat, Ricardo, 95–6

Halberstam, Jack, 193, 218n15
Hale, Dorothy J., 12, 156
Halfon, Eduardo, 39–40, 208n3,
    212n15; autofiction by, 212n15;
    within Central American
    literature, 67–8; on Guatemala, 74;
    The Polish Boxer by, 213n20. See
    also *Tomorrow We Never Did Talk
    About It*
Hall, Stuart, 26
Hamburger, Cao, 4, 35
Harbury, Jennifer, 100
Hardin, Michael, 94
Harlem (New York), 3–4
Hatuey (Pinis), 140
Hebreo, León, 94
Hebrew Hammer (film), 175
Hecht, Michael L., 61
Heirs of Columbus, The (Vizenor),
    34, 61, 81–2, 93–6, 211n10;
    cultural memory challenged by,

97; epistemologies of knowing
    recreated and scrutinized in, 98–9;
    Sephardic Jews emphasized in, 118
hemispheric thinkers, 207n19
Herskovits, Melville, 204n5
heteroglossia, 11–12, 53
Hill, Jonah, 200
Hirsch, Marianne, 75, 211n14
historical memory, 69–70
History of Sexuality (Foucault), 80
Hitler, Adolf, 160–1
Hoffman, Gaby, 187, 192
Holocaust, the, 28–9, 146, 160–1;
    genocide of Native Americans
    linked to, 59–60, 79; Israeli–
    Palestinian conflict and, 197–9;
    possibility and reality of, 29, 104,
    145; slavery contrasted with, 3, 29,
    151, 158–9, 207n15
Holocaust and Modernity, The
    (Bauman), 145
homosexuality, 189–90
Hooker, Juliet, 171, 204n7, 207n19
Hopkins, Anthony, 214n1
Horowitz, Sara R., 208n1
Hotel Bolivia (Spitzer), 30, 40
How Jews Became White Folks
    (Brodkin), 5, 216n4
"How the Jews Became Japanese"
    (Lesser), 16
How to Be an Antiracist (Kendi),
    150–1
Human Matter (*El material humano*)
    (Rosa), 212n15
human rights fiction, 95–6
Human Stain, The (Roth), 119, 127,
    129–35, 214n1, 215nn2–6; *Days of
    Awe* compared with, 137–8; Glaser
    reading, 136; racial categories
    deconstructed by, 128
humour, bias disarmed by, 194
hybrid ancestry, 80

hybridity, 100, 112, 206n13; intergenerational relationships and, 116–17; Jewish-Indigenous, 81–2, 84–5, 88, 94, 107; *The Long Night of White Chickens* depicting, 105; *The Master Butchers Singing Club* depicting, 63–4; surrealism and, 99; syncretism linked with, 137

I, Rigoberta Menchú (testimonial account), 105
I Am a Man (play), 204n5
Iberian Peninsula, expulsion from the, 23–5, 40
identity politics, race and, 128–9
"If I Were a Negro" (Faulkner), 204n4
Imagined Communities (Anderson), 80
I Married a Communist (Roth), 127
immigration, queer identification coupled with, 193
imperialism, place of enunciation linked with, 101
Incomparable Atuk, The (Richler), 87
Indigeneity: Jewish encounters with, 40–1; Jewishness and, 16–17, 33, 39–40, 50–1, 79, 82–3, 88, 117; mestizaje erasing, 18
Indigenous–Jewish encounters, 4–5
Indigenous–Jewish hybridity, 81–2, 84–5, 88, 94, 107
Indigenous Peoples: connection to the land of Jews compared with, 15–16; Jaime Nissán sexualizing, 46; tropes fetishizing, 121. *See also* Native Americans
Indigenous populations, Jewish populations identifying with, 76–7
Innocent Voices (*Voces inocentes*) (film), 70
Insensatez (Castellanos Moya), 67, 77, 212n15

intergenerational relationships, hybridity and, 116–17
intersectionality, *Transparent* falling short of, 184
Irizarry, Guillermo, 101
Isaacs, Jorge, 17
Israel, 85, 107, 110, 112, 114–15, 197–9
Israeli–Palestinian conflict, 197–9
Itzkovitz, Daniel, 15, 132

Jaime Nissán (fictional character), 44–6
Jakobsen, Janet, 53, 183, 184
James (Everett), 201
Jameson, Fredric, 206n14
Jáuregui, Carlos, 91
Jefferson, Cord, 203n2
Jewish Americans, Black folks contrasted with, 3
Jewish–Black relations, 9–10, 174–5, 199–200
Jewish Central American literature, 43
Jewish community: absorption in, 5; in Boyle Heights, 35, 178; Latinx civil rights supported by, 35, 178; whiteness avowed by, 216n4
Jewish Currents (magazine), 199
Jewish difference, in cultural models, 32
Jewish encounters, with Indigeneity, 40–1
Jewish experiences: in Bolivia, 40; exile defining, 30–1, 144; in Latin America contrasted with North America, 205n11
Jewish gaucho (archetype), 18
Jewish groups, First Nation groups enmeshed with, 89–90
Jewish identities, Blackness absorbed into, 130–1
Jewish–Indigenous encounters, 4–5
Jewish-Indigenous hybridity, 81–2, 84–5, 88, 94, 107

242 Index

Jewish investment, in whiteness, 6, 204n3
Jewish literary blackface, 152
Jewish masculinity, nationalism and, 49
Jewish–Native American encounters, 65–6
Jewishness: allegory of difference and, 15; Blackness contrasted with, 126–8, 133, 135–6, 163; colonization and, 97; cosmopolitanism associated with, 101–2; within Cuban identity, 144; gender and sexuality and, 183–4; Indigeneity and, 16–17, 33, 39–40, 50–1, 79, 82–3, 88, 117; inevitability and, 141–2, 146; land in relation to, 86–7; in Latin America, 22–3; Latinidad intersecting with, 139–40; mestizaje and, 23; mutability of, 113–14; race intersecting with, 200–1; in race relations, 177; racial alterity and, 16, 52; racial mixture and, 206n13; secret, 78, 118; syncretism compared with, 7–8; Vasconcelos depicting, 51–2; whiteness and, 5–6, 130, 132–3
Jewish otherness, racial alterity contrasted with, 47
Jewish populations, Indigenous populations identified with by, 76–7
Jewish spirituality, Catholicism contrasted with, 55–6
Jews, 5, 129, 184, 206n13, 216n4; Castro supported by, 146; connection to the land of Indigenous Peoples compared with, 15–16; in Guatemala, 66–7; Iberian Peninsula expelling, 23–5; Latinx, 103; Mexican, 210n6; Native American culture fascinating, 114–16; Native

Americans compared with, 38; political sphere in relation to, 68; Protestant schools attended by, 85; race relations between Afro-Brazilians and, 164–5. See also Sephardic Jews
Jodorowksy, Alejandro, 49, 210n5
Joel Fleischman (fictional character), 37, 41, 77
Johnson, James Weldon, 203n1
Jones, Nicholas, 12
José María de Pereda Prize for the Short Novel, 67
Joyrich, Lynne, 217n10
Judaism, 185–6. See also crypto-Judaism
Judeo-Indigenous, crypto-Judaism contrasted with, 141

Kakutani, Michiko, 60
Kalin, Betsy, 35, 178
Kandiyoti, Dalia, 25–6, 55, 141
Kaplan, Deborah, 180
Kaye/Kantrowitz, Melanie, 24–5, 129
Keeping Up with the Steins (film), 216n2
Kellet, Calderón, 189
Kendi, Ibram, 150–1
Keveney, Bill, 189
King, Martin Luther, Jr., 204n5
King, Rodney, 163
Kings County Hospital, 159
Kittleson, Roger Alan, 167
Klezmer America (poem), 16, 52, 133
Koffman, David S., 33, 41, 84, 89
Krupat, Arnold, 97–8

Lacandons, 45
La danza de la realidad (film), 49, 210n5
La frontera. See Borderlands
Las Casas, Bartolomé de, 107, 205n12

Index 243

Last Report on the Miracles at Little No Horse, The (Erdrich), 62
Latin America: Jewish experiences in North America contrasted with, 205n11; Jewishness in, 22–3; settler colonialism in, 40–1
Latin American literature, 95–6
Latinidad: Jewishness intersecting with, 139–40; sexuality and, 190, 216n2; in US, 109, 139
Latinx civil rights, Jewish community supporting, 35, 178
Latinx communities, in Boyle Heights, 216n2
Latinx Jews, Goldman writing, 103
Latinx representation, in *One Day at a Time*, 188–9
Lazarus, Emma, 16
lesbian existence, 181–2
Lesser, Jeffrey, 6, 16
Levinson, Hilary, 75
Lévi-Strauss, Claude, 115
Like a Bride (*Novia que te vea*) (film), 209n4, 210n6, 211n8
limpieza de sangre, 23–4
Lindstrom, Naomi, 120–1
linguistic syncretism, 53
Lispector, Clarice, 34, 119, 121–2, 125, 148. *See also* "Smallest Woman in the World, The"
literary figures, 14–15
London, Lauren, 200
Long, Crispin, 190
Long Night of White Chickens, The (Goldman), 81–2, 99–100, 101–4, 107, 109, 214n3; *The Art of Political Murder* contrasted with, 108; cultural schizophrenia evoked by, 106; hybridity depicted in, 105; Irizarry interpreting, 101
Los Angeles (California): Boyle Heights in, 178–9, 188, 192, 216n2;

Echo Park in, 178; *Fires in the Mirror* and, 163; Franco focusing on, 150
Los gauchos judíos/Jewish Gauchos (Gerchunoff), 17
lost tribes theory, 61, 210n7
Lott, Erik, 153
Lugones, María, 10, 154, 172
Lush, Rebecca, 98

Machuca (film), 212n17, 213n19
Madsen, Deborah Lea, 211n8
magical realism, in *Spirits of the Ordinary*, 57
Maguire, Geoffrey, 213n21
Mañana nunca lo hablamos. See Tomorrow We Never Did Talk About It
marginalization, 46–7
María (Isaacs), 17, 88
marrano (figure), 24, 53, 63–4, 138
Martín Cabrera, Luis, 213n18
Martínez, María Elena, 23
Marx, Karl, 21
masculinity, Jewish, 49
Massey, Doreen, 205n9
Master Butchers Singing Club, The (Erdrich), 14, 33, 39, 58, 60–2, 66; atrocities depicted in, 59; competitive memory undone by, 65; hybridity depicted by, 63–4
Masters and the Slaves, The (Freyre), 8
Maya, 97, 100
Médici, Emílio Garrastuzi, 164
Mendel Schneerson, Menachem, 152
Merchant of Venice, The (Shakespeare), 202
mestizaje, 8, 141, 213n23; Indigeneity erased by, 18; Jewishness and, 23; *Rites* fetishizing, 44–5; Sephardic Jews intertwining with, 25–6; Sephardism dovetailing with, 143
Mestizo (Feierstein), 18, 214n1

244 Index

metaphors, 80; Franco on, 20; metonymy and, 20–1, 150, 174; of settler colonialism, 19

metonymy, 16, 20–1, 63–4, 133, 150, 174

Mexican Jews, Tarahumara identified with by, 210n6

Mexico, 31, 50, 197–8

Mexico–US border, 31, 197–8

Miles, Elaine, 208n2

Miller, Michael, 160

Momaday, M. Scott, 97–8

Monkey Boy (Goldman), 99, 103, 107, 109, 214n3

Montreal (Canada), national belonging in, 84–5

Moore, Deborah Dash, 216n4

Moran, Kristin C., 181, 190, 215n1

Moreno, Rita, 189

Morrison, Alastair, 92, 141

Morrison, Toni, 5–6, 216n4

Moss, Joshua Louis, 183, 187

Movement for Black Lives, 163

Muhammad, Khalid, 157, 158–9

mulatto football (*futebol mulato*), 167

multiculturalism, 131

Multidirectional Memory (Rothberg), 157

My Mexican Shiva (*Morirse está en hebreo*) (film), 209n4

myths, of national identities, 16–17

national belonging, 48–9, 84–5, 118

national identities, 92; crypto-Judaism and, 51; *Days of Awe* focusing on, 139; myths of, 16–17; racial mixture informing, 91

nationalism, Jewish masculinity, 49

Native American culture, Jews fascinating, 114–16

Native American identity, 60–2

Native American–Jewish encounters, 65–6

Native Americans: the Holocaust linked to genocide of, 59–60, 79; Jews compared with, 38; *Northern Exposure* portraying, 208nn1–2

Nazis, 104

"Negro and the Warsaw Ghetto, The" (Du Bois), 20–1

Netflix, 188, 200

Neto's Silence (*El silencio de Neto*) (film), 70, 208n3

New York City, Guatemala City contrasted with, 107–8

New Yorker (magazine), 132

New York Times (newspaper), 3, 162, 201

Nora's Will (*Cinco días sin Nora*) (film), 209n4

North America, Jewish experiences in Latin America contrasted with, 205n11

North American fiction, 95–6

Northern Exposure (television program), 37, 41, 208nn1–2

Novia que te vea. See *Like a Bride*

Oakland (California), 170, 172–3, 175

Obejas, Achy, 34, 119, 148. See also *Days of Awe*

Ocasio-Cortez, Alexandria, 207n15

"Oh Sister" (song), 195

Ojibwe, 58, 60

One Day at a Time (television program), 35–6, 178–9, 182, 190, 215n1, 217n12; feminist innovations furthered by, 183; Latinx representation in, 188–9; rites of passage in, 180; *Transparent* contrasted with, 192–6

One Hundred Years of Solitude (García Márquez), 87–8

On Subjectivity and Survivance
  (Madsen), 211n8
Oppenheimer, Mark, 180
Ortiz, Fernando, 26, 27
Osborne, Stephen D., 93
Ostrov, Reuven, 159
OyamO (playwright), 204n5

Palestine, 114–15, 197–9
Palestinian–Israeli conflict, 197–9
Park, Shelley, 189
passing, 130–1, 132, 141, 217n12
"Passing Like Me" (Itzkovitz), 132
de Paula Rabelo, Adriano, 124
Pedro Pan Operation, 193
Perera, Victor, 33, 39–40, 41–50, 100;
  The Cross and the Pear Tree by, 42;
  ethnic identity of, 43–4; Spanish
  Conquest evoked by, 47–8. See
  also *Rites*
Pérez Firmat, Gustavo, 214n2
Perkowska, Magdalena, 211n12,
  213n21
Peters, Clarke, 11
Pinis, Oskar, 140
Plot Against America, The (Roth), 4–5,
  63, 127, 203n2
Pocahontas, 93–4, 100
police brutality, 163
Polish Boxer, The (*El boxeador polaco*)
  (Halfon), 213n19
political conflict, childhood
  perspective on, 212n17, 213n19
political correctness, 131
political sphere, Jews in relation
  to, 68
political violence, Goldman on, 108
Pop Network, 189
Portnoy's Complaint (Roth), 49
Posse, Abel, 94
postmemory, 75, 211n14
Pratt, Mary Louise, 111

Pridgeon, Stephanie, 206n14
Princeton University, 132
Pron, Patricio, 213n21
Protestant schools, Jews attending, 85
pureza de sangre. See blood purity

queer identification, immigration
  coupled with, 193
queer identity, 60–2
queering, of rites of passage, 192–6
"Queers Are Like Jews, Aren't
  They?" (Jakobsen), 184
queer sexuality, whiteness and, 182
Queer Theory and the Jewish Question
  (Jakobsen), 53, 183
Quinceañera (film), 216n2
Quiroga, José, 217n11

race, 26, 142; academic
  understandings of, 148–9;
  Appiah on, 205n9; gender and,
  32–3; identity politics and, 128–9;
  Jewishness intersecting with,
  200–1; sexuality and, 32–3
race relations: cities reflecting,
  151–2; Jewishness in, 177; between
  Jews and Afro-Brazilians, 164–5;
  Telegraph Avenue depicting, 169
racial alterity: Jaime Nissán
  fascinated by, 45–6; Jewishness
  and, 16, 52; Jewish otherness
  contrasted with, 47; relationship
  between centre and periphery
  and, 122; *Solomon Gursky Was Here*
  emphasizing, 91
racial categories, 108–9, 202, 205n12;
  The Human Stain deconstructing,
  128; organizing logics of, 119; Roth
  on, 135–6
racial democracy (*democracia racial*),
  123–4, 165, 167
racial difference, 167, 181

246 Index

racialized memory, 148
racial mixture, 177; in Brazil, 166; Jewishness and, 206n13; national identities informed by, 91
racial Others, in fiction, 9–11
racial politics, 134–5, 173
racial ventriloquism, 10–12, 105, 122, 140, 204n5; diglossia exemplified by, 156; double consciousness and, 152, 170–1; in "The Smallest Woman in the World," 125; Smith inverting, 157; testimonial theatre compared with, 154; by Twain, 201
racism, 130, 135–6, 160–1
Rama, Ángel, 27–8
"Reflections on Little Rock" (Arendt), 152
Reid, Alastair, 42
Reinelt, Janelle, 153
Repeating Island, The (Benítez Rojo), 7
Revolutionary Visions (Pridgeon), 206n14
rhetoric as persuasion (vertreten), 21
rhetoric as trope (darstellen), 21
Rich, Adrienne, 181–2
Richler, Mordecai, 34, 85, 87. See also Solomon Gursky Was Here
Riggs, Damien, 218n15
Rites (Perera), 33, 39–43, 48–50; marginalization depicted in, 46–7; mestizaje fetishized in, 44–5; upper-class as focus of, 208n3
rites of passage: father-daughter relationships impacted by, 194–5; in One Day at a Time, 180; queering of, 192–6; sexuality understood through, 187–8; in Transparent, 180
Roach, Joseph, 153–4
Robinson, Emily, 187
Rocha, Carolina, 165
Rock, Chris, 151
Rodó, José Enrique, 91

Rorabaugh, W. J., 172
Rosenbaum, Yudith, 122
Rosenberg, Roberta, 187–8, 218n16
Roth, Philip, 34, 148; American Pastoral by, 127; I Married a Communist by, 127; The Plot Against America by, 4–5, 63, 127, 203n2; Portnoy's Complaint by, 49; on racial categories, 135–6. See also Human Stain, The
Rothberg, Michael, 29, 157, 159, 207n15, 215n1
Rottenberg, Catherine, 203n1
Rubinstein, Rachel, 140

"Sabra" (Villanueva), 36, 197–8
Safdie, Benny, 199
Safdie, Josh, 199
St. Louis affair, 136, 145
Salcedo Mitrani, Lorry, 200
Sanders, Susan, 208n2
Santiago (Chile), 213n19
São Paulo. See Bom Retiro, in São Paulo (Brazil)
Sarmiento, Domingo Faustino, 204n7
Schechner, Richard, 154, 162
Schyfter, Guita, 210n6, 211n8
Sedgwick, Eve Kosofsky, 33
Seminet, Georgia, 208n3
Sephardic Jews, 24, 43, 78; Ashkenazim contrasted with, 44; in the Caribbean, 9; The Heirs of Columbus emphasizing, 118; Maya and, 97; mestizaje intertwined with, 25–6
Sephardism, 9, 143
settler colonialism, 18, 86; Israeli–Palestinian conflict parallelling, 198–9; in Latin America, 40–1; metaphors of, 19
sexuality, 60, 80; compulsory hetero, 181–2; homo, 189–90; Jewishness

Index   247

and gender and, 183–4; Latinidad and, 190, 216n2; queer, 182; race and, 32–3; rites of passage and understanding of, 187–8
Shaft (film), 175
Shakespeare, William, 202
Sharpton, Al, 156, 159, 162
Signifying Monkey, The (Gates), 12–13, 95, 204n5
Silverstein, Stephen, 27
Simpson, O.J., 151
Sitka (Alaska), Zion in, 109–11
Skidmore, Thomas, 166
slavery, 3, 29, 124, 151, 158–9, 207n15
"Smallest Woman in the World, The" (Lispector), 34, 119, 120–3, 126; biblical illusions in, 121; racial ventriloquism in, 125; slavery evoked in, 124
Smith, Anna Deavere, 9–10, 35, 172, 214n1; "The First Time a White Person Wrote 'Love' to Me" by, 154; racial ventriloquism inverted by, 157; *Twilight* by, 155, 163; Washington compared with, 162–3. See also *Fires in the Mirror*
soccer, 164–7
Socolovsky, Maya, 136
Solomon Gursky Was Here (Richler), 34, 81–6, 88–90, 92–3; Casteel reading, 87; Morrison reading, 141; racial alterity emphasized in, 91
Soloway, Joey, 184
Sommers, Doris, 17, 88, 94
Soviet Union, 144–5
Spanish Conquest: of the Americas, 22–3; Jewish-Indigenous hybridity and, 94; Perera evoking, 47–8; religious thinking influencing, 107
Spanish identities, Sephardism within, 143

speaking for oneself, 21–2
spirit of chiasmus, 14
Spirits of the Ordinary (Alcalá), 25, 33, 39, 50, 53–4, 56–8; cosmic race not explored in, 51; Delgadillo reading, 55; Freedman on, 52; magical realism in, 57
spirituality, 186; in adoption narratives, 106–7; diaspora contrasted with, 188; Jewish, 55–6
Spitzer, Leo, 30, 40, 207n17
Spivak, Gayatri, 21
Staging habla de negros (Jones), 12
Stanfield, Lakeith, 199
state violence, 42, 67, 69–71, 76–7, 105, 108
Stavans, Ilan, 18, 50–1, 74, 211n13
Stein, Shawn, 165, 167
Storyteller, The (*El hablador*) (Vargas), 38–9
superheroes, 170
surrealism, 81, 99
syncretism, 82, 95; Alcalá pivoting to, 55–6; fiction and, 9–10; Goldman addressing, 109; hybridity linked with, 137; Jewishness compared with, 7–8; linguistic, 53
synecdoche, metonymy moved to from, 16

Taking Their Word (Arias), 43
Tally, Robert, 206n14
Tambor, Jeffrey, 182, 195, 218n15
Tarahumara, 53, 55, 57–8, 210n6
Tarica, Estelle, 30, 40
Taylor, Breonna, 163
Taylor, Diana, 32
Ted Talks, 157
Telegraph Avenue (Chabon), 10–11, 35, 150, 170–5, 196; competitive

248   Index

memory avoided in, 176; race relations depicted in, 169; Simpson inspiring, 151
television, racial difference represented on, 181
testimonial theatre, racial ventriloquism compared with, 154
Theorizing Race in the Americas (Hooker), 204n7
"Third-World Literature in the Era of Multinational Capitalism" (Jameson), 206n14
Thirteen Ways of Looking at a Black Man (Gates), 132
Tomorrow We Never Did Talk About It (*Mañana nunca lo hablamos*) (Halfon), 39–40, 66–77, 208n3, 211n11, 211n13, 213n21; childhood perspective in, 70–1; exile shown in, 68–9; Perkowska reading, 211n12; silence centred in, 74
"Tomorrow We Never Did Talk About It" (short story), 211n13, 212n16
Toronto International Film Festival, 184
Trail of Tears, 4–5
transculturation (*transculturación*), 26–8, 95, 111, 214n2
translation, 136–7, 142–3, 147
Transparent (television program), 35–6, 215n1, 216n5, 217n6, 217nn13–14, 218nn15–17; Boyle Heights depicted in, 178–9, 188, 192; coming out narratives in, 182–3; intersectionality fallen short of by, 184; *One Day at a Time* contrasted with, 192–6; rites of passage in, 180; Rosenberg on, 187–8
Treuer, David, 201
Tropics of Desire (Quiroga), 217n11

Tuck, Eve, 19, 80, 205n8
Tumin, Melvin, 132
Twain, Mark, 201–2
Twilight (Smith), 155, 163

Uncut Gems (film), 199–200
United States (US), 31, 197–8; ethnic categories of, 102–3, 108–9; Guatemala differentiated from, 101–2; Latinidad in, 109, 139. *See also* Los Angeles
United States Holocaust Memory Museum, 207n15
upper-class, *Rites* focusing on, 208n3
US–Mexico border, 31, 197–8
Uzendoski, Andrew, 95

Vargas Llosa, Mario, 38–9
Vasconcelos, José, 8, 31–2, 50–2, 143, 207n19
ventriloquism. *See* racial ventriloquism
Veracini, Lorenzo, 19
verbatim theatre, *Fires in the Mirror* as, 152
Verdín, Azucena, 217n7
vertreten. See rhetoric as persuasion
vicariousness, consumption conveying, 92–3
Vida (series), 216n2
Villanueva, Luz Alma, 36, 197
Villarejo, Amy, 180, 184
Vinson, Ben, 23, 54, 141
Virgen de Guadalupe, 7
Vizenor, Gerald, 34, 61, 81–2. See also *Heirs of Columbus, The*
von Vacano, Diego, 205n12

wandering signifiers, 12–13, 22, 34
Warren, Kay, 43
Washington, Michael Benjamin, 10, 162–3, 215n2

Index   249

Way, The (*El camino*) (film), 70
Weeping Woman (Villanueva), 197
Weimar Germany, 180, 185, 188
whiteness: Blackness converging
  with, 125; Jewish community
  avowing, 216n4; Jewish
  investment in, 6, 204n3;
  Jewishness and, 5–6, 130, 132–3;
  queer sexuality and, 182
white privilege, crypto-Judaism
  and, 142
white supremacy, 5–6, 23, 128, 133
"Why Did Cup Foods Call the
  Police on George Floyd?"
  (Bayoumi), 177
Williams, Claire, 121
Winant, Harold, 124
Wood, Andrés, 212n17
World Cup (1970), 164, 167

World War II, 34, 59–60, 62–5, 115,
  127–8, 132
Wounded Knee Massacre, 59
Writing across Cultures (Rama), 27–8

X, Malcolm, 161

Yanders, Jacinta, 191
Yang, K. Wayne, 19, 80, 205n8
Year My Parents Went on Vacation, The
  (film), 4, 35, 163–9, 176
Yiddish Policemen's Union, The
  (Chabon), 34, 81–2, 109–17, 119
You People (film), 36, 200

Zamora, Lois Parkinson, 87
Zion, in Sitka, 109–11
Zionism, 115
Zivin, Graff, 22, 34